IN FASHION

IN FASH

FROM RUNWAY TO RETAIL, EVERYTHING YOU NEED
TO KNOW TO BREAK INTO THE FASHION INDUSTRY

HION

Annemarie Iverson

CLARKSON POTTER | PUBLISHERS | NEW YORK

All rights reserved. Published in the United States by Clarkson Potter/Publishers,
an imprint of the Crown Publishing Group, a division of Random House, Inc., New York.
www.crownpublishing.com
www.clarksonpotter.com

CLARKSON POTTER is a trademark and POTTER with colophon is a registered
trademark of Random House, Inc.

Library of Congress Cataloging-in-Publication Data
Iverson, Annemarie.
  In fashion / Annemarie Iverson.
    p.   cm.
  Includes index.
  1. Fashion—Vocational guidance.   2. Fashion design—Vocational guidance.   3. Fashion
merchandising—Vocational guidance.   4. Clothing trade—Vocational guidance.   I. Title.
  TT507.I87 2010
  746.9'2023—dc22   2009048121

ISBN 978-0-307-46383-8

Printed in the United States of America

Design by Debbie Glasserman

10 9 8 7 6 5 4

First Edition

Dedicated to the memory of Liz Tilberis

The brightest star of the fashion constellation,

Liz allowed many of us to shine in her orbit,

her sparkle, elegance, and warmth forever inside us.

Special thanks to …

All the cool people I've ever worked with, for, alongside, above, and below.
I hope you find my vision of our time together accurate, maybe even amusing.

All my new fashionista friends who were open and generous to share their stories with me.

Diane Reverand, for believing in me; David Vigliano for making this book happen; Rosy Ngo for bringing it to life.

I thank my mother, Mary Ellen Iverson, for helping me get my first break in magazines all the way from Wisconsin, and my two sons, Francesco and Giacomo, whose passion and enthusiasm fuel and inspire me. Lastly, I thank my husband, Alberto Finali, for sharing with us his love and impeccable vision of a fashionable life.

CONTENTS

FOREWORD
BY DIANE VON FURSTENBERG

I first met Annemarie Iverson at my then-offices at 757 Fifth Avenue in the early 1990s. She was working in creative at Revlon, which held the license for my fragrance Tatiana, and had accompanied one of its suits to the meeting. For my part, I was thinking to restart my fashion company, bringing everything I'd once created back together again. It was clear to me then—and I probably communicated it rather directly—that Annemarie needed to find a way to get herself out of Revlon and more directly in fashion, so to speak.

It didn't take long. A year or so later, Annemarie rode with me to my country house to interview me for a fashion feature she'd started writing for *New York Woman* magazine. It was called "In Her Closet."

Then, coming full circle a few years later, Annemarie, now the fashion and beauty news director of *Harper's Bazaar,* attended a fragrance launch in my then-new Twelfth Street showroom. We were both on our way.

I started doing runway shows on Sunday evenings at the start of fashion week, and Annemarie was usually there. I ran into her at the Couture in Paris one January: The very American optimist who was taking on the fashion world had married a handsome Italian banker and was pregnant with her second son.

Her path intertwined over the years with many others, as well. Through a combination of Midwestern pluck and sheer dumb luck, Annemarie has found herself in the presence of other fashion icons, people like Diana Vreeland, Jackie Onassis, Yves Saint Laurent, Liz

Tilberis, and Gianni Versace. Not to mention, my peers, Calvin, Ralph, Karl, and Donna. This access bestowed on Annemarie a rich understanding of the global fashion milieu allowing her to take on in *In Fashion* a topic enticingly impenetrable to many: *How to get your start in the Fashion Industry.*

In Fashion is a chunky, humorous, insider-y, but ultimately accessible, manual that will help focus and guide the next generation of young people dreaming of entering this world. My story is embedded here—how I became a designer nearly four decades ago and how I made my retrun just one decade ago to become an even larger force in fashion thanks, in part, to my role as president of the Council of Fashion Designers of America (CFDA)—but there are also the stories of window dressers ("visual merchandisers"), public relations people, department store fashion executives, and editorial and celebrity stylists here. Through targeted and amusing dossiers of people in these roles, Annemarie plots out lots of different career paths—where they started and how they arrived in the world of fashion.

The point is that there is likely to be a mentor here with whom each reader can relate. Highlighted throughout are the hot twenty-first century jobs (in public relations, online fashion journalism, accessories design, visual merchandising, retail fashion management), where to go now for the best start to your career, and up-to-the-minute advice for navigating in fashion's ever-changing landscape.

In addition, Annemarie charts out the precise educational path you should follow: If you want to be *Vogue*'s next cover hairstylist, for example, there is no compelling reason to go to Harvard or Brown or the University of Geneva. If you want to be the next me, however, it wouldn't be a bad idea. While fashion is big business and involves big brands, it is also craft, handmade and artisan; at any given moment, fashion pivots around a handful of key individuals, but it also touches everyone. Fashion is everywhere, but the heart of fashion is centered in a few fashion capitals of the world. Also, while fashion itself is highly accessible today thanks to the Internet, fashion careers are not. *In Fashion* understands all that.

Almost every day, I receive letters from students all over the world looking to apprentice with me. I try to hire as many of them as I possibly can. The United States has this amazing institution called *the internship* that gives young people practical skills and something on their résumé to help them get their first job. In fact, I created the DVF studio in the Meatpacking district in Manhattan as a creative lab in which young people could learn.

But first you must know what to write and to whom to send the letter. I believe this important book will inspire help young people do just that, to find their way or feel invited into the world of fashion: With *In Fashion* and your own passion, discipline, and persistence, you can find your way.

IN FASHION

PREFACE: AN UNLIKELY FASHONISTA

From the time I was four or five growing up in deep, dark, desolate Wisconsin, I collected those annoying blow-in cards from magazines that all arrived from the same place—New York City. I filled Stride Rite shoeboxes with my cherished postcard-size offers from *Good Housekeeping*, the rare *Glamour* that fell into my hands, *House & Garden*, *Mademoiselle*. It was my crude attempt to connect with the fashionable world.

I found *Vogue* at the Port Edwards two-dryer hair salon. I used these pages to instruct my mother how to knit and sew a collection of couture Barbie doll clothes. She did so, amazingly well. I still treasure these tiny creations. Nail enamel, makeup, hair color, according to this same good conservative mother, were *not* for ladies. But I instinctively ignored her. I knew I belonged to a different world, one where style and color and elegance mattered, where women were fresh and sleek and well groomed all the time.

I secretly groomed my inner city girl and, eventually, found my way to that magic world of magazine chic where beauty closets bulge with (free!) lipsticks, miraculous mascaras, and weird gadgets that promise to eviscerate cellulite; where models, writers, and photographers roam the halls looking fabulous and original; where editors go click, click teetering on the most dangerous never-worn-out or soiled shoes; where fashion closets spill out the dresses and shoes and bags that are the bright new vision for next season and for how we want to look now; and where sleek publishing executives package and sell everything editors touch and photograph and write about as the latest, best, and brightest. This is a world where you, like me, might find yourself in the same room with superstars like Kate Moss, Calvin Klein, Tom Ford, Courtney Love, Hugh Grant, Sting, Madonna, and Robin Williams or legends like Yves Saint Laurent, Jackie O, Diana Vreeland, or Princess Diana, as I unexpectedly did. Strangely, the superstars inspired less awe in me than the people with and for whom I worked.

I finally did arrive at the epicenter of the magazine universe, but getting there was not easy or obvious. What has motivated me to write *In Fashion*? To help others as clueless and unconnected as I was find a more direct path while making sense of my twisted journey.

I have experienced more and I have done more than I knew to even expect of myself. I was wooed. Courted. Hired. Lauded. I hired, lauded, congratulated, promoted others. Early on, I was dubbed by *Adweek* the "fashion girl to watch." And . . . I've been fired, gently—"There's this 'other job' at Ca-fugly Un-fashion Magazine that we think you'd be great for!"—and much more publicly and brutally.

I sat through my most recent—and let's hope last—firing as editor in chief of *Seventeen* magazine while lapping up frozen fat-free yogurt with Heath bar topping, trying to appear as cool as a cucumber. I'd been called back to the city from vacation for an "important" meeting that turned out to be a sham. My termination was carefully planned by the company's "management team." As it turned out, no one would survive much longer than I did with the bigger corporate mess they had created. My immediate, annoyingly smug boss, who had been imposed on me only recently, was soon fired herself. The boss's boss lasted not much longer and is now pursuing a career in either sporting goods or packaged goods, I don't remember which. None of the rest would be pictured "slipping up" in the *New York Post,* as I was, which felt brutal at the time but was, in fact, a kind of honor, I suppose. As they say, there is no such thing as bad publicity.

In a twisted, back-glancing way, I guess I won. I never sold out. I didn't allow myself to be turned into a rat in a maze trying to put out a magazine that some committee of executives determined would sell best, second-guessing every picture and forgetting about The Reader. I left with what I value most about myself—my gut, my passion, and my honesty. All three, I'm happy to report, are still intact.

There's nothing like deadline therapy to get me past lingering hurt feelings. After several quiet years of freelancing and consulting, I experienced the weirdest twist of my career: I was asked to return to *Harper's Bazaar* in my original role of beauty director for six months. While my husband was trying to talk me out of going back to a position I had held a lifetime ago, I saw it more cosmically, like time travel, and going back to a title that was golden for me. It would allow me to leap forward to next season, months before the rest of the world would get there.

Humbly and happily, I returned. It helped that *Bazaar* is now housed on the twenty-fifth floor of New York City's most glamorous and green skyscraper, the Hearst Tower. I found I still loved the nutty creative world of magazines, with its mix of young talent and swirl of creative businesses around them. I discovered that things just don't throw me anymore and that I can write fast, *really* fast.

Back where the universe clearly wanted me, sitting on a rich heap of advice, products, the newest and the latest, with an eye that can't help itself but to critique the looks and grooming of nearly every person strutting by my office, I had a great, soothing epiphany: Regardless of where I am physically, fashion is so deeply ingrained in my soul that, come what may, I will always be *in fashion*.

INTRODUCTION

So, YOU want to be the next greatest fashionista on earth. Maybe you imagine yourself taking the big honors on *Project Runway* and launching your design career in the footsteps of stars like Marc Jacobs, Stella McCartney, or Tom Ford. Or maybe you see yourself in the realm of *The Devil Wears Prada,* striking out in the world of fashion editorial and training yourself to be a great fashion editor, like Anna Wintour. Maybe you are the next Rachel Zoe, styling stars like Kate Winslet and Jennifer Aniston, and in the process, transforming yourself into a front row, red carpet star in your own right. Or do you see yourself ON the runway? Are *you* the next Kate Moss, Tyra Banks, or Gisele Bundchen? Or are you more the behind-the-scenes type—quietly, creatively producing the iconic images of fashion as the next great fashion photographer, a Steven Meisel or Mario Testino? Maybe you want to live it and loosely fictionalize yourself like Candace Bushnell did when she wrote about her modern fashion adventures in *Sex and the City*?

Or there's always the high-power corner office you could occupy as a fashion executive wearing crisp white suits and reptile-skin platform sandals twelve months a year, collecting contemporary art, designer bags, and important jewelry, and employing your own team of hair stylist, makeup artist, personal assistant, chauffeur, and housekeeper, all while hauling in more digits than you ever dreamed.

In Fashion is first and foremost a career manual—everything you need to know to enter the fashion business, and then to climb up the ranks and make it. Though I've spent the bulk of my career in magazines, I've had extensive firsthand experience in the related worlds of design, photography and styling, public relations, and events planning, as well as fashion retail and advertising. When my own experiences wouldn't give you maximum insight and mentoring, I've created profiles, or dossiers, of individuals who've struggled just as hard as I did and have landed just where they aimed on the global fashion freeway. Their career stories are filled with highs and lows and very detailed advice for people starting out in fashion today. People like Marc Jacobs' former assistant from Louis Vuitton, celebrity stylists, Prada U.S.A.'s visual merchandise director, the fashion director of Bergdorf Goodman, a highly recruited Internet fashion writer, Michael Kors' accessories genius, art directors, fashion photographers, the head of Vince's global sales, and more. See for yourself whether you feel aligned with these personalities.

Embedded in these stories are nuggets of advice you won't learn at Parsons, the Columbia Graduate School of Journalism, the State University of New York's Fashion Institute of Technology, the Wharton School, Brown University, the Rhode Island School of Design (RISD), or Sarah Lawrence College. My conversations with these friends, or friends of friends, or people I found and turned into friends, have always included this one question sent back to me: "Why didn't this book exist when I was trying to get into fashion?"

The reason I have felt *compelled* to write this book is that fashion follows no rules. If you want to be a pharmacist, teacher, engineer, doctor, or lawyer, the path is straight and obvious. In fashion, there is no clear path. That's the reason for *In Fashion*. Each of us—a total package of education, upbringing, ethnicity, innate style, looks, personality, sexuality—must find his or her own way. If you are blessed with luminous NYC-Paris-London-Milan connections and A-list cool parents, your career might just fall conveniently into your lap.

If, like me, you are an obscure mortal from nowhere—with good Lutheran parents, a math teacher mother and a paper-making chemist father—things are not as clear. You might just feel like a mouse (albeit a chic lab mouse) in a maze. I am here to light your way and to add some humor, mostly at my expense, along the way.

I served as editor in chief of *Seventeen* and *YM* magazines, and for seven years, I worked under the legendary Liz Tilberis as the fashion and beauty news director of *Harper's Bazaar*. I have written two *New York Times* bestsellers—*Bobbi Brown Beauty* and *Bobbi Brown Teenage Beauty*—and I aided Tilberis in writing her autobiography, *No Time to Die.* For years, I covered the Milan, Paris, New York, and London fashion shows, and I count among my friends industry power brokers from these worlds.

Besides its central mission as the essential career guide for a quite daunting industry, *In Fashion* captures the best and the worst events of my career. I feel lucky for the sweet highs and I accept complete responsibility for the blinding lows. I treat both with self-effacing humor, a survival tactic if there ever was one. My hope is that *you* benefit or learn from or are amused in some small measure by my telling of these episodes. That, for me, is the biggest prize.

In the telling of my experiences, it is not my intent to skewer others; I apologize in case my words bring pain or grief. I harbor no bitterness and know of no enemies. (Okay, maybe there was *one,* but I've long considered us made up.) This is supposed to be funny (!!!) and really useful.

Everything here is true and it absolutely happened, though I sometimes disguise exact places and/or identities. I am often struck by details unnoticed by others; I also get the feeling that I sense things more profoundly than others. These traits have helped me develop into a good reporter, but they have also burdened me with too much information. I'm a classic fashionista type C, a Critic, one who comments on the world around her. You'll hear more about this later.

HOW TO USE THIS BOOK

In Fashion is a *slash* kind of book: Glam career manual *slash* fashionista memoir. Writing instructional copy was my earliest training. Here I've applied the how-to format to the daunting exercise of breaking into and succeeding in fashion. I've sometimes felt I could find the essential how-to in any topic, and here I condense learning from my twenty-year career into lists of essential dos and don'ts. My intent is to share my story with fellow fashionistas, inviting their most brutal scrutiny while encouraging the next generation to passionately, deliberately go for it.

We'll start out, of course, with YOU! Explore the Fashionista Aptitude Survey (see page 13) to try to understand exactly what *sort* of fashionista you're likely to be and *where* you're most likely to fit in and find happiness and success. At the end of the survey, you'll see which of the four key fashion tribes you were born into, although no one bothered filling you in until now.

Creator Visualizer Critic Seller

Creators are fashion designers and their courts. They exist at the center of the fashion universe around which all the other planets orbit.

Visualizers bring fashion to life. Stylists are Visualizers, occupying what is probably the fastest growing, most appealing new role out there. Also among the Visualizers are photographers, illustrators, models, hair stylists, and makeup artists. Together, these people are charged with the task of capturing the imagination of the consuming audience by presenting next season's clothes and accessories in advertising and editorial in a compelling way. Sometimes their visuals inspire. Other times, they scandalize. The point is that you notice.

Critics are those who have opinions about what the Creators create. Critics express those opinions in fashion magazines, on fashion television, and over the Internet.

Sellers comprise the business end of fashion. The guy helping you "find your size" in jeans at the Gap is called a "retail sales associate," but he's a Seller. So are the entire publishing staffs of fashion magazines and the parts of advertising agencies that scare up business and maintain relationships with clients. While admitting that there's a lot of creativity and originality that goes into their work, I've also taken the old-fashioned view that public relations, merchandising, and marketing fall under this category: Ultimately their performances are judged by what *sells*.

These are not perfect blunt unyielding categories—just useful lenses through which to see the fashion world. Using these categories will help you make sense of things and, hopefully, avoid false starts and frustrations. If you find that you don't fall neatly into one or even two of the categories, don't be discouraged. You might just be one of those rare übertalents whose biggest decision is where to begin his or her most amazing career.

    In Fashion is organized according to these four key sectors of the fashion world. But don't just read about your specific career. Flip through the other sections of the book for general help on doing the perfect résumé, creating a concept book or portfolio, interviewing, what to wear on your first day, and every other little thing that might trip you up.

    My dream is that this book will help people realize *their* dreams. Of course, times are different from when I was growing up in central Wisconsin. Everything is more accessible and open to view. By logging in to www.style.com, you can see Derek Lam's fall collection online the same chilly February night it is presented in New York. With limited research, you could discover how many Diet Cokes designer Karl Lagerfeld has for lunch with whom, at which table in which restaurant in which city. The next "cool" band or trend or shoe or nail color takes milliseconds, *not* years, these days to beam into Wisconsin. Thanks to style-democratizing stores like H&M, IKEA, and Target, anyone, anywhere can live with good design, style, and "cool." If your hometown is anything like mine, Hollywood celebrities are discussed with the same intimacy as the local football team. Yet, while it might *feel* like this whole shimmering world is at your doorstep, the realization that it *isn't* and that you are missing it makes becoming a real fashionista all the more enticing.

FASHIONISTA APTITUDE SURVEY

What's *your* fashion fantasy? Do you love clothes and design so much that you dream of becoming a famous fashion designer? Are you obsessed with shoes, endlessly sketching heels and soles and researching trims, buying vintage stilettos at flea markets for your collection? Or do you devour fashion magazines and envision yourself as an exquisitely dressed editor at *Vogue*? Maybe you secretly imagine yourself in front of the camera, the smoky-eyed model in the Chanel ad, bringing next season's designs to life for the whole world to admire? Or maybe you see yourself behind the scenes as the fashion photographer or the stylist who brings his or her own original twist to clothes and accessories or as the hair stylist or makeup artist on the shoot. All of these people—and thousands more—populate the world of fashion. Each of them is *In Fashion,* and that's where you want to be too. But how can you get there?

Well, you're already on your way: The *passion* that's in your heart and mind for your future career is essential and will help shape your success and happiness almost more than anything else. While your fashion dreams may quickly become reality and you will soon be touted as the next Donna Karan, Anna Wintour, or Kate Moss, chances are there are years of education, tough work, highs, but mostly lows between you and that happy ending. Wouldn't it be a lot easier to know up front what path to follow? Or at least to know of a path or two that would be so wrong for your personality, so abhorrent to your tastes, that you shouldn't bother exploring them?

Beyond the passion (or obsession), *where* do you start? What's the right educational path and best possible schools, internships, and summer jobs? To get you started, we first need to understand: *What sort of fashionista are you?*

To answer that question, we need to delve deep inside *your* DNA to see how *your* personality is hardwired: What inspires you? And, conversely, what makes you glaze over? Shut down?

Just as millions of young people take the Myers-Briggs Type Indicator (MBTI) test to help determine their best possible career paths, you are about to take the *In Fashion* Fashionista Aptitude Survey to see where you might best fit in the ephemeral, glamorous, exhausting, and unpredictable world of fashion. The survey explores whether you are naturally outgoing or introverted; whether, when faced with information, you take it in on face value or, instead, you interpret it and add new meaning; whether, in dealing with the outside world, you tend to instantly judge a situation or you prefer to allow elements and details to seep in slowly.

Since there are no right or wrong answers to these questions, go with your first instinct and don't *overthink*. It is best to take a couple of quiet minutes to do these questions *on your own*: Doing the survey out loud with friends will inevitably skew the results. Given that fashion is a visual industry driven by image, creativity, and illusion, even in the hardest of economic times, this survey is designed for those who are naturally drawn to glamour. If you think the survey questions are inane and/or you don't identify with any of the responses, you might want to seriously question your inclination to the field itself. Let's face it, if you need something more concrete, there's always engineering, accounting, medicine, IT . . .

Those fields aren't for you? Okay, then. Let's begin.

1. **WORD THAT BEST DESCRIBES YOU:**
   a. Outrageous
   b. Sensitive
   c. Insightful
   d. Ingenious

2. **AS A CHILD, YOU MOST LIKED:**
   a. Performing
   b. Drawing
   c. Reading
   d. Socializing

3. **PERSONALITIES WHOSE BIOGRAPHIES YOU'D MOST WANT TO READ:**
   a. Karl Lagerfeld, Oscar Wilde, Princess Diana, Stephen Sprouse
   b. Leonardo da Vinci, Andy Warhol, Lou Reed, Lee Miller
   c. Diana Vreeland, Nora Ephron, Carmel Snow, Anna Wintour
   d. Donald Trump, Niccolò Machiavelli, J.P. Morgan, Warren Buffett, Diane von Furstenberg

4. **EXPRESSION YOU'RE MOST LIKELY TO OVERUSE:**
   a. "Heaven"
   b. "Cool"
   c. "Genius"
   d. "Perfect"

5. **PERSON YOU'D MOST LIKE TO HANG OUT WITH:**
   a. Sofia Coppola
   b. Kate Moss
   c. Christiane Amanpour
   d. Madonna

6. **ON SUMMER BREAKS DURING HIGH SCHOOL, YOU WERE MOST LIKELY TO BE:**
   a. Starring in a summer stage production
   b. Developing black-and-white prints for a photography class
   c. Winning the prize for the most books read at the public library
   d. Running a lemonade stand by day and babysitting by night

7. **HISTORIC PERSONALITY YOU'D MOST LIKE TO MEET:**
   a. Marie Antoinette
   b. Joan of Arc
   c. Queen Elizabeth I
   d. Catherine the Great

8. **YOUR BIGGEST WEAKNESS:**
   a. Meeting deadlines
   b. Making conversation
   c. Being impatient
   d. Letting go

9. **WHAT YOU VALUE MOST:**
   a. Originality
   b. Creativity
   c. Truth
   d. Results

10. **IF FORCED TO PLAY ONE OF THE FOLLOWING SOCIAL SPORTS, YOU'D CHOOSE:**
    a. Bowling
    b. Croquet
    c. Tennis
    d. Squash

11. **YOUR FACEBOOK HABIT:**
    a. You sometimes forget you're signed up.
    b. You log on once or twice a week when you have downtime.
    c. You compulsively sign in every morning to check flagged photos from last night's parties and film openings.
    d. You use it as a research tool, to vet potential new friends or learn more about future clients or bosses.

12. **BAD QUALITIES PEOPLE SOMETIMES ASCRIBE TO YOU:**
    a. That you're in outer space, unconnected to daily life, a total dreamer
    b. That you are unresponsive, inarticulate, lazy
    c. That you are unfeeling, insensitive, judgmental
    d. That you're always "on," too aggressive, and lacking in basic human values

13. **YOU ARE MOST LIKELY TO LOSE TRACK OF TIME WHEN YOU ARE:**
   a. Making something
   b. Watching something
   c. Reading something
   d. Planning something

14. **TRUTH ABOUT PETS:**
   a. My little dog comes with me everywhere.
   b. I love animals, but I'm allergic.
   c. I love cats because they have evolved personalities and are low maintenance.
   d. I travel too much to have a pet.

15. **FAVORITE WAY TO SOCIALIZE:**
   a. Go out, dropping by as many different kinds of parties as possible, ending up at dinner at 11 p.m. at a cool restaurant with a big group of old and new friends.
   b. Invite a few close friends over for a low-key dinner at home, then watch a new-release film together.
   c. Stage a dinner party with heady conversation and an interesting mix of guests.
   d. Attend a few important cocktail parties, then invite a group of business friends to dine at a good table at a hot restaurant.

16. **ALWAYS IN YOUR POSSESSION:**
   a. Pashmina or cashmere sweater
   b. Brush, lint remover
   c. *New Yorker*, lip balm
   d. Electronic agenda, money

17. **WHEN SOMEONE COMPLIMENTS YOU, YOU FEEL:**
   a. Energized
   b. Embarrassed
   c. Deserving
   d. Suspecting that there *must* be an underlying motive

18. IN HIGH SCHOOL, YOU ARE VOTED:
  a. Most Likely to Be Famous
  b. Most Likely to Travel to Faraway Places
  c. Most Likely to Rule the World
  d. Most Likely to Be a Billionaire

19. IN RELATIONSHIPS, YOU:
  a. Tend to be the more dominant partner, looking for adulation, support, and structure
  b. Seek to find your creative equal and would rather stay single than compromise this vision
  c. Want an accomplished mate, but one who has succeeded in a totally different field, like finance, architecture, or medicine, so you don't get competitive with him or her
  d. Love to go out with different kinds of people, but you have a hard time committing

20. YOUR DREAM WORKSPACE:
  a. It is not a traditional office but rather an open space, with the walls filled with inspiration boards; there's music playing, people are coming and going, and there's a nice buzz.
  b. I hate offices.
  c. It's a tidy corner office, with white Barcelona chairs and fresh flowers.
  d. It's a war room brimming with charts and presentation materials.

21. RELATIONSHIP WITH YOUR MOTHER:
  a. She's supportive and inspiring.
  b. She's practical and likes to nurture me.
  c. She's proud of me, but she knows I'm too busy to chitchat.
  d. She complains that I don't have a life.

22. RELATIONSHIP WITH YOUR FATHER:
  a. He's proud of me, but he's not that involved.
  b. We're a lot alike.
  c. He's the one who pushes and encourages me.
  d. Sadly, he doesn't have much faith in me.

23. RELATIONSHIP WITH YOUR iPHONE:
   a. You like making videos and texting friends but keep losing it.
   b. You use the camera and e-mail capabilities much more than the phone itself.
   c. When not at your desk, it's your lifeline: You keep lists, jot notes, take calls, and write e-mails.
   d. It's never out of hand, and the ringer is never silenced, but you actually prefer your BlackBerry.

24. BIGGEST INFLUENCES ON YOUR LIFE:
   a. Tom Ford or Yves Saint Laurent
   b. Helmut Newton or Richard Avedon
   c. Anna Wintour or Liz Tilberis
   d. Calvin Klein or Bernard Arnault

25. IF YOU COULD GO BACK AND DO ONE THING DIFFERENTLY, YOU'D HAVE:
   a. Continued with piano lessons
   b. Continued with French lessons
   c. Learned to cook some basic meals
   d. Taken more history and art classes

26. SECTION OF THE SUNDAY PAPER YOU FIRST WANT TO READ:
   a. Arts
   b. Style
   c. News
   d. Business

27. THE BEST DESCRIPTION OF YOUR CLOSET:
   a. This is one area of my life where I cannot bear clutter—I limit myself to one half-empty rack of clothes.
   b. It is endless, and its contents spill out into every inch of my personal space.
   c. Outfits are organized by day, with shoes and extras attached to the hangers.
   d. Current season is front and center; last season is pushed to the back.

28. **CLASS YOU *LEAST* WANTED TO SKIP:**

    a. Home economics

    b. Art

    c. English

    d. Econ

29. **KIND OF CAR YOU PICTURE YOURSELF DRIVING:**

    a. Restored antique Aston Martin or Citroën

    b. Jeep or urban SUV

    c. Mercedes

    d. Porsche

30. **YOUR PREFERRED HIGH SCHOOL EXTRACURRICULAR ACTIVITY WAS:**

    a. Drama or glee club

    b. Yearbook or sports teams

    c. Debate team or school newspaper

    d. Prom committee or student council

31. **SECTION OF A TABLOID PAPER YOU FIRST WANT TO READ:**

    a. Gossip

    b. Horoscopes

    c. "Media Ink"

    d. "Madison Avenue"

32. **ON YOUR BEDSIDE TABLE WHEN YOU GO TO SLEEP AT NIGHT:**

    a. Sketchbook

    b. French *Vogue*

    c. Notepad

    d. *Women's Wear Daily*

33. **RECURRING NIGHTMARE:**

    a. You are drowning in a sea of tulle.

    b. You are frozen speechless in front of a large group of expectant people.

    c. You are walking down a fashion runway nude.

    d. A series of obstacles prevents you from reaching your office or school for a big meeting or exam.

34. **YOUR FANTASY WAY TO SHOP:**

a. You shop at vintage couture auctions, estate sales, and European flea markets.

b. You shop at showrooms and sample sales to acquire unique pieces that were designed but never produced.

c. You preorder ready-to-wear with designer showrooms and then fill in your wardrobe using editorial discounts at Prada, Dior, and Gucci.

d. Your trusted personal shopper identifies ten to twelve current season looks and four current season evening looks with shoes, bags, and accessories.

35. **AFTER YOU'VE LEFT AN EVENT, YOU TEND TO BEST REMEMBER:**

a. The overall mood, colors, fabrics, smells, tastes

b. One amazing or novel thing

c. Names dropped and catchphrases spoken

d. Specific numbers or market trends revealed in conversation

Results: So Where Do I Fit In?

More A answers than anything else means you were born to be a **Creator**—a designer, a creative force, possibly even the Name on the Label. Characteristics of the Creator type:

You are an extrovert.

You are outgoing.

You love life, beauty, and material comforts.

You are needy and seek out constant reaffirmation from others of your talent, work, and abilities.

You can be spontaneous and unpredictable.

You shield yourself from criticism: It could slow your creative process.

You thrive on being the center of attention.

You dislike structure and are frustrated with strict routine in any aspect of your life.

You enjoy being dramatic.

You are extremely verbal and can express yourself in powerful and original ways.

For you, the process of creation is far more motivating than a deadline.

You are a perfectionist.

If you have mostly B answers, you are destined to be a **Visualizer,** bringing the world around you to life in a medium like film, video, photography, or illustration. You will be physically participating yourself as a model or, possibly, acting as an agent, representing models or photographers. Characteristics of a Visualizer:

You are, by nature, introspective.

You tend to be quiet, until you feel comfortable with the people you are with or the situation.

You are hypersensitive to criticism.

You "beat yourself up," anticipating negative comments about your work even as you are in the midst of doing it.

Goals or expectations that are stated too clearly make it hard for you to produce.

You are tolerant of different kinds of people and ways of thinking, and you are flexible to others' ideas when working in a group.

You prefer to work in a "creative" time frame: nine-to-five isn't for you.

You are strongly defined by your values and your cultural or religious identity.

Your EQ (emotional intelligence quotient) may well surpass your IQ.

If you are in your comfort zone, you are a tireless, cheerful, and creative collaborator.

You are extremely loyal to the small group of people that is most important to you.

The idea of making a presentation or speaking in front of a large audience is terrifying.

You possess a subtle sense of humor that not everyone gets, and you look for this trait in others.

You are self-contained, on time, and dependable.

To others, you seem to possess a Zen-like calm.

You like to express your originality in the way you dress—cool but slightly off, broken, surprising, or original.

You love to travel and to experience new landscapes, foreign cities, and their cultures.

You trust that "if you do what you love, you'll love what you do," more than five-year plans and long-term "objectives."

You trust individuals, not companies.

You loathe conflict and disagreements, preferring to talk things out calmly.

If you have mostly C answers, you would fit nicely in the editorial world in a function that would allow you to play the **Critic,** commenting on the world around you and educating others about it. Blogging or teaching would be another avenue to explore, as you like to be an authority and enjoy the challenge of filtering events and personalities in an original way. Characteristics of a Critic:

You are direct and frank.

You love learning, researching, and synthesizing information and then communicating what you've learned to others in new and creative ways.

Conflict and competition motivate you.

You are highly verbal and are clear and forceful in presenting ideas.

You *connect the dots* and are able to see larger social or cultural trends from individual pieces of disparate information.

You feel that you were born to lead.

You like to be the boss, to see your name in print or on the door.

You are judgmental and critical, in the sense that you enjoy dissecting the merits of an object, opinion, or runway creation.

You like order, and you sort ideas and objects to obtain a clear order.

You thrive in structure, routine.

You absorb tremendous amounts of information quickly; you are able to take in and later verbalize countless details after just a glance at a person or a picture.

You take pleasure in long-term planning and goal setting.

You love to read and always want to know what others are reading.

You like to be in the know culturally.

More D answers than anything else means that you have the fierce and irrepressible qualities of a **Seller.** This is a vast category that encompasses working at a retail store, selling advertising at a magazine, working on the client side at an ad agency, and merchandising and/or selling a fashion line from the designer. Characteristics of a Seller:

You are good with money—how to spend it and how to make it; you get commerce; you get other people.

You are an extrovert: You'd much rather be social and with other people than home alone pondering the problems of the universe.

You were born with thick skin and don't easily get discouraged by rejection or refusal. Sometimes you actually feel more motivated to get what you want after someone tells you no.

You are realistic.

You are driven.

You are a rational thinker.

You are motivated more by money than ideas.

You value efficiency.

You are practical and matter-of-fact about life.

You are decisive and move quickly to implement decisions.

You are able to organize people and projects in order to get things done.

You don't dwell on mistakes or embarrassments.

You are open and responsive to criticism and see it as a catalyst for personal and professional growth.

You are ambitious.

You like deadlines and meet them *no matter what,* often working backward from a drop-dead date to map out your strategy to complete the project.

You like to look sleek, spotless, and well manicured.

You work out obsessively.

You trust institutions and like being associated with a respected company.

You work best with clearly stated goals and objectives.

You could easily put work ahead of all other elements in your life—family, friends, and homelife.

Mixed Results?

The fashion world is, by definition, extroverted, and extroverts dominate Creators, Critics, and Sellers.

Visualizers stand alone in that they make up the only introverted group. If you have a majority of B responses (ten or more), you are a clear-cut B—don't make yourself miserable trying to convert yourself into a social butterfly. Nevertheless, you should strive to develop your extroverted side to succeed in the fashion business and be a balanced person in general. (The impossible question for me to answer is this: Am I naturally friendly, or have I taught myself to be social in order to be effective at what I want to do?)

A and C personalities adore being the center of attention—the critical difference is that A's function is to create in a three-dimensional world of forms, patterns, and fabrics for three-dimensional customers while C's function is to communicate and celebrate the work and creations of others. The message for both is to find time and ways to explore the inward-thinking side of your personality

C's and D's are both driven and highly disciplined, which serve them well in the business of fashion.

Unlike A's, B's, and C's, D's alone possess the divine ability not to take things personally. D's have removed their egos from the process. If you are clearly a D, you'll never be an A. But a smart A could partner with you.

Potentially Powerful Combos
When A + C = ME

If you find yourself with nearly equal numbers of A and C answers, you have all the makings of a leader, a communicator, and a creative force in popular culture. Your challenge is to explore in yourself whether you prefer physical expression of yourself via the creation of clothes or bags, or verbal or visual communication of your vision in print or online via words and pictures. Examples of designers who write include Isaac Mizrahi and Josh Patner; editors who design are rare, but include Glenda Bailey, whose early dream was to design her own collection and have it produced in Italy. Either way, the world is your oyster.

When A + D = ME

If you have an equal number of A and D answers, you possess the dual abilities to create and to sell, which will help you no matter which direction you choose. If your heart is really in design, start there. Luckily, you can always fall back on your business smarts down the road. Master designer/marketers like Calvin Klein and Ralph Lauren evidence equally developed A and D sides of their brains.

When C + D = ME

If you have an equal number of C and D responses, you have both the intellect and mental flexibility of an editor and the buttoned-up smarts of a money person. As with the previous combination, it is best to focus your energies on the area you love the most, without thinking about your salary. If you are a great editor, you'll be paid a great editor's salary. If you start as an editor and then move to the business side, you'll understand the process more thoroughly than most anyone else. But beware: There are very few examples in this world of a person who started as a D and then was able to switch to a C. First jobs *do* matter.

Quirky, Rarer Combos
When A + B = ME

You are truly an artist and an introvert and capable of great genius. But since you won't want to live your life in public, resentfully under a media microscope, you might consider designing for a label that's not your own or not your own name. Or consider being a photographer who travels between the worlds of art and fashion.

When B+ C = ME

These two qualities work very nicely together and could actually describe a lot of the most talented stylists (or fashion editors) I know at magazines. They are introverted and visually oriented, but they love the structure and prestige of a magazine. Similarly, photographers who develop a regular gig with a publication can play both sides of their personalities—relaxed and creative in the studio and more professional and formal in business dealings and relationships.

When B + D = ME

This is a most unlikely pairing of traits. Living in a big-league business world would prove tough for an introverted artist like you. Yet you may not find true success or satisfaction on the visual side of fashion either. Your best path may be on the business side of visuals—that is, as a photographer's studio manager or agent, or as a model agency booker or scout, running a retouching business for photographers, for example, or staging runway shows. Explore internships and classes in both fields and see where your interests and talent take you.

Note: If you want to explore career typing beyond the fashionista survey, go to www.myersbriggs.org.

FASHIONISTA BOOT CAMP

In this section is the scoop you need to drive your career forward. From these few short pages, you will get far better information about the degree or degrees you need to earn to go where you want to go in fashion than you would get from your guidance counselor, well-meaning granny, and know-it-all top fashionista frenemy. (No need to be cocky, but you *will*.)

It's natural that people who care about you want you to do the *safe* thing for your future. School types feel safer recommending that people *stay in school*. School is *what they know*. Parents and grandmothers think *more school* means *more money* and security for your future. But (here's the sentence to highlight for them), *it doesn't necessarily work like that in fashion*. To be a designer or photographer, you need to be in the *right* design or photography schools. To be a model, hair stylist, or makeup artist, you probably shouldn't be in school at all: The world is your education! To be a fashion writer or store buyer? College is your ticket. So . . . think about what you *really* want to do, and read on, to find out how long you should stay enlisted in school to get there.

The Education of a Fashionista: Degrees You Need

High School

Probably the coolest thing about fashion is that there are so many ways to play in this world where degrees or education (or lack thereof) make not a whit of difference. With the right apprenticeship or on-the-job training, you can learn to be a studio fashion photographer, or a runway photographer. Attach yourself to a great makeup artist or hair stylist, and your career has begun. The same is true for styling personalities. Your credentials are in your hands. Literally. (See the Visualizer section.) Success in this realm is typically in an inverse relationship to formal education.

Similarly, working in retail sales or at a fashion label's showroom doesn't require a college degree. That might eventually be considered if you move up the ranks into management, but, by then, your performance would be the more weighted consideration. (See the Seller section.)

Beyond these areas, there are lots of top fashionistas, including *Vogue* editor in chief Anna Wintour, for example, who never finished college. Ironically perhaps, for her own staff, she hires only young people who have a college degree, typically from the most prestigious schools in the United States and the United Kingdom.

College

A bachelor of arts (BA) degree with almost any major (art history, political science, English lit, French) is sufficient for an entry-level position in magazines, fashion companies, TV program and advertising studios and producers, and ad agencies in either editorial or sales. For graphic design, you'll need additional training in graphic arts and understanding of key design software.

"Status" colleges feed top fashion magazines. But the work is anything but privileged: In an unspoken apprenticeship system, you are lucky to find a job as a low-paying slave as an editor's assistant, for example, and lucky to work your tail off until the day two years later that you're named assistant editor. The two words are the same—but the order is everything. (See the Critic section.)

A bachelor of fine arts (BFA) degree is another way in, most likely into the art or photo department or, possibly, fashion. Top "design" schools, like Parsons or Central Saint Martins, feed the top design houses, LVMH, Chanel, and so on. (See the Creator section.)

Entering the executive training program of a major retailer such as Macy's, Bloomingdale's, Nordstrom, or Saks Fifth Avenue requires a college degree, preferably in business, economics, or something useful sounding. (See the Seller section.)

FASHIONISTA EDUCATION	HS DEGREE	SOME COLLEGE/ SPECIAL TRAINING	COLLEGE BA/BS/BFA	MBA	MS JOURNALISM
Retail Sales Associate	icing				
Store Manager	icing	icing	icing		
Showroom Sales	icing				
Stylist		icing	icing		
Fashion Photographer		icing			
Studio Makeup Artist		icing			
Studio Hair Stylist		icing			
Pattern Maker	icing	essential	icing		
Illustrator		icing	essential		
Fashion Production		icing			
Designer		icing	essential	icing	
Fashion PR			icing		
Fashion Advertising			icing	icing	
Fashion Editor			essential		icing
Internet Fashion Editor		essential	icing		
Art Director		essential	icing		
Graphic Designer		icing			
Production		icing			
Editor in chief			icing		
Ad Sales Exec			essential		
Publisher			essential	icing	
Retail Buyer			essential		
DMM			essential	icing	
GMM			essential		
Retail Fashion Director	icing		essential		
Corporate Officer			icing	essential	
Company President/CEO			icing	essential	
Fashion Entrepreneur		essential	essential		

☐ = expected   ▨ = icing on the cake   ▩ = essential degree to get in the door

Journalism School

I have a bias against undergraduate journalism degrees. I have never found that this trade school–like training prepares you for anything that happens in the Real World, and meanwhile you've managed to avoid reading basic literature, you don't know history, and, thus, you are basically ignorant. If you are especially focused or keen as an undergraduate, keep your hands in journalism through the school newspaper or blogging.

Personally, I was so clueless about getting a job after earning my expensive liberal arts degree that I decided to delay the inevitable by getting a graduate journalism degree. In doing so (and I cannot take credit for understanding this beforehand), I managed to leap-frog past the assistant world of magazines and start my career as a writer/reporter at a small trade publication. This training was key to my magazine mojo. It gave me my reporter's nose and balls to get the story, plus the research skills to back it all up. My confidence that I can always inhabit my profession is empowering: Drop me in Anytown, U.S.A., any day, and I can get a job.

BEST-BET J SCHOOLS

New York University (in New York City, undergraduate or master of science program)

Columbia School of Journalism (New York City, only graduate work, after work in the field)

University of California, Berkeley, School of Journalism (Berkeley, California)

Kent State University

State University of New York, Syracuse (Newhouse School of Journalism)

Washington University, School of Journalism (St. Louis)

When hiring, I (as does, apparently, Laurie Jones at *Vogue*) harbor a bias for those with an Ivy League edge, but many bosses have a prejudice *against* those lofty institutions because those bosses say that those schools produce young graduates who are too cerebral, polished, and privileged to jump in blindly and do the dirty work. It's a question of one's own background, I suppose. Find out as much as you can about an interviewer—schooling, hometown, other jobs, and those most recently hired—more as a filter to the interview than as an opportunity to repackage yourself.

Fashion School

If you know you want to be a designer and cannot imagine anything else for yourself, go to fashion school. Best bets are Parsons or the State University of New York's Fashion Institute of Technology (See the Creator section), both in New York City, or Central Saint Martins in London. If, on the other hand, you have diverse interests and are academically able to do so, attending a four-year liberal arts college *before going to fashion school* (either in BFA or MFA programs, depending on your skill set) would give you a stronger foundation and a lifetime of references upon which to base your designs. Indeed, admissions officers at both Parsons and Central Saint Martins have noted an increase in graduates from schools like Vassar and Brown entering their core fashion design BFA programs.

Advanced Degrees

Earning an MBA or, as in my case, an MS in journalism doesn't buy you much in fashionista land. Large fashion conglomerates (LVMH or Jones New York) or large retail organizations (Nordstrom, Neiman Marcus) may find a business degree helpful in analyzing data or working on mergers and acquisitions. Smaller designer brands do things in such quirky individualistic ways that an MBA might go bonkers with the lack of process.

A master's in journalism says that a candidate is serious and that he or she better understands the rules of journalism than a kid just out of college. In my case, it just meant that I loved being a student and that I was terrified to get out in the real world and earn money. Clearly, I had no clue how much fun it would be. Beauty school might get you the license you need to work in a salon, but it's not necessary for runway and studio hair stylists.

Homeschooling

Instead of whiling away your underage exile on the couch *dreaming* about the fashion world, *learn* about it instead. References from the past are a constant source of inspiration for every type of fashionista, designers, stylists, journalists, and retailers. Research, read, form a bond with an icon who inspires you.

Players

The following is a list of key fashion personalities, past and present. It's not exhaustive (you'd need an encyclopedia), but it's a start. You should be able to pronounce and spell these names as well as understand their unique contribution to fashion. You'll definitely grow from their experiences and examples.

Adrian

Azzedine Alaia (A-lie-uh)

Giorgio Armani

Kevyn Aucoin

Richard Avedon

David Bailey

Glenda Bailey

Cristóbal Balenciaga

Fabien Baron

Cecil Beaton

Geoffrey Beene

Manolo Blahnik
(BLAH-nick)

Bill Blass

Isabella Blow

Hamish Bowles

Alexey Brodovitch

Bobbi Brown

Naomi Campbell

Pierre Cardin

Mary Randolph Carter

Paul Cavaco

Coco Chanel

Jimmy Choo

Grace Coddington

André Courrèges

Bill Cunningham

Carrie Donovan

John Duka

Hubert de Givenchy
(Jee-von-she)

Loulou de la Falaise

Inès de la Fressange

Oscar de la Renta

Patrick Demarchelier

Christian Dior

Stefano Dolce and
Domenico Gabbana
(Dolce & Gabbana)

Carrie Donovan

Simon Doonan

Alber Elbaz

Arthur Elgort

Perry Ellis

Fendi Sisters

Salvatore Ferragamo

Patricia Field

Tom Ford

John Galliano

Garren

Jean-Paul Gaultier
(Go-Tee-A)

Nicolas Ghesquière
(JESS-Key-Air)

Madame Grès

Tonne Goodman

Guccio Gucci

Jerry Hall

Edith Head

Halston

Hiro

Cathy Horyn

Lauren Hutton

Iman

Marc Jacobs

Norma Kamali

Donna Karan (Care-on)

Rei Kawakubo

Kezia Keeble

Calvin Klein

Elsa Klensch

Michael Kors

Christian Lacroix

Karl Lagerfeld

Helmut Lang

Jeanne Lanvin
  (LON-van)

Ralph Lauren
  (LAW-ren)

Christian Louboutin

Alex Liberman

Phillip Lim

Claire McCardell

Alexander McQueen

Stella McCartney

Jack McCollough &
  Lazaro Hernandez
  (Proenza Schouler)

Craig McDean

Pat McGrath

Tomas Maier

Didier Malige

Martin Margiela

Raymond Meier

Steven Meisel

Polly Mellen

Suzy Menkes

Grace Mirabella

Isaac Mizrahi

Issey Miyake

Kate Moss

Helmut Newton

Camilla Nickerson

Norman Norell

Dick Page

Irving Penn

Phoebe Philo

Stefano Pilati

Orlando Pita

Paul Poiret

Zac Posen

Miuccia Prada
  (Me-ooo-cha)

Emilio Pucci

Mary Quant

Paco Rabanne

Narciso Rodriguez
  (Nar-sis-o)

Carine Roitfeld

Yves Saint Laurent

Jil Sander

Elissa Santisi

Elsa Schiaparelli
  (Sha-per-elle-ee)

Jeremy Scott

L'Wren Scott (La-REN)

Eugenia Sheppard

David Sims

Ingrid Sischy

Hedi Slimane

Paul Smith

Carmel Snow

Carla Sozzani

Franca Sozzani

Amy Spindler

Stephen Sprouse

Anna Sui

Juergen Teller

Mario Testino

Olivier Theyskens

Liz Tilberis

Isabel Toledo

Ruben Toledo

Philip Treacy

André Leon Talley

Stella Tennant

Twiggy

Emanuel Ungaro
  (UNG-arrow)

Dries Van Noten

Valentino

Donatella Versace
  (Vair-sah-chee)

Gianni Versace

Roger Vivier

Matthew Williamson

Diane von Furstenberg

Diana Vreeland

Alexander Wang

Melanie Ward

Bruce Weber

Linda Wells

Vivienne Westwood

Anna Wintour

Charles Worth

Jason Wu

Yohji Yamamoto

Zoran

MUST-READ BIOGRAPHIES

D.V. by Diana Vreeland

Front Row: Anna Wintour: The Cool Life and Hot Times of Vogue's Editor in Chief by Jerry Oppenheimer

Chanel and Her World by Edmonde Charles-Roux

No Time to Die by Liz Tilberis

A Dash of Daring: Carmel Snow and Her Life in Fashion by Penelope Rowlands

FASHIONISTA FICTION

Bergdorf Blondes by Plum Sykes

The Devil Wears Prada by Lauren Weisberger

Little Pink Slips by Sally Koslow

MUST-READ NEWS DAILIES

Women's Wear Daily

New York Times Style section

Gossip and "Media Ink" pages from the *New York Post* and MediaBistro.com

MUST-READ GOSSIP DAILIES

MediaBistro.com

New York Post

WWD Memo Pad

WEEKLIES THAT'LL MAKE YOU SMARTER

New Yorker (or at least the twice-yearly fashion issues)

Statistics page from *Harper'*s monthly (genius—this is all about editing, packing in great knowledge in small spaces.)

T Magazine: The New York Times Style Magazine

ESSENTIAL MONTHLIES

Vanity Fair

W Magazine

American, British, French *Vogue*

FLIP-THROUGH WEEKLIES

People

US Magazine

OFTEN-REFERENCED FILMS TO NETFLIX

The Blue Angel

Citizen Kane (especially if you work for Hearst)

Metropolis

Nanook of the North

The Ice Storm

8½ by Fellini

Eight Miles High (about 1970s German supermodel Uschi Obermaier)

Pillow Talk

The Birds, Psycho, North by Northwest, Vertigo, Rear Window (all by
   Hitchcock)

Belle de Jour

Office Killer (Cindy Sherman's 1997 horror film about the actions of a
   disgruntled former copy editor at *Constant Consumer* magazine)

Out of Africa (a Ralph Lauren fantasy)

Pretty Face

Swept Away

The Getaway (Ali MacGraw and Steve McQueen, very Michael Kors)

The Great Gatsby (especially if you work for Ralph)

Factory Girl

Prêt-à-Porter (Robert Altman send-up of 1994 Paris season)

Sabrina

FASHIONISTA DOCUMENTARIES

Grey Gardens (the Maysles brothers' 1976 original)

Unzipped (Douglas Keeve turns the camera on Isaac Mizrahi at the peak
   of his stardom.)

Valentino: The Last Emperor (Matthew Tyrnauer)

The September Issue (R. J. Cutler tracks Anna Wintour as she and her team
   build the biggest *Vogue* of the year.)

FASHIONISTA TELEVISION

It's always important to have one tacky TV show to which you're addicted. This
helps you fit in, allows for funny asides, and keeps you real. It was once *Ab-Fab,*
then, *Friends, Sex and the City, Project Runway* (first three seasons), *Ugly
Betty, Mad Men.* Stay tuned because there's sure to be something new soon.

Getting Your Manolo (Flip-Flop?) in the Door

Whether you are still in high school or midcareer in finance and looking to make a switch, the following information should set you up. (If too first-step for you, go directly to your career focus category: see page 68 for the Creator; page 118 for the Visualizer, page 172 for the Critic; or page 220 for the Seller.)

How to Get Your First Fashionista Internship

- Schedule appointments with your current teachers and past teachers (don't start this process in the last week of school), and take notes at these meetings. Be serious about getting their suggestions, and keep them in the loop if you explore the contacts they share with you.
- Visit your school's career or internship office frequently. Develop relationships with these people. Don't be shy—your tuition helps pay their salaries.
- Keep in touch with friends who have graduated and now work in fashion. They may need help where they work, and they will have already established a network in the business.
- Use your personal networks. Ask members of your family and friends of your parents whether they know anyone who works in fashion. Call all the contacts you have—your mother's childhood friend, your boyfriend's step-uncle—because a personal connection is always the best way in.
- Look online for internships (see "Online Fashionista").
- When you've run out of the above options, don't be afraid to cold-call.

Online Fashionista

Fashionistas would be smart to avoid generalist job search engines like Monster.com and loosey-goosey ones like craigslist.com. It's best to launch your searches with fashion-focused career sites like *Women's Wear Daily*'s wwd.com/wwd careers or fashion.net, or the site that is the most specific to your field that you can find. And don't disregard the obvious: Posting your portfolio on your school's website (most institutions invite graduates to continue to do so regardless of when they've graduated) can produce surprising big-time results.

MediaBistro.com. This is the hands-down best source, especially for non-first-job-level positions.

Ed2010.com. Great for REAL internship listings and entry-level assistant jobs. If you can get past the "let's havvanother beer" sense of camaraderie. Look for the cheat sheet on e-mailing almost anyone in the business.

Condenastcareers.com. The company's website warns that the Condé Nast Publications summer intern program is (hello) highly competitive. It is designed for rising college juniors or seniors who have a demonstrated interest in media and publishing and are available to work for the entirety of the program (June and July) working alongside professionals in editorial, advertising, and online or corporate departments. Résumé, cover letter explaining why you are seeking an internship at Condé Nast Publications, and professional or scholarly letter of recommendation. Deadline for internship applications is March 1.

INTERVIEW NOTES	INTERN	FULL-TIME
Length of interview	20 minutes	30 minutes to 1 hour
Number of people you meet	1 to 2	1 to 4
Number of times you come to the office (before being hired or not)	Once	2 to 3 times
Don't	Be late; make excuses; change your shoes in the lobby	Mention other companies where you'd rather work
Portfolio factor	Important that you have something to show—sketches, clips, blog, web design, etc.	Critical that you have a brilliant portfolio—it's how your eye and abilities will be judged
How long before you'll hear if you got the job	Within 1 week	From 2 weeks to 2 months or longer

INTERVIEW NOTES	INTERN	FULL-TIME
Interview assignment	None	Critique four issues of a publication. Write ten headlines. Sketch and think through a small collection for the current season
Who you'll meet	Design assistant, plus possibly a more senior buyer, designer, or editor	Buyer, editor, head designer, assistant designers, production head, business manager, owner
What to wear	Current season; good shoes	Current or next season, something of your own design; new shoes
Questions to ask	"With whom will I be spending most of my time?" "How can I be of the most help to the team?"	"What's working really well currently?" "What's working less well?" "Is the brand or publication looking to change direction?"
Questions NOT to ask	"Do I get my own computer?" "When can I take vacation?"	"Whom am I replacing?" (That person may still be working there.)
Good sign	If they ask when you can start; if you meet the interviewer's boss	If you're asked to do an assignment and told that they like it; if you meet the owner
Bad sign	If the person you're supposed to meet isn't around; if interview is over before it starts	If you're not asked to do an assignment; If the interviewer stops looking halfway through your portfolio
Follow-up	Short handwritten thank-you notes to everyone you meet mailed within 24 hours	Typed or handwritten note to key person(s) attached to beautifully executed interview assignment
Best possible outcome	That you adopt your boss as a mentor; that you develop lots of friends and contacts; that you eventually land a job here and love it	That you get the job, love it, and make your indelible mark on the publication or brand; that the company offers to launch your own

The Real Deal: How to Get Your First Fashionista Job

Seven Sacred Rules of the Search

1. Know who you know. When I moved to New York City from Stevens Point, Wisconsin, my mother knew only one person in the city. Well, actually, she knew the mother of one person, who happened to work in magazines. My mother wrote her acquaintance on her tasteful Crane stationery, and within a week, I was seated in front of Miss Jean Pascoe, senior editor of *Woman's Day* magazine, at the time a six million newsstand circulation powerhouse owned by CBS. Miss Pascoe worked for the glamorous and high-profile Ellen Levine.

Your contacts are usually more impressive than you realize. Use the people you know to find an in into the business you're craving to enter: friends, family, former classmates, classmates' parents, friends of friends, and alumni organizations. Former teachers or professors can be valuable sources. Don't be too proud, jerky, or snobbish to ask. One professor with a friend willing to speak with you is worth ten thousand blind letters to HR offices.

Chat with everyone to find out if anyone knows of anything. Ultimately any personal contact, however distant, is going to work better than responding to job postings in a trade journal, general HR department requests for résumés, or a craigslist entry.

If you worked as an intern, send frequent quick e-mails to assistants you cultivated as contacts to see if they know of any openings. When a new assistant needs to be hired, the first thing a smart editor does is to ask the top assistants for recommendations.

2. Your résumé and cover letter must be compelling and honest, clear, elegant, and mistake free, while managing to put you in the best possible light. Both résumés and cover letters are expected, and routinely ignored. Regardless, you must put thought and care into these two documents to ensure that they are polished, mistake free, and compelling. Tweak them for every potential job.

Do you print your name in Day-Glo orange? Maybe, if that says who you are. Or frame your name in a box? Why not, if it's well done. Or add a design element that stands out and helps interviewers remember who you are. Sticking to the formula in every other way is essential. See Résumé Creativity box.

Your résumé and cover letter must be easy to read and nicely structured. Nix the paragraph about what you did on your year abroad in Florence (everyone knows you did very little that had anything to do with academics) or your hardship summer in Costa Rica (everyone also knows it's a privilege to go on the same hut-building expedition Prince William did over his gap year). Work hard to make it look like you know how to work hard.

Don't mention that you prefer to work on a Mac. (Spoiled.) Or that you are willing to move to New York City. (Deal with that like an adult if you get the job!) Make finding you easy: e-mail and cell phone. Check your e-mail daily, and change your voice mail message to something normal. No heavy metal. No bitchy innuendo. No naughty sounds.

3. No little white, red, or blue lies. It's a huge, thorny issue plaguing résumés. Rounding up your grade-point average from 2.8 to 3.2 is a lie. Expanding the dates that you interned at the David Letterman show from one summer to one year would qualify as a total fib. Some experts blame e-mail for the rampant cheating in résumés, saying that the impersonal nature of cyberspace entices otherwise honest people to take liberties with the "facts." Some blame increased competition for cool jobs. You wouldn't be alone if you fudged the facts: You'd be part of a giant cheating epidemic that seems to have grown like mold on the job market. Don't do it.

In 2005, the Rutgers University Career Services office did an audit of résumés, and the audit revealed that 20 percent of students submitting résumés had inflated their grade-point averages. Résumé Doctor, a Vermont firm that helps people write their résumés, randomly pulled one thousand documents from its website to check them for easily identifiable facts like education, job titles, dates of employment. The results? 42.7 percent of them had significant inaccuracies.

The bottom line? Lying is the fastest way to sabotage your job search because the fashionista world is small and incredibly inbred. Chances are, there is a staff link back to almost anywhere you may have worked. That person will be asked about you and her voice will help determine how you are viewed. This is the great leveling force of creative businesses. Even former interns have the power to ding or cement the deal for a much more senior person. If you are panicked about a less-than-stellar GPA, don't list it. Most interviewers don't care that much to

RÉSUMÉ CREATIVITY: HOW FAR CAN YOU GO?

- You must make your résumé one page in length. NEVER under any circumstance, *no matter how fabulous you are,* let it creep onto a second page.
- It should be easy to read. Don't oververbalize to justify what you were doing in Bucharest on your junior year abroad. White space is not a bad thing.
- You must adhere to the conventional format: name on top, then, depending on which is more impressive at this point in your life, an education section, then experience section, brief personal data at the end. When in doubt, stick to a conventional format.
- Where you can, add subtle touches of personality.

    1. Use an interesting typeface for your name (say, Bodoni) and a highly readable conventional typeface for the body of the document, like Ariel or Times New Roman.
    2. Print your name in a color that expresses who you are—Day-Glo orange if you're a hipster, apple green if you're a prepster, navy blue or chocolate brown if you are understated and chic.
    3. Find an icon that represents you. A feather. A dolphin. A turtle. A swan. A falcon. A crab. A moon. A shell. Nothing daft or immature like a smiley face or daisy. A shoe, bag, lipstick tube, or dress form could be cute. Use the icon at the top of the résumé just to the left or right of your name. Postage-stamp size is good—don't make it so huge that it overpowers the page and don't make a big deal of it. This could be a good conversation piece, so be prepared to discuss what it is, how you got it (legally, but free), and what it says about you. "I swam with and attempted to learn the language of dolphins during a semester at sea." "I always loved the Aesop fable of the hare and the turtle. In life, I'm the turtle, deliberate and steady, and I always get the job done." Use the same icon on stationery or e-mails to consistently telegraph your personality.

Leave plenty of time for proofreading and tinkering with these documents. By this, I mean days, even weeks. Ask your mother, friend, grandmother, boyfriend, sister, *someone* to read whatever you send out very carefully. When you are working closely on a document, you stop seeing the mistakes.

RIGHT TIME, RIGHT PLACE: TEMPING AND VOLUNTEERING YOURSELF INTO A JOB

During my first week as editor in chief of *YM,* I caught a glimpse of a cute young girl with great style—a relief to my eye since I'd found few staffers who seemed to have a natural connection with the reader. I introduced myself and asked her if she was "in fashion," that is, if she worked as an assistant in the fashion department. A tad confused, Nicole Fasolino explained that she was a corporate temp for the summer. She'd just graduated from college and was planning to move out west in the fall to live the life of a ski bum for a year or so. But I had other plans for Nicole, and, I'm happy to report, she's been a successful magazine fashionista ever since. Lucy Wallace Eustice, a high school dropout shop girl at age fifteen first at Agnès B. then at Manolo Blahnik, also temped her way into publishing. "I joined a temp agency thinking I'd go back to school at night. My first assignment was at *Mirabella* magazine. I walk in and they take a look at me, and they set me up answering phones at the front desk." Before long, Lucy was drafted into the fashion department; then she slid into her real calling, the accessories department. After increasingly senior assignments at *Harper's Bazaar* and *Elle,* Lucy left to found an accessories company, M Z Wallace, with her partner Monica Zwirner.

Then, there's working for free. Atoosa Rubenstein was so set on a magazine career that once she started interning at *Sassy* magazine, she never left. The thinking is that if you show up and make yourself super-useful, you'll soon be indispensable.

ask because they know that good grades don't necessarily translate into good employees. In all résumé-related items, you can hedge and you can delete. Whatever you do, just *don't lie.*

4. *Go through the front door, and the back.* That means following the rules—sending your nice, neat, honest résumé to HR departments—*and* writing, calling, e-mailing everyone you know or have connections with inside the business. Be thorough. Keep records of whom you've written to and when and whom you've called and when.

5. *Be part of the community you're trying to join.* Don't call it an "informational interview," but that's what it is. *Show your face.* Get a feel for the vibe of an office. Write down every name of every person you meet and follow up.

If you are in Boston and all magazine and TV internships are in New York, do some groundwork, then go to New York. Showing up will separate you from 80 percent of the other candidates. Volunteer at the tents for Seventh on Sixth fashion shows (early September and early February each year). Dress models, meet people backstage.

Offer yourself up for free as an intern. If there's a designer you're crazy about, write to him or her. Put yourself in the milieu.

6. *Believe in providence and magic, and be on the lookout for the infinite collaborations of the universe.* Look for doors that open to you. Believe that everything can change in twenty-four hours. The magical and mysterious *do* happen. Look for your moment, then grab it and run with it!

7. *Find your fairy godmother and/or godfather.* There's this sweet story of a young male design student in the back of the plane, flying from Miami to New York City. He saw Anna Wintour boarding the plane, and he sensed correctly that she is not the kind of person who cozies up easily with strangers. During the flight, he wrote her a letter, explaining his passion for fashion and his particular admiration for Michael Kors. This was pre-9/11 and pre-heightened airline security so the young man was able to walk from his back-of-the-plane seat in economy up to the first-class cabin in the front of the plane during the flight, slipping the

JOB SEARCH DON'TS

- *Don't put yourself on the wrong side of the business.* You might be able to go from design to sales. But NOT the reverse. You will be setting yourself up for disappointment if you go into advertising, sales, or public relations at a big company thinking that you will be able to jump to design later. Better to start where you want to start at a nothing company and learn some useful skills.
- *Don't think you can outsmart the system by presenting yourself with one set of qualifications and aspirations to one potential employer and then rolling out another entirely different set of qualifications and aspirations to someone else.* That's naïve. And confusing. Be true to yourself. And consistent about what you want and your story. The world is too small to spin different versions of your own reality. Trust me: Even if you don't realize you're getting caught, you will be.

note into Wintour's bag, again politely choosing not to disturb her as she was at this point resting or pretending to be resting behind large sunglasses. Wintour made no contact with the young man, nor did she acknowledge she'd received the note. Nonetheless she must have been struck by his words. In her anonymous fairy godmother way that few give her credit for, she gave the note to Kors, and the young man was called in for a job. The fairy godmother thing? I never would have believed how far it could take me. Liz Tilberis, who was once my fairy godmother/boss/friend, is now my angel.

Fashionista Frontline: The Interview—Ten Things to Do in Ten Minutes or Less

Congratulations! You landed an interview. Now what? First find out from the assistant of the person you're meeting if there *is* an actual job opening and, if so, everything you can find out about that job. Don't be deflated if it's called an "informational" interview: They wouldn't be seeing you if they weren't interested, and staffing needs, especially at the entry level, change all the time. Here I've distilled the advice of dozens of high-powered friends in TV, magazines, retail, fashion houses, and agencies to guide you through this process. Together with my own experience, it's your blueprint for what you need to achieve during the loaded six hundred seconds that you sit in the interview chair.

1. Show a Spark, a Passion

This is the ephemeral, energetic quality that you need to find a way to project. It comes from a fascination with a place or a business. A dash of sheer fear, perhaps. It's a twinkle in the eye. A positive energy. A palatable sense that you want to be here—a childhood dream about to come true!

Many bosses are actually looking for a younger version of themselves—before they became so fabulously successful and jaded. Spark cannot be faked.

Note: You want your eyes to sparkle so if you wear contacts or suffer from dry eyes, be sure to put drops in your eyes just before the interview. Projecting an attitude of "why did I agree to this loser interview anyway?" will get you back out on the street in your fab new shoes faster than you can say "world weary."

2. Demonstrate a Sense of Humor

Displaying humor needs to occur opportunistically. It could be a simple play on words. If your last name is Caddish, for example, you might say, grinning, "Yes, it rhymes with *raddish*," as the interviewer struggles with the pronunciation. The high point of my interview with Rebecca Onion (yes, her real name) was her funny way of explaining how she dealt with her surname. That sparkling moment won her the job.

Humor in the interview situation shows that you don't take yourself too seriously. If the interviewer mentions that you're from Wisconsin, as I am, you might say that you left your cheese-head at the door. It could be expressed in light sarcasm. "Yes, I'm from Fargo, North Dakota. I spent my first eighteen years trying to get out." Humor should occupy only a millisecond of the interview. Like a dash of smoked paprika on the perfect deviled egg. Under no circumstances should you be glib about getting the job or boastful about how great you are. That's not humor; it's arrogance.

3. Give Evidence of Your Hunger and Ambition

This will come across in how you present your qualifications for the job. Frame your résumé in terms of preparing yourself for the job you're interviewing for. Give examples of how you've overcome obstacles in your life. Sick as a child? Stuck in bed looking at art books for your entire seventh year? Always good material. The influence of a great-aunt photographer, designer, or nun.

4. Be Convincing That You Will Work Hard

Drop in the conversation that you're no prima donna. Then back this up with specific examples of long hours and hard work even if it was community service in Colombia when you were a college sophomore. Convey that while the job sounds glamorous from the outside, you understand that there's lots of organizational, clerical, and administrative donkeywork that supports the real mission of the place. That you'd feel privileged to play a supporting role so that you know what goes into making a magazine (a collection, the season's numbers, an ad, or a TV show). That you understand the notion of an apprenticeship to learn the ropes.

Detail what you learned performing community service. How, for example, you managed to collect unused computers from businesses in your home town, then how you convinced a service to refurbish them gratis so that you could give them to schoolchildren whose families couldn't afford them. Talk about the obstacles and how you overcame them. How you cut red tape and developed follow-through skills.

5. Prove That You Know Your Stuff

While your background understanding of the business may never be directly displayed, it'll be obvious in how you articulate your responses to questions. Check online. Read everything posted about the business and the top boss during the past year. This is called *research*.

Sometimes, the most daunting thing about an interview situation is that there is an entirely new language and customs. It's as if you've crossed the frontier to a foreign land. Sure, the new tongue and the energetic bustle can be disorienting. But do yourself the favor of orienting yourself as much as possible. Go online and read about the company on its official website. Its owners, sister companies, founders, history, staff, successes, mission, global presence, Web presence. Who would be this company or brand's most natural competition? Read about that company or title, as well. When the interviewer refers to others on staff using their first names, or other properties the company owns, or key brands, you'll know what she's talking about.

6. Show That You Are a Team Player

Simply asking about the team you'd be part of conveys your understanding of the team nature of a workplace. Every creative company wants team players, but it's one of the toughest things to evaluate about a person before bringing someone on board. Team players love to be included in headline and idea meetings, brainstorming and building on others' concepts; they love the spontaneous spurt of ideas that somehow add up to much more than any one's original thought. Loners want to sit at their computers and e-mail in their thoughts. Team players love the energy of a bullpen; loners dream of quitting and working freelance at home with their cats. During my years as an editor in chief, the kiss of death for a new hire was always when I'd call an idea meeting or a cover line meeting and this person would never perk up or engage. She'd drop that she was better sitting in front of her computer alone.

How do you convey that you deserve a spot on the team? If you've ever played team sports, you might mention how your training might translate to an office setting. Don't say that you're a "people" person—a deadly cliché. Say that part of your motivation in seeking the job is to collaborate with "the team." Give an example of satisfying teamwork at an internship or class project.

7. Bring a Visual Aid

No matter what job you are applying for, bring something you've made to ensure that you're the one in one hundred who is remembered and called back for the next stage of interviews. It'll calm you down to talk about something familiar and clearly direct the conversation to you while humanizing you to the interviewer. What you bring can be an idea book, clips, photos, sketches, college newspaper clips, or your journalism school magazine project. Or you can print out a series of your best blogs. Be humble when discussing, but also proud. You are proving that you have the ability to produce.

8. Nail the Pet Question

The pet question usually pops up in the second half of your interview. It'll seem innocuous, but nothing matters more. In my interview to be the beauty editor of *Harper's Bazaar,* Liz Tilberis asked me how well I knew Evelyn Lauder and Calvin Klein. She cared a lot about how connected I was because, being new to the States, she needed someone with built-in ties to the business. Beauty advertising was a big revenue stream—my connection with advertisers was crucial. I made it through the question, but I wasn't well prepared for it. That stung.

Joanna Jordan, head of her own booking agency, Central Talent Booking, asks those she's interviewing who their favorite guests on TV shows are, and why. Then she asks what the dream booking would be for a show they might possibly work on. She's gauging how they'd do the job they're applying for.

People say that Laurie Jones, managing editor of *Vogue,* quizzes potential candidates about their favorite magazines, then zooms in to ask about their favorite writers for that publication, then their favorite works by their favorite authors, then wants to know very specifically why. Her honing strategy probably reveals for her how someone thinks, whether they really *read* magazines or simply *flip* through. The *flippers* don't get in. Even into the fashion department closet.

HOW TO DEVELOP YOUR CRITICAL EYE AND CRITICAL VOICE

You're tuned in to the Super Bowl. Or, you're parked in front of the flat screen for the Oscars. Just your average couch potato night? No. These are the two most-watched televised events in the United States for which the most anticipated, creative, and expensive new advertising has been generated. Either represents a perfect forum in which to develop your own critical eye. Typically, you, in your civilian hang-out role, watch a succession of Budweiser, IBM, Ford, Revlon, and Pepsi commercials while IM'ing friends, listening to music, nursing a beer, downing Doritos. Or most likely, you catch the first one, then mute the set or leave the room to grab more salty snacks.

Next time, try this. Really *watch* the commercials. Listen to the dialog and watch the images. Instead of letting the football game or the red carpet be the main course, it's all about the commercials. And you're the judge. Strap on your groovy-insider goggles, and pretend just for once that the world is standing by waiting to hear what you think!

Consider how the spot works. Is it trying to be funny? Does it succeed? Is it trying to pull your heartstrings? Does that work? Is it comfortably or uncomfortably nostalgic or patriotic or pandering? How long is it? Is that too long or too short? If a celebrity is featured, does that person fit the brand image, help communicate the message? Does he or she flop or, conversely, steal the show? Does the production quality feel cool or conventional? Like a movie? Like a video? Overall, is a strong,

Women's Wear Daily's Pete Born apparently always asks job candidates for writing positions whether they prefer the researching of a story or the writing of it. If the candidate says "research," they don't get the job. Writing, he believes, must be the first passion.

SAMPLE PET QUESTIONS

Where do you want to be in five years?

Why are you the best person for this job?

What has been your biggest disappointment in life, and how did you get past it?

Whom would you put in our next ad (on our next cover, on a company T-shirt)?

Who are your favorite authors? Photographers? Why?

What's the coolest new book (magazine, brand, ad) out there and why?

clear message communicated? Does it make you *like* the brand better? Does it have anything to do with the brand? How long does it take for you to understand which brand is being advertised? Is it generic feeling or fresh? Ultimately the only question that matters is this one:

Does it break through the clutter of your living room, get inside your brain, and make you want to buy it?

That doesn't happen very often, so don't be surprised if your answer is usually "no."

The next day, check online at the *New York Times* and *Adweek* to hear what the "experts" have to say about the commercials. Trust me, your opinion is just as valid as theirs. Probably even more important since you are more closely aligned with the targeted profile than they are. Sad thing is that this exercise may well be more entertaining than the game itself.

When you read the newspaper or look at a magazine, you do so as a consumer. Scan and flip. Scan and flip. In the trash. Chances are, you are gathering information or news interesting or entertaining to you. Sometime when you're not rushing, take the time to read a newspaper or magazine story *critically* from top to bottom. What draws you into the story in the first place? Does the story deliver the promise made in the headline and display copy? Does the story give you what you need to act on the subject in your own life? (Say, a website, phone number, or address for additional information.) Is it helpful? Complete? Do the pictures or illustrations make sense with the words? Look at the lead of the story. Is it compelling? Why or why not? Practice using words like *derivative, original, breakthrough, fresh, generic, flat.*

Why do you want to be in magazines (books, advertising, TV, PR)?

What's the best way to communicate with your generation?

9. Show That You Have a Critical Eye

One of a creative professional's most basic assets is his or her critical eye. This is your ability to separate yourself from the great masses of the consuming public and put yourself in the mindset of creating words, pictures, stories that would interest key segments of the population.

10. Say You Want the Job, and Explain Why You Are the Best Person on the Planet for the Position

At the end of every interview, the interviewer will ask whether you have any questions. I cannot remember anyone ever asking a great question. This is actually code for "your time is up so say something important or get out." If you have not yet made it perfectly clear that you want the job, this is your moment to say that clearly. Even though your brain is probably scrambled eggs at this point, you need to spit out that you are absolutely undaunted by the job's demands and that, in fact, you'd like very much to be considered. Consciously shift your voice to a lower, more confident octave, not a squeaky screech.

Next, make a swift and polite exit. Say something straight on your way out the door like "I'd love to be part of your team" or "I'd love the chance to work with you." Shake hands firmly. Make eye contact. Smile. Stop talking. Breathe. You did it.

Foolproof Interview Looks

Everything about you will be scrutinized—your hair, nails, shoes, bag, picked-over and badly covered up pimples, teeth, and, of course, the most obvious element: your outfit. You need to withstand the scrutiny, leaving nothing to chance and still feeling like yourself. It's so important, and it has taken such a huge amount of planning, that I remember what I wore to every interview of my life. To my Ellen Levine interview, I wore a lemon linen Perry Ellis suit with an orange 7UP T-shirt underneath to prove I wasn't dull, but I missed with boring navy pumps. I wore black platform Prada sandals, a crisp white blouse, narrow black trousers, and a Prada backpack (it was a Prada-meets-Pilgrim moment) to my first Liz Tilberis interview.

Dressing right for the interview is the budding fashionista's opportunity to portray something unique about her- or himself—in a way that isn't pushy or offensive.

For a Guy

A narrow-fitting, single-breasted navy, gray, or black suit with an open-collared shirt or sweater underneath. Loafers, monk strap, or wing tip shoes. Use a roller-tape lint remover before you leave the house or your current job to make sure the shoulders of your jacket are spotless.

Carry a neat, clean backpack (solid dark color) or a postman's-style bag.

Don't wear sneakers or grungy T-shirts with writing or designs on them.

Don't wear jeans, team jerseys, ball caps, flip-flops, sweats, or shorts.

For a Woman

The best and easiest possible look is well-tailored wool trousers (white, black, navy, or gray) with a neat shirt and high boots, sandals, or pumps depending on the season. A snug-fitting jacket worn on top is fine as long as it doesn't match the trousers. Show your creativity in how you layer a thin sweater over a patterned blouse, which is over, say, a shimmery tank top. If it's spring or fall, wear a trench coat on top. If it's winter, wear a fitted knee-length coat. Skirts or dresses make it seem like you're trying too hard. Plus, you'll have the more complicated issues of wearing stockings, or not, and a more frightening exposure of your choice of footwear.

Carry one purse big enough to hold your portfolio, if you have one, plus all your personal necessities—lip gloss, comb, tampons, and so on.

WOMEN'S DON'TS

Don't wear a suit to a creative interview.

Don't wear anything that isn't well pressed.

Don't carry multiple bags or shopping bags.

Don't drape on too much jewelry—no major bling.

Don't wear head-to-toe one obvious designer—you'll be tagged a fashion victim, and your résumé will be in the bin before you're out of the building.

Interview Wardrobe Don'ts

1. Don't dress too casual. What you threw on to make your 9 a.m. art history class is *not* what you should wear to an interview.

2. Do not wear more than one excitement piece. Either carry your most fabulous orange Dior bag *or* your most excellent high-altitude gold Prada sling backs *or* throw on your grandmother's orange A-line Courrèges coat. Gold metallic ballet slippers, white leather and gold metal-trimmed Prada bag and gold mesh Marc Jacobs trench coat: Fashion overload invites ridicule, not job offers.

3. Don't show too much skin. Not wearing stockings is fine in warm weather, but wear opaque tights if it's freezing outside.

4. Avoid showing off piercings. No nose rings, tongue rings, toe rings. Navel rings (see skin warning, above). Just take them out for the day. Or, better yet, forever!

5. Never chew gum. Even if you think they won't see it floating among your molars, they will.

6. Never show up late. (Duh!)

7. Do not be in a rush to leave. Do not look at your watch. You might be asked to budget one hour for an interview, but if things are going well, you may be asked to hang around and meet others on the staff. This is a GOOD SIGN. Don't be a nerd and say you need to get back to your unpaid, comparatively pointless internship!

8. Never have cigarette breath. A robin's-egg-blue pack of Indian Spirits stuck in the outside pocket of your roommate's grooving Marc Jacobs white bag is *not* a status symbol in this situation. Even fashion people these days don't like smokers. Smokers take more sick days and need long breaks to indulge in their habit on the streets outside the office when they could be inside answering phones. If you smoke, whatever, that's your choice. Just be wise enough not to reveal it at the interview.

9. Do not bother to explain why you need the month of July off for the extended family cruise to Alaska. Or why you need a week off in August to attend your best pal's wedding. Deal with this stuff once the job is offered to you. Right now, no one cares. Really.

10. Avoid asking personal or "career path" questions of the interviewer. Don't ask about personal effects in the office. This is neither the time nor place. If you don't already know everything about this person's background, you didn't do your homework.

11. Do not babble on. Keep your answers crisp and clear. Remember, you have only ten minutes.

12. Never be arrogant about where you went to school or all the fabulous people you know or are related to. Never be arrogant about anything. Yuck.

13. Do not ask about title, salary, benefits, laptop, BlackBerry, office or cubicle size, vacations, or perks.

14. Never wear a blank, passive face. Blasé is the kiss of death.

Practiced Sound Bites

When you have a series of interviews at the same place, make sure you stick to your story with a few well-rehearsed lines. Use the same sound bites with everyone.

WHAT MAKES YOU UNIQUE?
- "I'm from Wisconsin so I understand how real American women think."
- "I'm an army brat and can quickly adapt and contribute to new situations."
- "My parents ran a printing shop so I've always been around words and pictures, editing, and proofreading. Seeing typos is my thing."
- "I grew up in Southern California with Asian parents and traveled globally, so I always see things from more than one point of view."

WHY CAN YOU HANDLE IT?
- "I've never been afraid of hard work."
- "I work best under deadline pressure."
- "I have thick skin and welcome criticism."
- "It's how I'm programmed: I played varsity sports and earned top grades while helping my mom at home with my little sisters."

WHY ARE YOU THE BEST PERSON FOR THE JOB?
- "Passion and training. Everything I've done leads to this position."
- "Discipline and gut. I'll work as many hours as it takes and create systems out of chaos."
- "Nothing you've described is new to me. I can take this position to the next level."

Follow-up

Immediately

Later the same day or the next day, do quick, topical e-mails to every assistant you met. Lots of people no longer use fine stationery on which to write the perfect thank-you note to the person doing the hiring. Handwriting, they insist, doesn't matter in the twenty-first century.

Dear Marc,

It was my pleasure to meet you yesterday at Vuitton. I was there to speak with Antoinette about an internship. Bumping into you in the hall afterward helped put the whole thing into sharp focus for me.

My internships at Lucky and NBC, as well as all the learning and hard work at Parsons, have prepared me for this challenge. I'd be privileged for the opportunity to work for you.

Thank you for your consideration.

Sincerely,
India Cosgrove–St. Pierre

I'm old fashioned on this count. A handwritten note will set you apart. It shows elegance and good manners. I also know that fashionistas *love* handwritten notes on good stationery. It's part of our genetic makeup. This is especially crucial if you meet someone stratospherically important in passing. Take the opportunity to pen a quick, grown-up note so they'll remember your name.

Within Three Business Days
Call the office of the person in charge of hiring. Say you are checking in, wondering if there is anything else you can do to support your application. Is there anyone else you should meet? Ask when the decision will be made. Best to call early or late in the day, so that you might catch the actual person (not a bored assistant or intern) at her or his desk.

When You Make the Cut

Imagine that you are now standing there with Miss California and it's her beauty contest to lose. Don't do anything stupid, aggressive, or cocky. This is your chance to ask someone you know who knows someone at the company to call on your behalf and put in a nice word. You might call your references to alert them to the fact that they might be hearing from someone at the company and to see whether they might make a call to a friend there, as well.

Now is also the time for you to make absolutely certain you want to commit the next twelve months of your life to this gig. Once an offer is made but before you say yes represents your turn to articulate any seemingly minor issues. These include start date, where you will sit, to whom you will report, what your title will be, what the pie chart of your day should roughly look like (that is, 60 percent of your time devoted to the regular business of the office and needs of your boss, 20 percent to reviewing unsolicited manuscripts and making recommendations about them, 10 percent to attending industry events or reading industry periodicals, 10 percent to special projects), whether you'll have someone to help you cover the phones when you need to take a break, who makes those schedules. What computer you'll be using. Vacation allowances. Benefits. *You are not being a nudge* by asking about any of this: You are showing initiative, reinforcing why you're the person for the job, and, most important, you are equipping yourself to succeed. The sad truth is that your future boss probably has not had a chance to think through all of these issues. By being proactive, you eliminate first-day awkwardness.

The Right Way to Accept the Job

When you finally hear that The Job you've been obsessing over is yours, you should calmly thank the person for the "excellent" news. Don't scream, gush, kvell, drop the phone, or in any way, act like you're on TV. This isn't *American Idol*. Calmly, then and there, review the particulars, including salary, title, benefits, and start date. Communicate *with words* that you are very excited but that you'd like one night or the weekend—if it's Thursday or Friday—to think it over before giving your final answer. By not gushing your acceptances on the spot, you show that you are a careful person, and you put yourself in control of the process. Full disclosure: I'm not sure I ever actually did this in my career—I was too enthusiastic and unedited. And whenever someone I have wanted to hire has asked me for a day to think over a job offer, I have been impressed and I have wished I'd been able to do this myself.

The person offering you a job probably has assumed that the matter will be tied up immediately and will probably take you more seriously for not jumping to yes. Since you've taken time to reflect, your future boss will probably be more open to little tweaks or requirements you may have in your new role. A delayed yes to a job provides you with time and space to carefully consider what might seem like minor issues before you start. And, trust me, issues that seem minor before you start can easily become the bane of your existence.

Standing Out from the Crowd: Job Fair Basics

Take any opportunities that come your way to attend a career fair at your school or in your community because we *all* have something to learn. I recently presented at such an event at the French high school in New York City (Lycée Français de New York) that seemed to me a bit like "speed dating"—twenty minutes with a group at a table with a bell ringing in between signaling the rush to a new group.

I admit that I approached the night with a smug fashion attitude that the event was in desperate need of *MOI* to save it from eternal boredom. Well, the superwoman in the Calvin-esque suit to one side of me was a producer at *60 Minutes,* and the chic French lady in a lace Chanel dress was the fashion director at Neiman Marcus. Just goes to show that, no matter how kind, Zen, and non-judgmental I strive to be, I find myself at times slipping back into *fashion bitch* behavior. #*&#!@@ (See "Fashionista Detox," page 316.)

What You Need to Bring to a Job Fair

- A notebook and pen to write down the person's name and company and to keep notes and jot down pointers. Having a pen and paper at the ready will also help you focus, show you're serious about the topic, and instantly create a good impression. If things are superboring, just *act* like you are taking notes—you can actually be writing a list, a note, maybe sketching someone's face—while occasionally nodding and making eye contact with the presenter. He or she will think you're way above average. And you are!

- Good questions (see below, a starter set).
- Business cards, even if handmade or supersimple.
- Portfolio or example of your artwork or writing.
- A résumé, no matter now simple or empty.

What You Need When You Leave the Job Fair

That presenter's business card or e-mail address, especially if there's a possibility you'd like to intern at his or her place of work.

A STARTER SET OF FASHIONISTA JOB FAIR QUESTIONS

1. What is your schedule on a regular day? How is your time allocated between internal activities at the office and external activities?
2. What education, degree, or training is required?
3. Does your career have an international flavor? Have you worked abroad?
4. Does your career provide opportunities for advancement in other fields? Has your career path changed over your professional life?
5. If you could, how would you prepare for your career differently?
6. What are the personality traits (say, effervescent and energetic versus serious and disciplined) that best fit with this job?
7. How did you get your first job?
8. What's the biggest mistake you've made at work, and how did you get past it?
9. Which areas in your field of expertise are in a growth mode, involve new technologies, are hot, so to speak, and offer the best opportunity for young people?
10. What computer applications or software do you use professionally? Is there a specific technology that is changing the way business is done in this field?

Shoving Your Fashionista Foot in the Door

If you're burning to get inside a presenter's company, take a minute at the end of your session to introduce yourself. Ask what the internship program is like and how you should apply. Offer the presenter your card and ask for his or hers. Politely ask if it would be okay if you used the presenter's name when applying for the internship and whether you might follow up on the conversation with an e-mail with further questions. Bingo. You have your lead. Be polite, tenacious, and don't take no for an answer.

THE FASHIONISTA GRAPEVINE

**gossip n. 1. Rumor or talk, of a personal, sensational, or intimate nature.
2. A person who habitually speaks intimate or private rumors or facts.
3. Trivial, chatty talk or writing.**

gossipmonger n. a person who relates gossip.
From the *American Heritage Dictionary*.

Let's talk about the irrepressible urge to dish. If you enjoy speaking cattily and light-heartedly with colleagues about other colleagues, you're not alone. It's a major global office pastime. Perhaps it's human nature—if together we denigrate another, we'll feel superior. Bonded. Pumped up. In charge.

The truth is, the more you communicate negatively about others, the more negatively those around you will view you. While you and the people around you whisper mean things about someone else, someone else may well be doing the same about you. Look inside yourself and find a way to change this behavior. Find something good to say when someone opens up a gossip topic. Or say absolutely nothing. Shut down the conversation with a simple "You think so?" Convert it to something positive: "Oh, I think she's really cool." In the end, you'll like yourself better for turning around this destructive behavior. Plus the world will be a nicer place.

I've heard some people argue that there exist situations in which gossip is good or useful. That if the intent is not evil, it is *good* gossip. In my book the very definition of gossip implies that there is a malicious undertone. That the impetus for gossip is thoughtlessness or an intentional desire to hurt others. It is essentially stealing someone's good reputation.

I don't believe in dull, robot-like human relations, however. There are well-intended means of sharing inside information. Juicy news *can* and *should* be shared.

CONFIDENTIAL OR SPECULATIVE INFORMATION THAT'S NOT OK TO SHARE

- Discussion of a person's declining health or shabby sex life based on gathered tidbits from unreliable sources and gossip.
- Discussion of a person's potential imminent firing or demise.
- Commentary about another person's weight, body type, style quotient.
- Unsolicited negative commentary about someone's writing, layouts, photographs, or ideas—let these efforts stand on their own merit.

CONFIDENTIAL OR SPECULATIVE INFORMATION THAT IS OK TO SHARE

The most useful thing anyone ever told me at Midge Richardson's *Seventeen* magazine was to stay away from Midge on days she wore her glasses to work. (Thank you, George! You totally got it!) When Midge appeared in the Third Avenue offices with her heavy framed glasses on, it meant that she was in a foul temper, would say no to whatever you asked or requested, and would not readily like any pictures or layouts presented to her. Had she stayed out too late the night before? Had a bad time with contacts in the a.m.? No one knew. The glasses would appear only a couple times a month, but word spread like wildfire: "It's a *glasses* day." That was code for "Stay in your chair." "Don't engage in idle conversation." "Look busy. Very, very busy." Another reliable barometer of her mood was her outfit. Skirts always signaled a good mood, pants, the opposite. Wearing black said she was down, whereas colors indicated she was up. Is the communication of these behaviors really gossip? No. Though not exactly empirically based information, I prefer to call Midge's mood meter the proper sharing of confidential information for the good of the community.

It is fine to share information of a personal nature that will help a new colleague through a tough situation. If the boss's assistant is sent out to fetch coffee and you know exactly how the boss likes it, you should pass it along. The benefit of your knowledge could save her neck. If you know that the business manager has an illness or just lost a family member and is acting incredibly cranky or remote with her new assistant, you might share this information in broad strokes to explain an unpleasant work situation to the novice. It is always fine to humanize an uncomfortable situation.

Communicating cultural expectations there'd be no way someone would know is an important contribution to the office. Like days when Big Bosses visit and everything should be neat, clean, and in control. It's important to know who gets what reports and when, who attends which meetings and why, when it's okay to dress down, when it's not, and when it's okay to take vacations or skip out early, and when it's not.

Exposure to businesswide gossip is an information system you'd be unwise to ignore. The power of this insider grapevine is mighty. What starts as a rumor, regardless of its truth, can so rattle the confidence of advertisers that a business may topple. Sometimes companies float rumors about themselves to see how the press or marketplace reacts to see if a sale or a purchase is viable. You'll be valued for adding meaningfully to conversations of this nature. Be warned that spending too much time keeping abreast of the last "word" on the street is a waste. Let someone else do that—someone whose *job* it is to think all day about that stuff.

Now You've Got It. How to Keep It.

Making Your Fashionista Job Your Own: Twelve Basic Steps

Yippee! The dream job is yours! Instead of blabbing your excitement or throwing a party, put your head down and get serious. Show that you deserve it.

1. Know the Code. Look the part. Act the part. BE THE JOB. "Nice pant," one editor reluctantly allowed another editor in the back of the elevator. In one glance, you need to learn to take it all in.

2. Don't take your job for granted. Be humble. The karma of kindness is unbelievable. Treat eager job prospects how you would like to have been treated. Ditto pesky PR people. There is no reason *ever* to treat others disrespectfully.

3. Always be on time. That means before your boss, at 8:30—not 9 a.m.—on the dot. Don't rush out of the office in the evening until you see that your boss and the big bosses have gone.

4. Keep coming up with new ideas. Find ways to renew your freshness— self-generate projects, ideas.

5. Volunteer to take on projects. Even the doggiest ones, like being in charge of the interns or handling some large and painful mailing.

6. Be the person who doesn't waste time gossiping. (See the Fashionista Grapevine, page 64.)

7. Be part of the team. Make friends—do not be a weirdo, loner.

8. Don't undermine colleagues. Give your bosses credit for knowing what's really going on. Your role is not to inform them. Everyone hates a rat.

9. Show that you are ambitious in an appropriate forum. When an opportunity comes up, throw your hat in the ring. Don't wait to be called upon. Even if you don't get the job, people will think of you differently for trying.

10. Admit when you screw up. Tell your boss it won't happen again and move on. Most people are unable to do this—taking responsibility shows character.

11. *Nothing beats hard work and talent.* That's the cocktail. If you possess obvious talent, maybe you won't have to work quite as hard. Remember: Everyone loves the brick that can always be depended on to get things done with a smile.

12. *Know your place.* You are not a peer. When you are a peon, act like one. That's the hardest lesson for new hires to absorb. What does it mean? You hold the door open. You go into the revolving door first to make it easier for the boss. You NEVER take the backseat on the passenger side of the car that's reserved for her. When she takes a serious call, you quietly leave the room. It's NONE of your business.

When Work Works: It's One Big Cocktail Party

The best work gets done when everyone is relaxed, but creating the illusion of happiness and relaxation isn't always easy. Never admit how hard you work. So you were in the office all day Saturday with rice crackers and your personal space heater finishing a project? Who needs to know? It's your secret and will get you nowhere but scorned, reviled, or despised if you admit it. Keep your gargantuan efforts private. Make it look easy.

Liz didn't call it a 10 a.m. Monday morning staff meeting but rather a gossip session on her giant cushy sofa (never say "couch" or "drapes"—it's "sofa" and "curtains"). She wanted to hear what films we'd seen, what restaurants we'd tried, which socialites we'd seen prowling about the dinner party circuit. Or she'd ask a few of us for lunch at Petrossian for no reason at all. Beluga and champagne all around. Extravagant? Sure. But Liz knew such spontaneous acts of extravagance earned her our eternal devotion.

In this cocktail party environment, **play bad news as good news**. Angelina Jolie dumps the gown you helped fit and tweak just minutes before leaving for the Oscars. Your editor kills the sixteen-page feature you've been working on for six months, and you hear about it from the art department intern. Big smile—that's the way it goes. Don't show the pain. Don't pout, stomp around, or go home early or angry. In my case, I bounced back by presenting a new, intriguing idea to my editor and discussing it with her. When doing this, be sure to communicate that you are sorry she didn't like your original piece. Then, in this positive context, she is more likely to give the information you really need to get it right the next time. Chances are you'll get a second chance. Weirdly, it's in your hands.

CREATOR

1

WHAT: | Designing clothing or accessories.

DEGREE: | Art, design, or fashion.

TRAITS: | Charismatic, creative.

ESSENTIAL ABILITIES: | To create something original that defines you (Dior's New Look, the Chanel suit, Diane von Furstenberg's silk jersey wrap dresses, Calvin Klein's tight jeans and branded briefs, Ralph Lauren's polo shirts, Halston's single-seam jersey dresses, Prada's minimalist uniforms).

ROLE: | Be the embodiment of your aesthetic.

WORKSPACE: | From cramped closet to posh Paris atelier.

PATH TO POWER: | Go to the right design schools, intern for the right designers, or wing it early with pure genius.

MOST COVETED JOBS: | In-house designer, eponymous designer, with the ability to expand label into bags, shoes, fragrances, lifestyle.

DOGGIE JOBS: | Don't be a snob—you can learn anywhere.

KEY BRANDS: | Chanel, Dior, Lanvin, Balenciaga, Louis Vuitton, Gucci, Prada, Ralph Lauren, Calvin Klein, Marc Jacobs, Yves Saint Laurent.

KEY PERSONALITIES: | Career angels like Anna Wintour, financial backers (that is, anyone with deep pockets), the people who get you best, to work with you and build your business.

KEY ALLIANCES: | Hip young stars, potential backers.

MODERN SUCCESS STORIES: | Giorgio Armani, Ralph Lauren, Calvin Klein.

MISCONCEPTION: | That every designer is a tailor or that you need to know how to sketch.

LANGUAGES: | Technical tailoring and fabric French helpful.

STARTING COMP: | Nada to negative (*somebody* has to buy the fabric).

POTENTIAL COMP: | $ to $$$$$.

PERKS: | "Friendships" with Hollywood actresses who love fashion connections. The possibility of dressing Michelle Obama, who has been hugely supportive of young, diverse Seventh Avenue talent. The chance of finding a patron or muse who invites you into her fab life and homes. Direct links to newspapers, magazines, photographers, stylists, models, stores—all the other realms of the fashion business.

How Can a Young Designer Make It Today?

"Cut a CD," advises Nicole Miller in answer to my question, only half jokingly referring to personalities like Beyoncé Knowles, Sean John, Gwen Stefani, Jennifer Lopez, Paris Hilton, Charlotte Ronson, Christina Aguilera, and Justin Timberlake who have launched their own clothing lines with automatic fanfare, built-in creds, and an instant audience because they're, well, *already* famous.

"The most fantastic thing in this country is the internship," enthuses Diane von Furstenberg, the designer as well as president of the Council of Fashion Designers of America (CFDA). She notes that she has a long waiting list of young people from all over the world wishing to be interns at her company. "It's old-fashioned advice, but it still works today. People will notice you if you are the first to arrive in the morning and the last to leave in the evening. That was the advice given to a friend of mine in Hollywood from his grandfather. He was from the South and knew no one there. He followed that advice and became very successful. If a job opens up and you have proven yourself, you might get the job. More important for you is the experience. You need that experience and having people around you who bring you up in your craft."

Unlike Diane or Nicole, I never dreamed of becoming a designer. Far from it. Sewing a button on a shirt is frustrating for me. In a pathetic attempt to be a liberated woman/intellectual snob, I treated home economics like the biggest time-sink on the planet. Because my mother is an excellent seamstress, creating for me pastel bouclé Easter coats with matching bonnets, smocked red velvet Christmas dresses, and Swiss dot summer shifts, and because I wanted to be *anything* but handy like her. Because I was impatient and probably actually left-handed but made to work with my right hand, I was patently bad and drew no pleasure at all from handiwork. Because of all of the above sorry excuses, I cut myself off from a world that I may have enjoyed exploring. Or, at the very least, I could have learned the essentials of hemming, ironing, and button sewing and saved myself a load of embarrassment, frustration, time, and money.

But because I'm sorely lacking in these skills, I admire all the more the vision, talent, endurance, and, ultimately, success of the designers I've known through the years, like my girlfriend Nicole Miller and longtime acquaintance Diane von Furstenberg, as well as Ralph Lauren, and Calvin Klein, with whom I've worked in various capacities and known over the years.

Sitting in Nicole's office over lunch one day, I witness a calm, assured designer in action. We first dissect the mock-up of a fragrance ad on her desk, and I dab a drop of the scent sample onto the inside of my wrist. Then, while we chitchat and shovel sushi into our mouths, a parade of employees slip in and out of her open door seeking direction or approval. A seamstress drops off a gorgeous pair of black leather paneled briefs with a back zip that *Vogue* had requested Nicole design at the last minute for a shoot. The designer gently asks the woman to place them on her armchair, away from the spray of soy sauce. Next, Nicole nods in approval as one assistant appears carrying large rolls of solid chiffons she'd chosen to line two different beaded chiffon fabrics. A print designer brings in three large square fabric samples, each different versions of a purple, black, and white spot print. Nicole says she wants the one with the white outlining the other colors, without really even looking. (I get the sense that it was the one she'd asked for at the beginning of the process and hadn't actually needed to review.)

Just then another assistant enters to ask whether she can give away a bunch of samples to the staff—never-produced items from a previous collection—holding up a teal cotton jersey top with bronze metal squares adorning the neck as visual evidence of the goods. The lovely lady who makes lunch for the staff every Friday slips in with an open Cuban cookbook so that Nicole can scan the recipes and okay that week's menu. Before long, Nicole's business partner Bud appears to comment on the pandemonium going on at the sample giveaway that apparently was already under way. In amongst the fabrics, samples, groovy girls, and seasoned seamstresses, Bud cuts a fresh, preppy figure. From Nicole's waste bin, I fish out the color printout of yesterday's top selling ten dresses that Nicole had probably scanned when she first arrived that morning with her coffee. Then, before I leave, Nicole slips on the paneled leather briefs (think 1960s, constructed bikini bottom) over her heels and lace pattern tights to check the fit before sending them off with an assistant for the four-block hike to the Condé Nast building: Not only does Nicole look model-hot in them, she has had the luxury of overseeing the entire process of making the item right here under one roof in her own Seventh Avenue offices, from her pencil illustration to patternmaking, cutting, and sewing and final fit. Together with Oscar de la Renta and Carolina Herrera, Nicole counts among the handful of designers who continue to have this capacity. How *much fun* and how satisfying must that be? And this has been just one hour in the creative professional life of designer Nicole Miller. By the time I gather up my things, Nicole has already moved on: She is leaning over a belted jacket, talking buttons.

To get the full picture of the world of fashion design, I also went inside fashion schools, roamed the halls, listened to conversations, sat in on classes, chatted with students. I spent days with fashion school deans, professors, and internship placement officers to learn about the fantasies of students' expectations and the reality of today's job market. I talked to the interns and to their bosses to hear the nitty-gritty of what really goes on.

So if you are *not* JLo or JT, how *do you* enter the world of fashion design? Let's begin by looking at some of today's best-known designers and see how they got their starts.

Halston, the son of an Iowa accountant, was first a milliner (made hats), then was a window dresser, before creating daring minimal, sexy, single-seam jersey dresses that have scandalized most good Midwestern folk, like his own. New York City was where he needed to be. Here, Halston, a strikingly gorgeous man, was a Studio 54 regular alongside pop culture luminaries like Andy Warhol and Bianca Jagger. While the same crazy nightlife that so clearly inspired his collections was likely his undoing, no great collection ever came from the mind of a recluse.

Donna Karan, whose father was a tailor and mother a model, graduated from Hewlett High School in Long Island, then attended Parsons School of Design, leaving after two years to work for Anne Klein. Donna rose to became head of the Anne Klein design team, finally breaking from the label after fifteen years to launch her own eponymous brand.

The catalytic concept behind the Donna Karan label "Seven easy pieces," bodysuits, knit skirts, and dresses was a feminine, but strongly empowered, vision for how modern women could dress. The fact that Donna herself was a young, modern, appealing woman dressing other professional women based on how she herself wanted to feel and look proved hugely appealing in a marketplace dominated by male designers. It was and remains her niche.

Calvin Klein, an FIT dropout, made a rack of clothes and rolled it right into a Fifty-seventh Street department store to get his first order. A marketing genius beyond compare, Calvin's defining trait was the ability to capture edgy, novel movements in popular culture in his collection and his advertising images. Calvin himself would be present at photo shoots directing the nuances of efforts as iconographic as his early jeans campaign starring Brooke Shields ("Nothing comes between Me and my Calvins") to Marky Mark in Calvin briefs to Kate Moss in Obsession fragrance campaigns. That Calvin, himself a tall, lanky, handsome guy, had at his side his best childhood friend, Barry Schwartz, running the business side of things was a key ingredient to his success.

Ralph Lauren had an unlikely fashion start. Born Ralph Lipschitz, the son of Jewish immigrants from Belarus, Ralph studied business for two years at Baruch College before serving in the U.S. Army. Ralph's first job in fashion was as a salesman for Brooks Brothers. He then opened his own necktie store, where, among other brands, he sold his own ties under the Polo label. Movie-star handsome, Ralph Lauren's singular genius is that he understands that the glamour of *his* fantasy world of *Out of Africa*–like safaris, the wild West, *Gatsby*-esque glamour, and grand English old-school style would translate into the pristine beauty and appeal of Polo Ralph Lauren. For Ralph, it's all about mining the past to push our highly sensitive buttons of cultural aspiration.

Ralph has had no formal design training and does not sketch his collection, but "dreams it" instead. Ralph Lauren has created a "family" business in which his brother, Peter Lauren (who, like his older brother, also changed his name), works on the men's business and his son, David Lauren, helped create the hugely effective Internet effort and oversees advertising and public relations. In addition, Ralph has a fiercely loyal core team whom he trusts completely.

A financial success beyond all others, Ralph Lauren, Inc., is a publicly traded New York Stock Exchange $13 billion juggernaut of a company, of which Ralph owns a large stake. Jackpot.

Miuccia Prada is the youngest grandchild of a respected Milanese luggage maker, Mario Prada, whose shop in Milan's famous nineteenth-century Galleria shopping arcade still bears his name. But Miuccia (born Maria Biancha; "Miuccia" is a name of endearment) was a child of the 1960s. She studied politics, earning a degree in political science, and did not envision a role for herself amid the fine goatskin Prada suitcases until she was well into her thirties. Together with her husband and business partner, Patrizio Bertelli, a Tuscan entrepreneur, Miuccia discovered high-tech parachute nylon and began designing simple black and navy windbreakers, rain jackets, and parkas that were soon discovered by locals and then the fashion cognoscenti at her grandfather's luggage shop. Almost overnight, the Prada brand ignited into an international powerhouse.

Giorgio Armani dropped out of medical school to become an assistant at the Milan department store La Rinasceute and then at Cerruti, starting his own label ten years later with the help of his partner, Sergio Galeotti. Armani created the label synonymous with corporate power and Hollywood in the 1980s, most notably as the uniform of choice of women who had risen to executive ranks in banking and industry. His distinctive understated grays and greens and fluid designs marked both his men's and women's collections, which continue to be both strikingly handsome, quietly luxurious, and tasteful. Today, still privately held by the famously shy Mr. Armani and a small number of family members, the company curates hotels, furniture, and home designs, as well as a custom collection show in Paris during the Couture. Guessing who will eventually succeed the seventy-something Armani is a favorite parlor game among fashionistas.

Gianni Versace grew up in Sicily helping his mother, Francesca, a dressmaker. His older brother, Santo, and younger sister, Donatella, proved instrumental in shaping the Versace fashion house. Versace's vision of women couldn't have been more different from Armani's: Where Armani explores androgyny in his designs for women, Versace celebrates sexy, unabashed, powerful, and sometimes extremely exaggerated femininity. Clean, optimistic color marks his clothing as did brash advertising campaigns shot by Avedon featuring 1980s' and 1990s' supermodels and music celebrities like Elton John, Prince, and Courtney Love. His life ended tragically at age fifty when Mr. Versace was murdered in front of his Miami mansion by a spree killer. Since then, Donatella has led the design of the collections, and Santo, the business.

Diane von Furstenberg, the daughter of a Russian father and a Jewish mother (who had survived the Holocaust), has had an amazing fairy tale life and brilliant career. A bewitchingly beautiful woman, Diane was born and raised in Belgium, and she studied economics at the University of Geneva. At eighteen, she married Prince Egon von Furstenberg, and she was thereby bestowed with the title of princess. In quick succession, she gave birth to two entitled children, Alexandre and Tatiana von Furstenberg. Determined not to let what would turn out to be the short-lived marriage and title define her, Diane, with no formal design training, created a sexy, easy, colorful knit jersey "wrap dress" in 1972 that would sell millions and land her on the cover of *Newsweek* magazine. Over this time of unbelievable success, Diane developed many lucrative licensing partnerships, but after many successful years, the fashion label itself took a decade-long break. In 1997, Diane relaunched her business to a new audience hungry for her feminine jersey dresses and iconic colorful prints to even bigger acclaim than the first time around.

Five Key Qualities That Great Designers Usually Possess

1. They Have Charisma

Nearly all designers are physically beautiful, appealing people. At the very least, they are audacious and original. In this highly visual world, it's hard to think of a designer who doesn't have a signature or recognizable look. In addition, most are natural self-promoters, and many possess an amazing verbal fluidity as well as exude an alluring quality akin to a rock star or movie star. The responsibility that comes along with public status is tricky and invasive. Once a designer puts her name on a garment and people are buying and wearing that garment, she is officially a public person on a public stage. Every time you go to the beach, run for a bus, buy a doughnut from a sidewalk cart, you need to embody the carefully

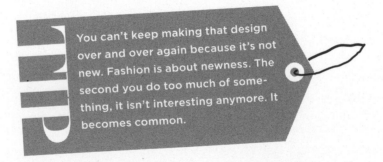

You can't keep making that design over and over again because it's not new. Fashion is about newness. The second you do too much of something, it isn't interesting anymore. It becomes common.

crafted persona that is your brand. And you need to be nice and genuine to people who want to connect with you.

2. They Develop a Defining Style

This is about owning a look that has never existed before, like Halston's single-seam jersey dresses, Donna Karan's jersey power dressing in separates, Diane von Furstenberg's wrap print silk jersey dresses, Galliano's bias-cut dresses, Calvin Klein's architecturally minimal designs, and Armani's flowing women's suits. This is about expressing a fresh, personal vision for how women or men will want to look and dress and to attract a group of people who want to work for you, partner with you, and buy in to this vision.

3. They Live in the Moment

The best designers on the planet surround themselves with other creators, artists, musicians, photographers. They see films, visit galleries and museums, and love to explore clubs and restaurants in cities all over the world. To create for a modern woman means being in touch with the popular culture of your time. They draw inspiration from their muses, take pleasure in dressing friends, and notice every little thing about Every Woman.

4. They Achieve a Balance of Art and Commerce

Fashion is the perfect balance of art and commerce. The best designers are not deaf to the likes and dislikes of the retailers or consumers who buy their clothes. The best fashion company CEOs are not blind to the beauty and purpose of creativity and cutting-edge design. The best designer understands the basics of business—and staying *in business*. The best business person understands fashion and that playing things safe is not the way to stay *in fashion*.

5. They Have Stamina and Courage

After catastrophic failure, instead of hiding or changing professions, a great designer returns to the skills that made him or her great in the first place: the foundation skills of sketching and draping; fabric expertise; tailoring; patternmaking—the process of turning a design flat, like a paper pattern, into muslin or silk jersey so that it can be made into a garment. He exhibits the stamina and resolve of an elite athlete. This is the essential quality that separates those who ultimately make it from those who vanish into the faculty lunchroom at a junior college in the suburbs. But no one talks about it because it's so *un*sexy. Plus, America loves a comeback. Moral makeover. Public rehabilitation. Look at Madonna and Michael Vick. You'll only be more successful for the footfalls.

The Ultimate Design Test:
How to Know If You Are a Designer

You see an ad in the back pages of *Women's Wear Daily* that says, "Top Dress Designer Wanted," e-mail in your résumé, and receive a standardized response that you'll be hearing more within two weeks. After ten days, you're asked to show up for an interview on Seventh Avenue on a Wednesday at 11 a.m. You enter and meet a business guy with a legal pad. Within minutes you realize that this isn't really a talking interview and the interviewer doesn't want to hear about your summer in Paris interning at Balenciaga with Nicolas Ghesquière. No. This is a tryout, a time to *show what you know* as well as give a sampling of your instincts, inclinations, energy, knowledge, and taste. Tougher than *Project Runway* because it's one shot and on the spot: No prep. No breaks. No retakes.

Bud Konheim's Signature Designer Interview

The dapper, preppy Bud Konheim was born into the dress business on both his mother's and father's sides of the family, attended an Ivy League school (Dartmouth), and tried his hand at many different professions, but ended up discovering what he loved the most was the closest thing to home. The process presented here is drawn from the approach Bud devised to hire Nicole Miller away from her then-company many years ago. At that time, he received 340 résumés, interviewed 170 applicants using this process, and identified three candidates who rose to the top before selecting Nicole.

OBJECTIVE
"When I need a talented top designer, I think about the interview for three to four months. You can't decide talent from a résumé. Design is not about talking."

PART 1. CHOOSE A FABRIC
"I have a pile of fabrics on the table, among them six or seven good ones. I ask the candidates to pick out the fabric they'd like to use. It is a test of their touch, fabrication know-how, understanding of fibers, weights, seasons. Most don't make it past this step."

PART 2. SKETCH AND DRAPE

"Next, I ask people to first sketch a dress and then drape the fabric to show the idea of the dress. I need to see what they'd *do* with the fabric. This is all about draping.

"I have a big pad. They sketch the dress on my pad. I then use the pad to grade the rest of the interview.

"Sure we can all name famous designers who don't know how to sketch, but you'll be much more believable if you can express your idea on paper. The language of a designer isn't words. Don't tell me—SHOW ME!!"

PART 3. UPDATE A BASIC AND/OR UPDATE A WINNER

"All companies have one style that's a real winner at retail, and they face the challenge of taking that winner into the next season. The challenge is how to evolve it so it's new but keep alive what consumers love about it. How to take a winner into the next season is what I call the 'evolution' of a design.

"So I have a dress hanging on the wall. I ask the candidates that made it this far to tell me what they'd do to move it forward. There are no good designers who do not possess this ability. Where would you look to change it?"

GETTING HIGH MARKS

"How was Nicole able to do so well? She had innate good taste, a French mother, and her RISD training. She was a groovy girl who went out to cool clubs and parties at night. She was in tune with contemporary culture and had lots of friends who were artists."

GET OFF YOUR JIGGLY BUTT

At some point in Nicole's interview, a patternmaker walked into the room with a question on a sample she was making of a dress that she was holding in her hand. Bud liked the fact that Nicole got up out of her chair to touch and examine the dress. That she got down on her knees to get the hem right (and still does!) showed that she understood what the job was and exactly what kind of energy she'd put into it.

Designing clothes is not a desk job. You must have mental and physical stamina and be mentally and physically fit. You are constantly moving. Given all that activity and the fact that the designer is often the *image* for a brand, it's not surprising that I can count on half of one hand the number of overweight designers I've ever met. Just an observation; not a judgment.

Designing Your Own Design Education

Unlike the careers of Ralph Lauren and Miuccia Prada, the words "No Formal Design Training" do not apply to many of today's most successful designers. Indeed, when you examine the paths followed by today's generation of successful designers, it is striking how similar they are.

TODAY'S TOP DESIGNERS & THEIR FASHION EDUCATION

DESIGNER	BRAND	EDUCATION	CITY
Mark Badgley and James Mischka	Badgley Mischka	Parsons Parsons	NYC NYC
Christopher Bailey	Burberry; Burberry Prorsum	University of Westminster; Royal College of Art	Westminster, United Kingdom; London
Luella Bartley	Luella Bartley	Central Saint Martins (journalism track)	London
Hussein Chalayan	Hussein Chalayan, Puma collection	Maarif College, Central Saint Martins	Nicosia, Turkey, London
Peter Copping	Nina Ricci	Royal College of Art, Central Saint Martins	London
Esteban Cortazar	Esteban Cortazar, Ungaro	Miami's Design & Architecture Senior High School (DASH)	Miami
Francisco Costa	Calvin Klein	FIT	NYC
Christophe Decarnin	Balmain	ESMOD (l'Ecole Superieure des Arts et Techniques de la Mode)	Paris

DESIGNER	BRAND	EDUCATION	CITY
Ann Demeulemeester	Ann Demeulemeester	Royal Academy of Fine Arts	Antwerp, Belgium
Peter Dundas	Pucci (previously Emanuel Ungaro, Cavalli)	Parsons	NYC
Alber Elbaz	Lanvin	Shenkar College of Engineering and Design	Ramat Gan, Israel
Tracy Feith	Tracy Feith, Tracy Feith for Target	Self-described "fashion school dropout"	Montauk, NY
Tom Ford	Tom Ford (previously Gucci, Yves Saint Laurent)	Parsons (interior design)	NYC
John Galliano	John Galliano Christian Dior	Central Saint Martins	London
Nicolas Ghesquière	Balenciaga	High school and internships at Agnès B., Corinne Cobson	Paris
Prabal Gurung	Prabal Gurung	Parsons	NYC
Lazaro Hernandez and Jack McCollough	Proenza Schouler	Parsons Parsons	NYC NYC
Marc Jacobs	Marc Jacobs; Marc by Marc Jacobs; Louis Vuitton	Parsons	NYC
Christopher Kane	Christopher Kane, Versace, Topshop collection	Central Saint Martins, BA, MA	London

DESIGNER	BRAND	EDUCATION	CITY
Michael Kors	Michael Kors; MICHAEL by Michael Kors; KORS by Michael Kors (previously Céline)	FIT*	NYC
Derek Lam	Derek Lam	Parsons	NYC
Nanette Lepore	Nanette Lepore	FIT	NYC
Phillip Lim	3.1 phillip lim (previously Development)	Cal State Long Beach	Long Beach, California
Martin Margiela	Martin Margiela (previously Hermès for women)	Royal Academy of Fine Arts	Antwerp, Belgium
Stella McCartney	Stella McCartney; Adidas by Stella (previously Chloé)	Central Saint Martins	London
Alexander McQueen	Alexander McQueen	Central Saint Martins	London
Nicole Miller	Nicole Miller; Chartreuse	Rhode Island School of Design; ESMOD	Providence, Rhode Island; Paris
Isaac Mizrahi	Isaac Mizrahi, Liz Claiborne (previously Isaac Mizrahi for Target)	High School of Performing Arts; Parsons	NYC; NYC
Kate Mulleavy and Laura Mulleavy	Rodarte; Rodarte Go International Collection for Target	UC Berkeley UC Berkeley	Berkeley, California
Rick Owens	Rick Owens	Otis College of Art and Design*	Los Angeles

DESIGNER	BRAND	EDUCATION	CITY
Thakoon Panichgul	Thakoon; Thakoon for Target	Boston University; Parsons*	Boston; NYC
Phoebe Philo	Céline (previously Chloé)	Central Saint Martins	London
Zac Posen	Zac Posen	Central Saint Martins	London
Tracy Reese	Tracy Reese; Plenty by Tracy Reese; Frock by Tracy Reese	Parsons	NYC
Patrick Robinson	Gap (previously Patrick Robinson)	Parsons	NYC
Narciso Rodriguez	Narciso Rodriguez	Parsons*	NYC
Cynthia Rowley	Cynthia Rowley	School of the Art Institute of Chicago	Chicago
Ralph Rucci	Chado Ralph Rucci	Temple University; FIT*	Philadelphia; NYC
Behnaz Sarafpour	Behnaz Sarafpour, Target	Parsons	NYC
Peter Som	Peter Som	Connecticut College; Parsons	Mystic, Connecticut; NYC
Anna Sui	Anna Sui	Parsons	NYC

DESIGNER	BRAND	EDUCATION	CITY
Vivienne Tam	Vivienne Tam	Hong Kong Polytechnic University	Hong Kong
Olivier Theyskens	Olivier Theyskens (previously Rochas; Nina Ricci)	École Nationale Superieure des Arts Visuels de la Cambra*	Brussels, Belgium
Riccardo Tisci	Givenchy	Central Saint Martins	London
Isabel Toledo	Isabel Toledo	FIT; Parsons*	NYC
Carmen Marc Valvo	Carmen Marc Valvo; CMV	Manhattanville College BFA; Parsons	Purchase, New York; NYC
Dries Van Noten	Dries Van Noten	Antwerp Fashion Academy	Antwerp, Belgium
Alexander Wang	Alexander Wang	Parsons*	NYC
Matthew Williamson	Matthew Williamson	Central Saint Martins	London
Jason Wu	Jason Wu	Parsons*	NYC

*Indicates that designer did not complete studies or earn a degree

Where to Go to Fashion School

You can see from Today's Top Designers & Their Fashion Education chart (see pages 80–84) that of this sampling of fifty-three young designers, widely considered to be among the most important in the world today, two-thirds attended only three schools: one-third studied at the Parsons School of Design in New York City; some 20 percent at Central Saint Martins in London; and 10 percent at the Fashion Institute of Technology in New York City. The only other schools to appear more than once are ESMOD (founded in 1841 in Paris), the oldest fashion school in the world, and the Royal Academy of Fine Arts in Antwerp, Belgium, which since the 1980s has been a hotbed of amazing creativity. When I've shared this chart with fashion insiders, they've all been stunned to see the impact on the world of fashion that such a small number of institutions has had.

The take-away is simple: If you are an English-speaking person, go to Parsons in New York or Central Saint Martins in London. If you are French, explain to us why there are so few French designers, s'il vous plaît. If you speak the three official languages of Belgium—French, Dutch, and German—and hold a Belgian passport, you may apply at the Royal Academy of Fine Arts, but beware: The attrition is high. Of the estimated 120 who start the first year, only 70 survive. After four years, only 15 to 20 students are allowed to remain in the program and graduate.

Like most New Yorkers, I'm biased and believe my city is the center of the universe. When it comes to fashion and a fashion education, it's hard to argue: New York City is the U.S. fashion capital. It follows then that if you do want to study design, New York is the place to do it. But I'm also a snob about a liberal arts education. If you have options and, say, have the choice to attend Brown University or FIT, I say there's no contest: Go to Brown. But when Zac Posen had the option of accepting a spot at Brown University or going to London to interview for a spot at Central Saint Martins, he did the latter. And things have worked out pretty well for this bright star. To my mind (and to many fashion academics), the absolute perfect education of a fashion designer would be to attend Brown University for a BA and then to continue on to Central Saint Martins for an MA or Parsons for an MFA.

In a perfect world, I'd recommend the path that Thakoon took—earning a degree from a liberal arts university, following up with technical and creative coursework at an amazing school like Parsons or Central Saint Martins in London. Steven Faerm, director of fashion design at Parsons, confirms that, increasingly, students come to Parsons having already completed a BA from schools as prestigious as Vassar, choosing to start the BFA program at Parsons. In addition, there is an increase in BFA graduates continuing to earn MFAs.

If you've narrowed your search to NYC, you have two main options. Below I've tried to condense the profile of these two top, but dramatically different, U.S. fashion schools according to your key issues and concerns.

PARSONS VERSUS F.I.T.

	PARSONS: THE NEW SCHOOL FOR DESIGN	FIT: FASHION INSTITUTE OF TECHNOLOGY
Check Out	www.parsons.edu	www.fitnyu.edu
Why Go Here?	You get the highest-caliber, most well rounded fashion education at this private institution, part of The New School. You join an elite group of graduates who blanket Seventh Avenue and populate design studios in Paris and Milan.	Technically a New York State community college, it's as tough and technical as the industry itself.
Star Alum	Edith Head, Claire McCardell, Adrian, Norman Norell, Reed Krakoff (Coach president and executive creative director), Tom Ford, Marc Jacobs, Donna Karan, Isaac Mizrahi, Anna Sui	Calvin Klein, Michael Kors, Nanette Lepore
Famous For	The Parsons Portfolio	Producing hard workers
Also Famous For	Star alum make themselves available to critique and guide senior projects, and often they hire favorite graduates.	Industry internships help you get your foot in the door.
How to Get In	A great portfolio, good SATs, ACTs, TOEFLs	Show up.
Hallmark	The clear, sequential logic of the four-year BFA design program turns out talented designers who are creative problem solvers.	A long, moveable menu of possibilities from full-time BA or MS degrees to flexible evening classes catering to people looking to move up in their careers or switch out completely.

Parsons: The New School for Design

Claire McCardell, the woman who practically invented American sportswear, Norman Norell, one of the first American designers to win the respect of the Paris designers, and Edith Head, the Hollywood costume design legend—if these famous graduates from Parsons are any indication, the bar is set high at this school. Academically, the school is looking for conceptual, technical, and well-rounded students. Standardized tests—SATs, ACTs, and, for foreign students,

	PARSONS: THE NEW SCHOOL FOR DESIGN	FIT: FASHION INSTITUTE OF TECHNOLOGY
Teaching Style	Highbrow, conceptual, referenced, but ultimately commercial	Lowbrow, hands-on, practical
Cost	$$$$	$
Perks	Parsons in Paris	Programs in Florence and London, among others
Toe-in-Water Test	Take an evening illustration class, or study with the Paris summer program (there's one for high school students).	Check out summer programs custom-tailored for high school students with fashion fever.
Vibe	Art school intensity	High school aura with lockers and an auditorium
Campus	Seventh Avenue between 41st and 40th Streets	Sprawling urban complex in Chelsea
Industry Dis	"Those people have their heads up in the clouds."	"It's the fashion factory."
Props	Established in 1896, the oldest fashion educational institution in the United States produces some of the greatest designers of our time.	Established in 1944, it takes nobodies and gives them a future in fashion.

the TOEFL—are required. Students who have shown high intellectual capacity coming in generally surpass those with outstanding drawing abilities within the first two years of study, says Steven Faerm, BFA director at Parsons. Once you do get admitted, the program builds in a straight line from the core skills of fashion illustration to creating a full-blown collection.

Year 1. Foundation classes. Rigorous focus on skills and tools of design. Special focus on fashion illustration. "We still use gouache," says Faerm. Every student does at least fifty illustrations per week.

Year 2. Skill building and fashion history. Moving into two dimensions—patternmaking, draping, sewing, color sense, proportion, exposure to every market including men's, women's, children's, teens', denim. "We still do 'flats,' and top stitching by hand, so students get the feel of the process."

Year 3. Concept and mini thesis collection. Shopping the marketplace for trends and direction. Determining the fabrics and concept for a small collection of looks, a process that is intended to be a warm-up to the much more sophisticated and professional thesis of year 4.

Year 4. Thesis collection. Each student develops a collection from 100 or more sketches. Famously, the duo already known as Proenza Schouler (Lazaro Hernandez and Jack McCollough) saw their entire senior collection snapped up by Barneys fashion director Julie Gilhart to be sold at that store.

The best students, Faerm says, come to Parsons with historical and cultural contexts to draw from and generally have very strong time management skills. Those who've been drawn to the field after watching *Project Runway* generally do not fare well. "Students who come here because of that fail out," says Faerm.

Fashion Institute of Technology (FIT)

FIT has something for everyone, including options for high school students who want to get a head start, as well as evening and weekend coursework for nontraditional, already working people who want to pursue their fashionista dreams. There's even a store on campus that sells students' creations. Talk about real! Like any school, FIT is only as good as you make it. While it is more practical than the more arty and theoretical Parsons, be careful of what you specialize in, because many of the most technical of these jobs have moved out of the United States to China.

Other Schools

Antoinette Westphal College of Media Arts & Design, Drexel University, Philadelphia, offers a five-year liberal arts program with a one-year co-op in which you work in the field. Visit www.drexel.edu.

Fashion Institute of Design and Merchandising (FIDM) is a private college with campuses in Los Angeles, San Francisco, San Diego, and Orange County, California. Its teachers maintain strong contacts in the West Coast activewear, sportswear, and swimwear markets. Visit www.fidm.edu.

Rhode Island School of Design, Providence, Rhode Island, offers high-concept education in architecture, art, music, film, fabric design. (Nicole Miller's alma mater, see page 71). Visit www.risd.edu.

Savannah College of Art and Design (SCAD), Savannah and Atlanta, Georgia, campuses, has a well-rounded, career-focused design program. Visit www.scad.edu.

Cornell University (www.cornell.edu), Texas A&M (www.tamu.edu), University of Georgia (www.uga.edu), and University of Wisconsin at Madison (www.wisc.edu) are among the state schools that previously had strong home economics programs that morphed their expertise into sexier formats like fashion design, fashion business, or fashion management. Don't automatically reject this option since, occasionally, there is one dazzling personality, dean, or professor who makes a program like this cool and rewarding.

Getting a Grip on Central Saint Martins (CSM)

Thank God for CSM Professor Sarah Mower, my former *Bazaar* colleague, for she can explain this fine, intimating institution for us *Ah-Mer-RI-cans.*

What is it? Central Saint Martins' design school in London, www.csm.arts.ac.uk.

Curriculum. "Creativity, not technical concerns, come first. You don't go there to learn pattern cutting or business. You go there to find out who you are and do something that is (if you're lucky) original, or at least very, very true to yourself."

How to get in: The interview. "You must know *absolutely everything* about the history of fashion. And if you can't quote chapter and verse on who's styled what for whom, on catwalks and in magazines and have an OPINION about current fashion, and why you should be in it, then forget it."

What it's like. "Incredibly multicultural, like London itself. And very competitive. The BA program now has a vast intake that has diluted the teaching since Galliano, McQueen, and Hussein days. You are very much thrown on your own devices, but that is what they have said about CSM for years: You teach yourself, find out how to operate, by having to operate."

Fashion, communications, and promotion (FCP) degree. "A fast track to fashion journalism, styling, PR. They always get jobs as everyone takes them as interns. Though of course they all have to slave unpaid for quite a long time too."

Master of arts (MA) degree. "The actual crème de la crème of world-class standards is run by Professor Louise Wilson. She is a phenomenon. She breaks them down, does not allow *anything* derivative, but sends them out to populate the great brands of the world: Lanvin, Chloé, Donna Karan, Louis Vuitton, Marc Jacobs. Or they become star designers in their own right like Christopher Kane, Jonathan Saunders, Marios Schwab, Louise Goldin, Sophia Kokosalaki. Verily, all the good young designers we have now are hers."

In my opinion, says Sarah Mower, visiting professor at Central Saint Martins: "If a person is serious about fashion, she or he could take a first degree [a bachelor of arts degree from a liberal arts college] anywhere, but if he or she is obsessed about getting on, save up to try for the MA, fashion's elite finishing school." Look at their graduation show on style.com.

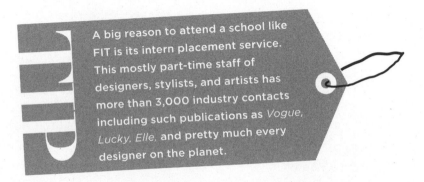

A big reason to attend a school like FIT is its intern placement service. This mostly part-time staff of designers, stylists, and artists has more than 3,000 industry contacts including such publications as *Vogue, Lucky, Elle,* and pretty much every designer on the planet.

Advice for foreign applicants? Be aware that CSM is part of the University of the Arts of London, which confoundedly also includes the London College of Fashion. CSM and the London College of Fashion operate completely separately with very different standards and studies. In addition, Sir Philip Green of Topshop fame owns something called the "retail academy" in London, which offers courses that may not be completely applicable to U.S. or continental European marketplaces. There's only one real CSM.

Design Competitions

Talk about breaking away from the pack. Winning a design competition is an instant way to get seen and be known where it matters most—in the marketplace. Stuff like this happens all the time so read the bulletin boards hanging around school. Keep your ears open. What do you have to lose? Go for it.

Some examples. Gap creative director Patrick Robinson, a serious designer in his own right, recently invited thirty Rhode Island School of Design students to have a go at designing a classic cotton cardigan for spring. Their work was displayed at Gap's rotating concept space on Fifth Avenue and Fifty-fourth Street in Manhattan. Henri Bendel, a store known for its *open call* system where accessory and jewelry designer hopefuls are invited to show their stuff, also sponsors a handbag competition with Parsons. Recently, of the thirty-five Parsons seniors who submitted sketches, the winner received $10,000 and the opportunity to sell the bag through the store; two runners-up received $2,500.

Also, check out the Council of Fashion Designers of America (CFDA) website, www.cfda.com, for information on the influential, annual CFDA/*Vogue* Young Designers Competition as well as the *Teen Vogue* Student Design Competition.

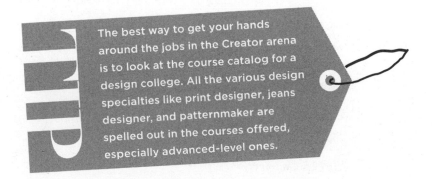

The best way to get your hands around the jobs in the Creator arena is to look at the course catalog for a design college. All the various design specialties like print designer, jeans designer, and patternmaker are spelled out in the courses offered, especially advanced-level ones.

Getting Your First Design Job

Think of your job search as a campaign to work where you really want. Be creative. Make yourself seem interesting. Here is some advice specific to fashion design that comes from lots of designer friends who combined have centuries of experience interviewing, hiring, and training design assistants on Seventh Avenue.

Finding a Design Internship

"Everyone is always looking for a good intern," says dress designer Ruth Ann Stanley. "The top designer companies are looking for students with exceptional design and sketching skills—there's a lot of competition for these internships. And the most talented students get them.

"I work for a small, unknown company, so I'm not the top choice for interns who'd much rather intern at well-known places like Marc Jacobs or Donna Karan. I'm looking for interns who may not have the most fully developed skills but who are smart and intensely interested in learning. Where I work, it's all hands on deck: You have to work and participate, and we are depending on you."

Ruth Ann hires interns who are available to work four to five days per week. "It's excellent practice for understanding the day-to-day life in an office," she says, adding that the interns are also able to see a project progress. "They are able to take the responsibility for a project and have complete ownership of it. And I've found by giving interns actual responsibilities and the ability to watch something they've worked on materialize, it helps build self-esteem."

RECEPTION = FIRST IMPRESSION LAND

One insanely funny, well-known Seventh Avenue designer told me that he sometimes doesn't even bother sitting down with assistant candidates for design jobs. His "time saver" method is to walk through the black-and-chrome reception area where the candidate waits, and, in a millisecond, based on how the person is dressed, he makes the decision whether he is interested enough in this person to do the interview himself or whether he'll pass it along to a top assistant. The outfit and how the candidate looks in the outfit tell him everything he needs to know about that person's taste level and eye.

Don't Dismiss the Small Labels

When you work at a small company, you are more likely to have the chance to interface with merchandising, production, the spec department, sample room, and maybe even accounting. Not only is it valuable to know how a company functions and how each division functions, you may discover that your strengths lie in another division. Perhaps you'll find that you love the pace of the later stages of work that happens in production. In this situation, you'd have time to adjust your studies and future internships to focus on just that so that when you graduate, you will be on the right track straight out of school.

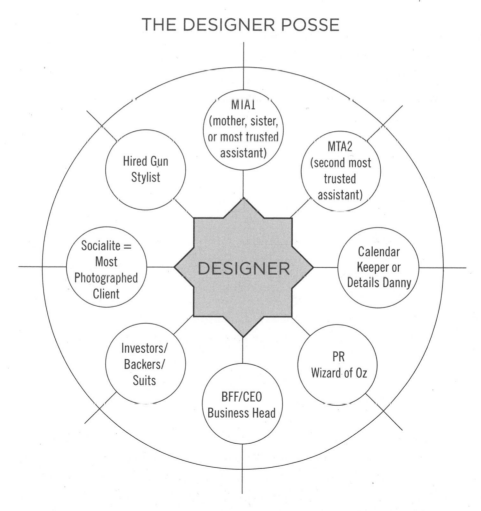

THE DESIGNER POSSE

A designer's inner circle looks something like this and functions more like a family or tribe than like a business.

WEB WARNING

Lots of websites promise the world. They then ask for your credit card number to cover your monthly fee. AVOID THESE SITES!

You shouldn't be paying for a service to help you find a summer job. The three listed here are among the ones worth checking out:

www.internzoo.com
www.dailyfashionjobs.com
www.freefashioninternships.com

How You Look at Your Interview

This is fashion. How you present yourself matters. "You need to look polished," says one friend in fashion HR, "but don't wear a business suit. That's too stiff."

Try to figure out what would be appropriate for the company you'd be working with. Let your look be influenced by that company's culture and style, slanting your look to the brand where you are interviewing. For example, if you have an interview at Calvin Klein, you'd blow your hair straight and dress neat and minimal. If you're interviewing at Betsey Johnson, you'd wear your hair curly and dress more crazy-creatively, like high tops and a touch of neon.

How to Express Yourself

You need to be relaxed enough that you can relate your passion and your good attitude toward work. Be prepared to talk about what you want to learn and what your goals are for the internship. Be specific. Make a mental list of these things beforehand so that you are prepared. A designer is looking for someone who is friendly and positive, who will pick up things easily and be positive about learning. Try to couch your comments about school and other work experiences in positive terms. Starting every sentence with "I hate it when . . . " won't help you make a positive impression.

How to Prepare for the Interview

Portfolio. Most art and design schools have classes to teach you how to prepare and present your portfolio. The irony is that many of these classes fall into a student's last year of studies, long after you are expected to interview for an internship. Start building your portfolio early (see pages 95–98). "I don't expect intern candidates to have wonderful portfolios," says Ruth Ann Stanley. "I want to see that they are trying to put it together in a professional way and that they are having fun with it."

Big picture. Take thirty minutes to research the company on your computer. Know the names of its different businesses and labels as well as the names of its top executives and designers. Go and see stores where the label is sold. Take notes on the type of people or personalities who wear the label and who would be considered its biggest competition.

How to Assemble Your First Design Portfolio

According to modern design school convention, portfolios can be presented either on a candidate's laptop or in a large black book filled with acetate covered pages. Most interviewers prefer the old-fashioned physical portfolio because they like to see the actual lines of illustrations and the weights and textures of fabrics, and

ART SPEAK

So you don't have to ask.

FLAT: A drawing or design that represents how a garment will be cut from "flat" fabric.

CROQUIS: A quick drawing of a figure or a design, made with the intent of communicating the big picture. Also called a "rough," the illustrator will often use it to help create a subsequent, more detailed work. Fashion illustrators typically produce a series of croquis to show an art director, after which the two will discuss how the final illustration would best work. The word *croquis* comes from the French verb *croquer,* which means "to sketch."

MAQUETTE: A rough representation or small-scale version of an unfinished work. The term is used in architecture, set design, and magazines where a "maquette" is a "dummy" of the final issue of the publication. This maquette is painstakingly created by hand in the art department. Each page of editorial (with final images and copy) and advertising is spray-mounted into a white "book" and given to the editor in chief and the publisher to review and make last-minute changes. See the scene in the 2006 film *The Devil Wears Prada* when the Anne Hathaway character brings the maquette to the home of the imperious Miranda Priestly.

they like to be able to flip through pages at their own pace. That makes sense since fashion people are tactile—it's all about touch.

Since I grew up in the editorial world of portfolios (where my black book holds my most recent cover stories, followed by favorite tear sheets of other feature stories I've written, and so on), I asked around Seventh Avenue to find out who possessed a most outstanding design portfolio. Troy Sanford (currently designing at Ann Taylor) was a name I heard repeatedly, so I pinned the guy down to share his secrets.

Over a martini ("dry and dirty, with extra olives"), Troy, a tall, elegant Nebraska native (blond and handsome like a young Halston), showed me his seemingly endless output of amazing sketches and then walked me through the elements of his great design portfolio.

HOW TO MAKE INSPIRED INSPIRATION PAGES

Inspiration pages = evidence of conceptual thinking = the difference between a drafter and a designer = the difference between getting the designer job or spec room job.

Yes, your illustration skills are paramount. But a strong portfolio strikes a balance between your sketches and the thought that inspired those sketches, or your *inspiration* pages. The elements of an inspiration page must be interesting, diverse, and original: A piece of lace, a ribbon, a matchbook cover, an iconic photograph, a quote, a flower petal, a pebble, a shell, or a collage of many of these elements, the print of a poem, canvas, sculpture that moves you.

- The living world around you. For example, an entire collection could pivot on the concept of fireflies.
- Allow a highly evocative city, like Paris, Prague, or St. Petersburg, or a particular highly evocative place, like Nantucket, the Swiss Alps, or Palm Springs, to be your muse.
- Express your collection via architecture: A picture of a steel and concrete building might inspire a collection of neutral colors in clean shapes.
- Dip into something very personal, like "I found this Moroccan tile when I was on vacation. The colors were so amazing I wanted to base my collection on that."
- Use provocative *swipe* (literally means "swiped" or stolen, like a tear sheet out of a magazine) of an incredible *forest scene* that serves as inspiration for a fall collection of mossy knits that look like they have little twigs in them.

BEST AND BRIGHTEST AT SKETCHING AND ILLUSTRATION

Seek out and savor line drawings from this group of designers. Note the extent to which what they create on paper (even in their earliest work) comes alive in fabric. And, if you can get your hands on any: The value of Saint Laurent and Valentino sketches will only go up.

Oscar de la Renta	Christian Lacroix
Karl Lagerfeld	Isaac Mizrahi
Valentino	Yves Saint Laurent

Page 1. Your résumé. Troy's showed that he started school in Chicago at the School of the Art Institute of Chicago to save money so that he could transfer to Parsons School of Design in New York to earn his BFA. I also see that Troy sketched for DKNY and CK while still in school and interned at Michael Kors. He has had his own decorative T-shirt business, Little White Lines, worked with Parsons classmate Alicia Bell in the creation of her shirt line (www.aliciabell.com), and has held design posts at Polo Ralph Lauren and Gap in women's wear.

Pages 2 to 3. Inspiration pages. These pages are based on a theme (a country, an adventure, a literary movement, an architectural style, a color, an artist—see box above) and can include scraps of fabric and/or current runway shots, as well as architectural drawings, or art or nature drawings that relate to the theme. These pages should showcase your unique creativity.

Pages 4 to 5, 6 to 7, 8 to 9, and 10 to 11. Spreads of the collection that you "designed" based on your inspiration.

Troy did four groups of illustrations of six models on each spread (twenty-four total looks). His sketches are beautiful, amazingly precise and distinct. He presented his looks so that one design followed naturally from the last with a very strong commercial logic. Other people do three to four groups of designs with ten looks in each.

What you choose to design should reflect what you'd like to design or, at least, the design job you're going after. If you want a job doing dresses, design

HOT TOPIC: ECO-COOL

Green chic. Stella McCartney took the stand early as the most self-consciously green designer on the planet. Regardless of the "trendiness" of the green movement, every designer is being judged increasingly by how environmentally correct his or her materials and manufacturing processes are. This is *not* going away.

Bike lane. Designing cool clothes for riding your bike to work is definitely a category of the future. Workplaces providing showers for biking staffers seems to be a key next step.

dresses. If it's a jeans line, do jeans. If it's more general, like sportswear, you need to cover all the basic elements, including a dress or two.

Seasonality is important. If you go into Oscar de la Renta with spring sketches when his entire organization is focused on fall, you'll look out-of-sync.

Pages 12 to 13. Here, Troy presented a condensed look at his process from the inspiration for a Ralph Lauren blouse from a vintage lace dress, then swatches of fabrics he found and hand painted. The rough illustrations, or croquis, of his design, are alongside the template or final drawing. He then showed the "flat" version of the shirt (necessary for patternmaking) and the actual "specs" that he provided production for the manufacturing of it.

Beware of using the term *haute couture* incorrectly. Strictly speaking, when it is capitalized as *Haute Couture*, it refers to the French syndicate that oversees the Haute Couture houses (including Dior, Chanel, and Gaultier) that present their collections twice yearly in Paris. The definition of *Couture* is that everything is made of the finest fabrics and is hand sewn and structured, involving a series of fittings.

Design Internship Crib Sheet

PREREQUISITES FOR DESIGN INTERNSHIPS
- Technical skills like patternmaking and sewing
- Artistic skills like drawing and illustration
- Computer skills like knowing the most current computer-assisted design (CAD) software

Note: If the above sounds like a foreign language, you might want to consider other departments like public relations, merchandising, or sales.

Interview Outfit

You need to wear a current season dress or outfit. If you need to buy something just to wear to the interview, do so! At places like Zara and H&M, you don't have to spend a lot of money to look current. Designers notice everything. Especially your *shoes!!!* If they aren't current season, make sure they are freshly polished and newly heeled.

Exude

Effervescence, good energy, a positive attitude.

Life *Is* the Interview

Sometimes it happens like this: "I met this girl on the E train," recalls Ruth Ann Stanley. "She was showing her portfolio to her friend. I had a quick look at the book and told her that she was really talented. I gave her my card and now she is interning for us."

HOT JOBS: ACCESSORIES DESIGN

NEWS FLASH: The lipstick index has just been replaced by the shoe index. Traditionally, when times were tough, women bought lipstick instead of clothing. Today, it seems, women are buying shoes. Indeed, both shoes and bags are hot categories today and offer fashion brands high profit margins and good street creds as well as giving consumers maximum satisfaction. In today's tough economy, these are the last things women are likely to give up.

THE MOST GLAMOROUS, NONPAYING "JOBS"

FASHION ICON

This isn't a job you can apply or study for, nor is it one you can inherit or purchase. To be an icon is to stand apart from all others in society with your own unique, alluring, and inspiring vision of yourself. It is to be outlandish, as Coco Chanel was when she dressed as a man, and liberating, as she was when she eliminated corsets and foundations from her designs, freeing women from a dressing tyranny that's hard for modern women to fathom. It is to be chic, as Audrey Hepburn was in life and in her, ahem, iconic roles as Jo Stockton in *Funny Face* (1957) and Holly Golightly in *Breakfast at Tiffany's* (1961).

Today's top modern icon is First Lady Michelle Obama, whose tall athletic frame and modern comfortable vision of dressing is inspiring women across the world and, specifically, U.S.-based designers of diverse ethnic backgrounds.

Icon Examples

Pop culture: Lady Gaga, Madonna, Blondie, Nico, Marianne Faithfull
Movie stars: Audrey Hepburn, Kate Hepburn
Supermodels: Twiggy, Veruschka, Kate Moss
Royalty: Princess Grace, Princess Diana
Presidential: Jackie Kennedy Onassis, who epitomized the ladylike dressing of the early 1960s and also the chic of the 1970s
Fashionistas: Divas like Carmel Snow, Diana Vreeland, and Coco Chanel; Georgiana the Duchess of Devonshire

Qualifications: An icon must possess a highly public role in society but exist above the commercial and day-to-day workings of the fashion world. Sources of income are born or married into or earned independently from the world of fashion.

Tenacity + If You're Not in NYC, Get to NYC

"This guy had come from Texas and just showed up at my company one day," says my HR friend. "He introduced himself to the receptionist, presenting himself in a really polite way. He knew enough to say that he wanted to meet the *design director*. She happened to be around and had enough time to sit down to speak with him. He asked to intern for three months; she said yes on the spot. After that, he got a job with us and has done brilliantly."

MUSE

A muse is a living person who on a regular basis inspires, leads, and animates and epitomizes everything a designer stands for or wants to be. Some designers have illusory muses, their idealized concept of a woman. Some designers switch muses as often as they change their socks or create a new collection. *Muse*, these days, is an overused word, but the role of the muse in fashion is enormous and elusive. Definitely *not* a job you'll see listed in *WWD*.

Some icons started out as muses, like Jackie Kennedy for Oleg Cassini, Audrey Hepburn for Hubert de Givenchy, Princess Diana for Catherine Walker. Among the pure muses is Loulou de la Falaise, who worked with Yves Saint Laurent. She supposedly inspired a tuxedo for women, *le smoking*, with see-through blouses and collaborated with the designer until his death. The late Isabella Blow played the muse to Irish hatmaker Philip Treacy and to English designer Alexander McQueen. Similarly, the late Carolyn Bessette-Kennedy once played this role for Narciso Rodriguez, who famously made her wedding dress.

Living, breathing muses include (the salaried) Lady Amanda Harlech, first for John Galliano for twelve years before joining Chanel where she's been now for nearly as long. Film director Sofia Coppola and model Kate Moss have been (unsalaried) sources of inspiration for Marc Jacobs and Calvin Klein, respectively.

SOCIALITE

With his famous "swans" Babe Paley, Marella Agnelli, C. Z. Guest, Gloria Guinness, Pamela Churchill Harriman, Slim Keith, Gloria Vanderbilt, and Lee Radziwill—Truman Capote etched the concept of a socialite onto the modern consciousness. Today one thinks of It Girls like Tinsley Mortimer, Tatiana Santo Domingo, Daphne Guinness, Charlotte Casiraghi, and Margherita Missoni. In ready-to-wear, a socialite is a living, breathing wearer (buys and borrows); in couture, she is a client (one who buys). See the latest socialites on the party pages of *WWD* and *Vogue*.

Once You Snag Your Design Internship

Don't be shy. You need to learn how to express your opinions and your own style and talents. It's about relaxing into being yourself. You have to learn to become part of a team. At the same time it's about being you and not being afraid.

How to Be

Proactive. Have a big sense of urgency.

HOT JOBS: REPURPOSED FASHION

We've just exited an era of conspicuous consumption and should all now have learned about our responsibilities to reduce our carbon footprints on this planet. This plays into the vague, but totally appealing, notion of reworking vintage jewelry, clothing, and bags in witty, new, and fresh ways. I've only seen a few, small successful attempts at this concept—a shop in SoHo, Flying A, that turned old Lacoste polo shirts into miniskirts—and a line of bags made from vinyl singles from the 1960s.

Stuff NOT to Do
- Show your belly with short tops.
- Wear flip-flops.
- Distracting stuff. One Seventh Ave. intern switched her silver tongue ring for a flesh-colored one thinking that that would make it acceptable. Well, it wasn't.
- Rude stuff, like calling in sick because you have your period. Showing up late because you were out late.

First Thing to Learn
Work out your office kinks. Learn the processes. Learn how to express yourself.

Besides doing the best job you can do, it helps if you are addicted to fashion. You need to shop. Always wear new, good-looking clothes. As a young assistant, you need to be inspirational in your look. In a perfect world, you would be an inspiration to the designer. Everyone is expected to bring something to the table. You need to express your personal style, appropriately to the label.

Be eager to learn. Show enthusiasm. Be passionate. Show you are engaged in what you are doing. Take ownership of what you're working on. Assume accountability.

Express your personal style, and allow your style to expand and develop with what you are seeing and learning on the job.

Mint Your Boss into a Mentor
Square 1 is that your boss knows your name. Next step is making yourself invaluable. After the internship, you need to keep in touch with everyone you worked with in a friendly, persistent way. Let them know you are looking for a job.

In the Meantime?

Keep interning as long as you can (even part time) until you can convert that experience into the job you want.

Besides Having Your Name on a Label, There Are Lots of Other Ways to Be a Designer

Jewelry designer, textile and/or surface designer (print design), lace and embroidery designer, woven designer, knitwear designer, package designer, sportswear designer, denim designer, and textile designer as well as high-tech textile designer.

Fashion Designer

With specialties in men's wear, women's dresses, women's tailoring, children's wear, intimate apparel, knitwear, special occasion, sportswear, swimwear, leather apparel, outerwear, performancewear (athletic), made-to-measure or custom women's clothing, millinery (hats).

PROFILE

RICHARD SINNOTT | Accessories Mastermind, Michael Kors

Today a driving creative force at Michael Kors, Richard Sinnott made his way up the fashion ladder the hard way, working tirelessly as a magazine assistant for years before his abilities were recognized with bigger titles and responsibilities, which ultimately resulted in a switch from critic to creator. That today his speed dial reads more like that of a Hollywood agent than an accessories designer speaks to his own star personality and comedic talents. Nonetheless, Richard presents himself modestly, poking fun at his upstate origins and finding humor in the sometimes ridiculous, sometimes sublime situations of his early career.

BIG BREAK

Getting a job at *Harper's Bazaar* first as a secretary to the fashion director. "I was a secretary and wore a tie. I made $17,000, which represented a pay cut from my receptionist's job at Macy's."

FIRST *BAZAAR* BOSS

"Miss Weir found me charming. Sometimes, after a long day, we would sit in her office and watch the sunset. She never got my name right; She always called me 'Robert.'"

NEXT STEP

Richard was then promoted to sittings assistant at *Bazaar*. "I worked like a slave seven days a week. Suddenly the kid from the Catskills was flying all over the world with actors and models, seated at dinner next to people like Cindy Crawford."

HOW RICHARD GOT INSIDE FASHION

"Hard work. I remember scraping gum off the floor of the photography studio at lunchtime. So very few people have that work ethic. I wasn't in it for the glamour. I just wanted to be present. I was soaking it all in. I'm like, 'Holy shit! This beats sitting in math class with the pig farmers' kids.' "

DRIVING FORCE

"It was a voyeuristic thing. Certainly not the money, honey. And it's not like I was planning for a future."

SLEEPING BEAUTY

"It was the tacky late 1980s and 1990s, and a lot of work was in California with [Los Angeles photographer] Matthew Rolston. I remember opening up jewelry cases in my hotel room and putting on gold Rolexes. Sometimes my bedroom would be filled with diamond jewelry. We'd put on all the jewelry. Or there'd be Fendi minks. Once I took all the fur coats, put them on my bed, and slept on them."

FAMOUS FASHIONISTA ACTS

The Richard Sinn character in *The Intern* (2000) by Jill Kopelman Kargman and Caroline Doyle-Karasyov is based on Richard Sinnott. In addition, the leonine-haired, small-framed Richard was famous for his office runway performances where he'd don Manolos and a sequined skirt to impersonate the runway walks of supermodels Naomi Campbell, Kate Moss, Carla Bruni, Linda Evangelista, and others.

HOW HAVING FUN HELPS THE CREATIVE PROCESS

"I like to have a good time. If you have a sense of humor and are freethinking, you do better work, you make better things. The people I most admire tend to work that way too. When your head is twisted with ugly thoughts, it doesn't work."

AIR KISSING BACKSTAGE

"I think Michael Kors first took note of me when, in Paris, after one of his Céline shows, a bunch of us from Liz's *Bazaar* went backstage to congratulate him. We were clearly having fun together and worked well together and that made a positive impression."

WHAT PREPARED RICHARD FOR THE BIG LEAP TO THE DESIGNER SIDE

"My experience. I'd seen everything any company had made for years. Also, designers and PR people began to ask my opinion on designs and collections. They'd ask me what would make a better style. I was able to walk into a room and to see clearly how to change designs and make them better. That others valued my opinion gave me confidence that I could design and succeed as the designer. People were always asking my opinion. I sometimes thought, 'I could do this for a living. This could be fun.'"

BAZAAR SURVIVOR = 11 YEARS, 11 MONTHS, 11 DAYS, 11 HOURS, 11 MINUTES . . .

Richard has the dubious distinction of surviving more editors and regimes at *Harper's Bazaar* than any other living soul. "After years at the magazine, I'd finally made it as the accessories director. I'd survived the Mazzolas [Tony Mazzola and Michelle Mazzola, who'd jointly run the publication in the 1980s], loved my time with Liz [Tilberis, 1990s], made it to Kate Betts [who succeeded Liz, but lasted barely a year]."

THE CALL

"One day, a year or so after we'd greeted Michael backstage at Céline, I was sitting at my desk with a bunch of assistants around me. Barbara was on the phone. Barbara who? I pick up the phone. It was Barbara LaMonica, the president of Michael Kors. She invited me in to talk about working on an accessories line with them. To go work there. I went to talk to them about it. Met with Michael. That was that."

ACCESSORIES EDITOR TO ACCESSORIES DESIGNER

"At the beginning, it was horrible. I realized I didn't know anything about production. I had to go and create something from nothing, not just walk into a showroom and critique what was already there. The Italians at the factories kept saying 'domani' 'domani' [*tomorrow, tomorrow*].

"You had to depend on other people to get your things. You had to go to the leather show in Milan that was like an airport hangar filled with the stuff. It was a rude awakening. I didn't *have* to be a designer. It wasn't at all like the fun accessories shows in Paris, where I'd walk through 'Yes, I love that. Send me one.' And 'Oh, can you make that in gold?'"

REALITY CHECK OR POP GOES THE EDITORIAL BUBBLE

"I heard the word *no* for the very first time, which was the biggest shock of my life. I couldn't have it in gold, and I couldn't have it for Monday. I wasn't shooting a bag for a magazine that translated into instant sales and status. I was *making* bags. It was emotionally frustrating. And the worst thing was that it was *not glamorous*. I got through it because that's the way I am. I don't give up.

"When you leave editorial and join a company, you go from receiving a hundred phone calls a week to four. In December, it was like 'What do they mean I have to *pay* for Christmas gifts?' But, in the end, it was a good thing for me to leave magazines. You get too caught up in it. It's really like cleansing your palate. Actually making something and knowing who your friends are: Somewhere it's kind of grounding."

EIGHT YEARS LATER

"Now it's like clockwork. I've learned the hardest lesson that not everything can be done when you want it to be done, or exactly how you planned it in your mind."

PROUD OF

"I created a business. In the process, I learned a lot about design and manufacturing, what can be made, how exactly things get made, and I learned a lot about myself."

Michael Kors has been nominated for the CFDA award for best accessories three times.

WHAT'S COOL ABOUT THIS JOB

"I can totally express myself. My sister wore high heel wooden clogs that I had bought her that felt so right again. I'd saved the picture of them all these years. My babysitter wore wedgie corkies. To do a luxe version felt personally satisfying and totally ironic to me. With Michael Kors, there is an irony to what we do. And intelligence. Taking something nostalgic and twisting it to make it modern."

LUCY WALLACE EUSTICE | Founder and Co-Owner of
M Z Wallace, Accessories Designer, Retailer, Fashion Business Owner

Lucy talks fast, thinks fast, and observes, digests, and personalizes visual trends fast. Born and raised in New York City, she is sharp and savvy with a biting sense of humor. The ultimate fashionista, Lucy has played in almost every arena of the business—as a seller, a visualizer, and a creator—and, as a result, she possesses among her most valuable professional assets, a mental reference library of the greatest shoes and bags of our time. You spot Lucy a block away—walking fast, her silky long dark hair flying—and she's likely to be brandishing the edgy prototype of a bag she's working on and wearing a vintage sample of some dizzyingly high Manolo boots.

BACKGROUND

A lifelong New Yorker, Lucy attended the prestigious Fieldston School, a private high school located in the Riverdale section of the Bronx.

FIRST CAREER: RETAIL

At fifteen, Lucy worked as a salesperson at the French clothing company Agnès B. in SoHo when it had just opened in the States and was hot. At nineteen, she worked for master shoe designer Manolo Blahnik in his Manhattan boutique, selling the chic, fantastic shoes long before his was a household name (and *Sex and the City* staple).

SECOND CAREER: FASHION MAGAZINES

"I started out at *Mirabella*, as a temp, because I was planning on going to college. *Mirabella* then asked me to join the staff as a fashion assistant. I liked fashion, but I was actually trying to leave this world to study psychology, so it was complicated. I said fine if I could leave at 5 p.m. to get to my classes. Of course, the hours were crazy since *Mirabella* was a start-up. We'd still be there at 3 a.m. After the first year, they transferred me into accessories under Elissa Santisi where I spent another three and a half years. I was completely obsessed with accessories.

"Then I went to *Harper's Bazaar.* I knew Paul Cavaco [a founder of the Keeble, Cavaco and Duka fashion agency, now KCD, and, at the time, fashion director of *Bazaar*] who was very good friends with my old boss, Amy Sullivan from Agnès B."

Lucy was named accessories editor, but after a year and a half, she left *Bazaar* to become the accessories director of *Elle*.

THE BENEFITS OF MAGAZINE TRAINING

"A true ability to edit, to recognize what works and what doesn't. Magazines honed my instincts for trends, and for spotting relevance in small details. I also got to see an incredible amount of accessories and work with some of the designers. I was lucky enough to be able to look through all of the old archived magazines [in the case of *Bazaar*], which was fantastic."

THIRD CAREER

After Lucy was dismissed from *Elle,* she moved into product development at Schwartz & Benjamin, which, at the time, held the footwear licenses for Yves Saint Laurent and Anne Klein. "I was in Italy half the year with people like Manolo Blahnik and Patrick Cox."

THE SWITCH FROM PUBLISHING TO MANUFACTURING

"The pace is much different. In manufacturing, it's hurry up and wait, but without the craziness." Lucy says she absolutely does not miss magazines. "There's a fair amount of manic craziness that's not necessary," she explains. "Yes, that energy keeps you going. It feeds the whole Center-of-the-Universe feeling" at a fashion publication.

NEXT STOP

"After that I went to work for Patrick Cox as vice president of North American operations to bring his shoes to the United States. That experience was a whole lot of everything: finding a showroom, identifying the right architect, establishing a wholesale division and a press office. It was like setting up a business. That gave me my MBA in fashion."

CHANGE OF PLANS

"Then Patrick Cox ran out of money. I was five months pregnant when everything shut down and everyone was let go. Then, I had my daughter, Pearl, and I hung out for a while." For the first time in Lucy's life.

KISMET AT THE UNION SQUARE FARMER'S MARKET

"I ran into an old friend, Monica Zwirner, whom I'd met while working at Manolo. I hadn't seen her in a long time. She had been living in Germany and was styling advertising campaigns and international magazines. She was now back in New York and wanted to start a business. I'd been approached to partner before, but it hadn't been the right person. It's a marriage that really has to work. So we set up the company to design bags."

M Z WALLACE

"Founded in January 2000, the mission of M Z Wallace is to create a handbag that is stylish, functional, lightweight, timeless, and affordable. An American classic."

MY VISION WAS TO HAVE A STORE

"During my time at Manolo Blahnik, I learned that if you have your own store, you can grow your business yourself and have control over your image." In May 2000, Monica and Lucy opened their own store, designed by Annabelle Selldorf, on Crosby Street in SoHo. Now M Z Wallace has two stores in downtown Manhattan, in addition to a store in Tokyo. M Z Wallace bags are also found at over three hundred specialty stores nationwide. Additionally they have a thriving e-commerce website that was started in 2003.

BUSINESS BALANCE

"There are two things going on when we look at what we create. There's the edit of what's really new and what we love. Then there's the business edit. That is, the edit ensures that we are staying true to our mission statement. Fashion balanced with function. You have to always strive to have both.

"The conversation is like this: 'Do we need this item on the line? Why does this need to exist? Is it addressing a missing element?' Sometimes it needs to exist because it is simply fun and great looking. Sometimes it needs to be there because it is addressing a need that we feel is not being met. Sometimes it doesn't need to exist, even if we love it.

"Paul Cavaco really helped me become a brutal editor. He taught me to really question 'why?' 'Do you really need it? Why?' We try to be really tough on ourselves."

THE CHALLENGE

"It all turns over so much faster than a few years back. There is no downtime."

DIVISION OF DUTIES

"We both design. Monica does more sourcing and production, and she works closely with our design assistant, while I do more press and retail operations, and I have oversight of the website."

NEW KIND OF STRESS

"Now I feel the stress of an owner with issues like sales, timely production, logistics, payroll, design, HR, and so on. This stress seems more real. It's different from editorial, where sometimes there was a freakout over shoes not being available, or a seat in the second or third row at a show, as opposed to the first. Looking back, that stress seems not as stressful as the stress I now experience."

FLIPSIDE
"I also have the freedom to go to all of my children's school plays, or to the farmer's market, and I know everything at work is fine."

THE DREAM
"To grow bigger and bigger organically. We've always made the harder choice. We invariably take the more painstaking road. We have consistently chosen quality and originality over easy fixes. Always."

MUSEUM STANDARDS
M Z Wallace's Jane bag is the only handbag sold at the gift shop of the Museum of Arts and Design (MAD) on Manhattan's Columbus Circle.

ADVICE TO PEOPLE STARTING OUT IN ACCESSORIES
"Keep your eye on the prize, be confident, and be prepared to work really, really hard. You have to really, really want it. Only the crazies don't quit. When it gets really hard, which it will, most sensible people give up—don't. Don't listen to ANYONE on how to do it. There are no rules. The only rule is that you have to do what works for you—and everyone, and every business is different. Always follow your gut."

M Z WALLACE SPOTTINGS
"It's always a thrill, I have to admit. It's seeing the end result of your intention as a designer: that someone *liked* the bag, *bought* it, and *is using* it. It's incredibly nice to be with my children when that happens because they really get excited and feel a connection to my work. Not to be grim, but I mostly like to try to find out what women *don't* like about the bag, what's *not* working. I never tell them who I am."

RUTH ANN STANLEY | Designer, Depeche Mode

Like many fashionistas, she never wears a lick of makeup. Her all-American style shines through via her perfect posture, tall, thin stature, and whatever dress she's thrown on that day. Her look usually falls somewhere between bohemian chic and country-club preppy. The midsized dress company for which she has designed for over fifteen years produces its own label, Depeche Mode, as well as other licensed brands. This is a case in which you may own a Ruth Ann design and not even realize it.

BACKGROUND
"I learned to sew when I was four when my mother made me start embroidery and cross-stitching. Both parents could draw. We would spend evenings together doing drawings. I also took art lessons." In Southbury, Connecticut, where the family lived, Ruth Ann's mother made all of her clothes.

EDUCATION
Graduated from Marymount Manhattan College, New York City, BS in fashion design (called *home economics* in the day). Later on, night classes at Parsons School of Design, New York City.

CHILDHOOD DREAM
"Beginning in the sixth grade, I wanted to be a designer. I knew this world existed from reading magazines, like *Vogue*. For me it was a straight path, from the Girl Scouts to Seventh Avenue."

BABYSITTER AND MENTOR
"My mentor was this beautiful blonde, who went to Marymount and also happened to be my childhood babysitter. She ended up in the most amazing job, managing the Calvin Klein brand inside Bloomingdale's, basically the in-store representative for Calvin, working for both the brand and retailer at the same time."

CANOEING OR CLUBBING?
"My mentor called to offer me an internship at Calvin Klein for the summer after my junior year in college, and I had no idea what that even meant. She called me all excited with the news. I said to her, 'I'm supposed to go to the Adirondacks to be a camp counselor.' My thinking was that this would be my last summer to be swimming and backpacking in the mountains and that I should enjoy it. I gave the internship to my roommate. Looking back,

CAREER CHANGER

To make this step, Ruth Ann took night classes at Parsons so that she could learn how to build a design portfolio. She also entered and won a sewing competition, which helped infuse her with the confidence she needed to go for what she loved.

I can't believe I didn't take that opportunity. I would've had such a leg up at the beginning of my career."

FIRST JOB
Dressmaking coordinator, editorial, at Butterick, which Ruth Ann describes as "the best job I ever had."

HOW RUTH ANN STOOD OUT
"I entered a sewing contest that was sponsored by the company. I won the suit category. The judge was the head of design. That's how I first got noticed. I spent a lot of time talking to her. Helping her with projects helped her get to know me. It was a good opportunity."

BIG BREAK
"Someone didn't come back from pregnancy leave. I got her job as a designer of Butterick patterns."

HOW DID YOU GET INTO READY-TO-WEAR (RTW)?
"After a few years at Butterick, I realized I *had* to get into ready-to-wear. I met a friend of my boyfriend's who was a buyer who had had a showroom appointment at [the Seventh Avenue dressmaker] Gillian that day. He told me that they were looking for a design assistant.

"I called Kay Unger, and she said, 'Can you come in tomorrow?' I said, 'Tomorrow is Saturday.' She said, 'Yes. Can you come in tomorrow?' I found out that Kay, and pretty much every other designer on the face of the earth, was famous for working crazy hours, and every Saturday.

"So, I went in to meet her on a Saturday. She looked at my portfolio and said 'You know, honestly, I don't like your taste level, but I think I can trust you.' She asked what I was making at Butterick. I told her $25,000. She gave me $27,000."

FIVE-YEAR PLAN AT GILLIAN
"I started by doing 'specials,' which meant updating designs that had been successful—working with everything that sells. I grew into the role of designer, Gillian Dress Company, and started to design for specialty chain stores, and other labels."

MOVE TO DEPECHE MODE
"When Gillian went out of business, I was able to take my contacts, experience, and relationships with the buyers to Depeche and continue the same business."

FOR THE PAST FOURTEEN YEARS
Ruth Ann has been a designer at Depeche Mode, managing the product development side of one of their private label divisions.

JACK TUNG | Designer

This cool, talented, personable, handsome young designer seems to have assembled a lot of qualities mentioned on pages 76–77 and might someday be the next Jason Wu or Zac Posen.

BACKGROUND
"My parents came to Baltimore, Maryland, from Taiwan with empty suitcases and $20. They've been working superhard—in groceries, restaurants—ever since."

JACK'S WAY OF LOOKING AT LIFE
"I am writing my own autobiography every day. I've only got my one little life, and I want my story to be exciting and compelling. You don't have chances to do rewrites, so take advantage of every opportunity to enrich your life story. If you want something, the only person who'll stand in your way is YOU."

PROFILE

CREATOR VISUALIZER CRITIC SELLER

JACK'S CATHARSIS

"I had always dreamed of working in fashion, but thought I lacked the creativity. On top of that, I'd never drawn in my life, and I knew nothing about fabrics or clothing construction. I saw some shows online and *thought* this world seemed glamorous and creative, but well out of reach. Despite that, at twenty-three, I looked in the mirror and asked myself: Was I happy in my heart? Was I fulfilled? I knew I was done with the wishing thing. My mom told me to wait until I was financially stable. But my window of opportunity was narrow, so I decided I couldn't afford to wait. I didn't want to lead a what-if life, so I made my move."

GUARDIAN ANGEL

"I first met Felicia DaCosta, the chairman of the Concept Development department at Parsons School of Design, when I was twenty-three, during an informational interview at Parsons. Two years later, in my sophomore year at Parsons, during my first year of concentrated fashion studies, Felicia DaCosta was my teacher. Then I kept in touch with her when I was at the Parsons program in Paris the following year. She made sure that I stayed in school (despite a job offer from Louis Vuitton) and learned as much as I could. I got a lot of great advice from her: how to quiet my mind, how to quiet my anxieties."

PARIS TERM

"I took advantage of the opportunity to go to Parsons in Paris for a semester during my junior year. Sometimes to be creative, you have to breathe different air. Eat different food. I didn't speak French. I'd never been to France. I went with a clean slate. Open, young, excited about opportunities. Pretty French girls everywhere. It was kind of cool. Never in your life can you be so free."

FIRST FASHION JOB = FIRST BRUSH WITH GREATNESS

A teacher at Parsons in Paris referred Jack to a colleague of his, Peter Copping, now head designer at Pucci, who happened to be Marc Jacobs' right-hand man at Louis Vuitton.

"I sent sketches of projects and my résumé in December, and by January, I was working there. I was a full-time paid intern, earning 1,400 euros per month as opposed to nothing. That for me was my entrée into fashion. Coming from New York, this was like the difference between playing in the Turkish basketball league and the NBA."

PINCH ME

"Sometimes when I was sitting in Paris, I'd ask myself how a kid like me could possibly have met as many talented people as I have."

CAREER CHANGER

STARTED IN: **FINANCE**
SWITCHED TO: **FASHION DESIGN**

To make the leap from his high-paying analyst job on Wall Street to new nonpaying beginnings in fashion, Jack Tung first took evening drawing classes so that he could build a portfolio and apply to Parsons. During his studies in Paris with Parsons, he landed his first design jobs, with Louis Vuitton (nonpaying, but prestigious) and then Ungaro (paying, and prestigious).

YOU SAID NO TO A JOB AT VUITTON?
"I understood I was breathing this rarefied air. But I ultimately declined when they offered me a continuation in textile design. Wherever you go next, you have to make sure you have all your skills and qualifications under wraps. Why be pigeonholed or stymied?"

INDEFATIGABLE INTERNING STUDENT
Internships with Patrick Robinson at Paco Rabanne and Gaspard Yurkievich followed. "Then I graduated from school, barely, receiving my second bachelor's degree." His last internship, with Parsons graduate Peter Dundas at Emanuel Ungaro, would turn into Jack's first design job.

BIG BREAK
"They gave me a shot at Ungaro. In three months, I went from intern to assistant designer to head designer of the jeans line."

THE WALLET FAIRY
One day while working at Ungaro, Jack lost his wallet. Before the end of the day, he found an envelope containing a stack of euros on his desk. That was the kind of boss Peter Dundas proved to be.

MILAN MEETINGS
After leaving Ungaro, Jack interviewed in Milan with Tomas Maier at Bottega Veneta and at Versace.

CREATOR VISUALIZER CRITIC SELLER

ADIEU, PARIS?

"I wound up interviewing at a lot of other places. At that point, I had a temporary visa tied to my job contract. In order to renew my visa, I needed a new contract, which in turn required a new work permit, which I couldn't get without a new contract. On the day of my appointment to renew my visa, with neither job contract nor work permit in hand, I went to the *prefecteur* and told them in my best French that I was waiting for feedback from really great companies, that this was the one opportunity in my life that I could work at this level. I literally begged them for more time, a few weeks at least, and they actually gave me four extra months. Life will never give you anything you won't ask for yourself. While I was awaiting feedback from the companies I'd interviewed with, I ran out of money."

HARD-EARNED (UNDERGROUND) EUROS TO KEEP DREAM ALIVE

"Because my work permit had expired, it was impossible for me to find legal gainful employment because nobody wanted to sponsor my visa. I wound up working illegally as a dishwasher and kitchen assistant in a Chinese restaurant in Belleville, one of Paris' two Chinatown districts. It was quite a humbling experience to be chopping vegetables, mopping floors, and taking out garbage, working thirteen-hour shifts six days a week. But it gave me a chance to keep my dream alive. I thought if I worked hard enough and believed in myself enough, my story of struggle might somehow turn into a story of success. In the end, my luck ran out, my options dried up one by one, and I realized I was fighting a losing battle. The United States is home; nonetheless, it was really sad to leave. I had basically the adventure of a lifetime. Closing that chapter of my life, acknowledging and accepting my failure, was an incredibly painful experience."

BACK TO THE USA

"After the incredible journey of the previous four years, it was quite sobering to move back in with my parents, with no money and no job prospects. Fortunately for me, I have amazingly supportive and understanding parents, who, despite their lack of education, means, and resources, nonetheless worked tirelessly in their unconditional support of me and my career. They truly believe in me, and made the pursuit of my dream into the pursuit of OUR dream. Based out of the bedroom I grew up in, I regrouped myself and started sending e-mails and making phone calls to try to land job interviews in New York, all the while doing more projects to keep my skills in place and stuff my portfolio with fresh work. I would wake up at 5 a.m. to catch a bus to New York, do three or four interviews, and catch the 5 p.m. bus back to Baltimore the same day. Sometimes I would have only one interview on a given day, which meant that I would spend eight and a half hours on a bus just to do a thirty-minute exploratory interview. In the meantime, I again had to bite the bullet and support myself as a part-time sales associate at the local mall."

GOOD-BYE, MALL; HELLO, ZAC POSEN
"After about twenty separate interview trips to New York, I found myself sitting in front of Zac Posen. I did a project for him and started working there right away. Then the market crashed, and I left. A couple weeks later, I met Nicole Miller, and she offered me a job on the spot."

WHAT NICOLE SAW IN JACK
"I thought he seemed very capable and talented and that he had a wide range of experience. I liked his illustrations. I hired him without hesitation."

WHAT MIGHT SURPRISE THOSE AROUND HIM
"I still see myself as a banker masquerading as a fashion person."

WHAT'S DIFFERENT ABOUT THE DESIGNS OF A STRAIGHT MAN?
"There aren't that many straight male designers. There's actually a pretty big difference between the designs of a straight guy and those of a gay guy or a woman. I have a different appreciation of the female form. Knowing the various women in my life and what they want to wear, I bring a unique perspective."

SURVIVAL INSTINCT
"I know when to shut up and step back and listen."

VISUALIZER

2

WHAT: | Clothes stylist, hair stylist, makeup artist, art director, photographer, graphic designer, model.

DEGREE OR STUDIES: | No degree to MFA.

TRAITS: | Visual, creative, versatile.

ESSENTIAL ABILITIES: | Natural charm. An ability to collaborate with your fashion family. An ability to see the next thing in fashion.

ROLE: | To generate the creator's desired image via fashion, accessories, hair, makeup.

WORKSPACE: | As various as the many jobs in this diverse category.

PATH TO POWER: | Apprentice with the best, have a good agency represent you.

MOST COVETED JOBS: | Super stylist, super model, top photographer, super hairstylist, super makeup artist

DOGGIE JOBS: | Cleaning toilets, lugging trunks, taping bottoms of shoes, fetching who knows what for whom at all hours of the day or night, searching 24/7 for the perfect prop, be it a rare vintage car or kitsch blow-up doll.

KEY ALLIANCES: | Editors, celebrities, other photographers, stylists, models, hair stylists, and makeup people.

MODERN SUCCESS STORIES: | Patrick Demarchelier, Mario Testino, Rachel Zoe, Steven Meisel, Bobbi Brown, Kate Moss.

MISCONCEPTION: | That because you're creative, you don't need to be organized.

LANGUAGES: | English or French.

TRAVEL REQUIREMENTS: | Not easily fazed by last-minute trips to far-off places. Long, unpredictable hours and loads of down-time. Passports always current.

STARTING COMP: | You'll gladly work for free.

POTENTIAL COMP: | $ to $$$$.

PERKS: | Hanging with supermodels and superstars; making your living in a relaxed, nonoffice atmosphere; rarely having to dress up; traveling to cool locations all around the world; teaming up with like-minded people and, in time, forming a professional "family" that can last your entire career.

Walk onto any fashion photography set—be it Mario Testino's, Patrick Demarchelier's, or Steven Meisel's—and you might think it was a cocktail party: The music is groovy and loud; there are lots of interestingly dressed characters who seem to be friends with everyone else; the atmosphere is relaxed, lively, and fun; there are no raised voices or barked orders; no hurry; there's a lovely spread of food and drinks. And they call this *work*?

Probably the coolest people in fashion and definitely the ones that seem to have the most fun are its visualizers   the image-making stylists, art directors, photographers, makeup artists, hair stylists, and models who bring fashion to life and populate fashion photography sets on a daily or weekly basis. As much as designers themselves, visualizers are at the heart of the fashion business.

I've broken down the visualizer world into three groups:

1. *Stylists:* The stylists hold the hottest jobs in fashion today.
2. *Photography team:* The photographers and hair and makeup artists, together with the stylists, form a fashion family, the members of which trust each other implicitly and work together beautifully. The photographer gets the assignment from an art director who, together with a graphic designer, creates the finished editorial story or ad campaign.
3. *Models:* Models are the focus of everyone's attention before and during the shoot. If you are a supermodel like Natalia Vodianova or Lily Donaldson, you are likely to have worked with pretty much every top stylist and photographer around. If not, you will be building your fashion creds, which, little by little, amount to insider status.

Visualizers comprise the most diverse cross-section of jobs, and because they can be so different, mini crib sheets for each of these main components follow.

Stylist

WHAT: | Stylist, personal shopper, fashion editor, artistic director, creative director, or merchandising director.

DEGREE OR STUDIES: | Art school or liberal arts degree.

TRAITS: | Visual, practical, patient, watchful, organized, unflappable, creatively flexible, ingenious.

ESSENTIAL ABILITIES: | To generate the desired image via fashion, accessories, hair, makeup, props; to be clever and versatile.

WORKSPACE: | Fashion closet or wardrobe trailer to darkroom or photography studio, TV or movie set.

PATH TO POWER: | Apprentice with the best.

MOST COVETED JOBS: | Stylist to TV show, major celebrity, stylist to major designer, top fashion editor (AKA stylist or sittings editor) at a fashion magazine, in-house stylist at fashion house.

DOGGIE JOBS: | Weeding the mommy jeans out of a client's closet. Otherwise, as long as there's a camera, current season clothes, and it's *not* porn, you're learning.

KEY ALLIANCES: | Editors, celebrities, other stylists, models.

STARTING COMP: | You'll gladly work for free.

POTENTIAL COMP: | $ to $$$$.

How to Be a Stylist

Sitting around the conference table with a group of FIT's placement advisors, I ask about the hottest jobs today: What are your students *dying* to get into?

"We like to call it the 'career du jour,'" explained Nancy Ross, chic in a short cashmere lavender jacket over black. "Everyone today wants to be a stylist." What makes things tricky for people who want to be stylists—and indeed for this team of highly connected professionals attempting to match students with their dream jobs—is that, like much of fashion, **there is no single, obvious path to becoming a stylist.** *Ce n'est pas très évident,* as they say in French. In some ways, it's a new profession.

At FIT's own Center for Professional Studies, you can focus on a certificate program called "Fashion Styling," which requires 165 hours of coursework including the following *required* classes (57 hours): Still-Life Fundamentals; Introduction to Fashion Styling; Fashion Styling II: Fashion Styling for Media; and Fashion Styling III: Launching Your Career. In addition, 99 hours of "related" classes are required: Hand Sewing, Mending, and Alteration Essentials; The Great Designers; Styling Tricks of the Trade: Pinning, Taping, and Clothing Care; and Introduction to Fashion Photography; as well as 9 hours from free-choice seminars, like Fashion Styling for Celebrity Images; Styling Career Options: Still Life and Soft Goods; and Advanced Styling: Tricks of the Trade. Or, if your skin crawls inside a classroom, check out (four hours each and $100 not including food or subway costs) on-the-street stylist tours like Star-Quality Vintage Shopping, or The Professional Stylist's Insider Resource Tour, which promises access to sources for fabric, vintage fashion items, trimmings, and flowers. FYI: All the above classes are offered every semester, so touch base with FIT's Center for Professional Studies at (212) 217-7715.

People, I haven't done the math, but if your parents are underwriting your fashionista education or, more important, if *you* are paying, I'll tell you what to do: If you have the resources and ability, go to a good liberal arts college and study history, art history, English, anything. Then go intern with one of the stylists I list here, or a stylist who's worked with someone I list here, and you'll have a broad context and rich references for your work, and (promise!) you'll learn the technical stuff on the job.

Further complicating matters, the actual job of a stylist often goes by different titles in different situations. At a magazine, you'd be called a *fashion editor,* or you'd work for a fashion editor. At a fashion company or large store, your position might be called *artistic director, creative director,* or *merchandising director. Personal shoppers* at stores like Neiman Marcus, Barneys, or Bergdorf Goodman work like stylists for their top clients, keeping track of their wardrobes as well as what items live in their Aspen, Palm Beach, East Hampton, and Paris closets. I know one personal shopper who actually maintains one client's Manhattan closet as well as packing her bags—each outfit prestyled on a hanger with shoes attached—every weekend and for all trips to her various residences. A parallel profession called *image consultant* involves an initial pressing of the reset button—a total closet and/or hair and makeup makeover—followed by seasonal updates.

Over the past fifteen years, as the world has become more celebrity centric and paparazzi stake out stars every day of their lives, personalities feel a need to dress on a regular basis for the camera. It's not just ego at work here, but a career imperative. To keep his or her buzz alive, an actress or pop star needs to be photographed and seen on a regular basis. In the olden days, when stars were making films, the wardrobe department or costume designer would dress them. When they were in their "private" lives, agents or managers would try to access gowns for them, or they'd dress themselves or ask assistants to help them with this process. When magazines like *In Style, People,* and *US* started doing heavy-duty documenting of the red carpet, star-studded parties and even Starbucks drive-bys and a day at the beach, dressing personalities quickly turned into a full-time job. Fashion houses, seeking to win the good graces of stars as well as clothing credits from these paparazzi photos in these publications, set up their own "personality" divisions charged with the task of reaching out to stars and their stylists. Suddenly the dressing standard zipped light-years ahead: Not only would Armani, Valentino, or YSL dress a personality but the fashion house would also dress him or her

TOP EDITORIAL FASHION DIRECTORS AKA "STYLISTS"

Emmanuelle Alt, French *Vogue*
Paul Cavaco, *Allure*
Lucinda Chambers, British *Vogue*
Anne Christensen, *T (New York Times)*
Grace Coddington, *Vogue*
Sashia Gambancini
Adam Glassman, *O, the Oprah Magazine*
Tonne Goodman, *Vogue*
Katie Grand, *Love*
Sarajane Hoare, *Vanity Fair*
Camilla Nickerson
Carine Roitfeld, French *Vogue*
Elissa Santisi, *Vogue* and commercial
Karl Templer
Melanie Ward, *Harper's Bazaar* and commercial
Alex White, *W*
Brana Wolf, *Harper's Bazaar* and commercial
Joe Zee, *Elle*

TOP CELEBRITY AND/OR TV STYLISTS

Cate Adair

Joanne Blades

Phillip Bloch

Michael Boadi

Tina Chai

Nicole Chavez

Jessica Diehl

Cristina Ehrlich

Patricia Field

Leslie Fremar

Andrea Lieberman

Kasum Lynn

Penny Lovell

Josh Madden

Joe McKenna

Bill Mullen

Amanda Ross

Estee Stanley

Maryalice Stephenson

Kate Young

Rachel Zoe

in *next season's* frock, so that the credit in the magazine could actually drive customers to buy that same dress. Ka-ching. It's a win-win. Everybody's happy.

Perhaps most famous for forging the Fashion-Hollywood connection and for wearing the stylist title is Phillip Bloch. In his wake, Rachel Zoe burst on the scene dressing A-list stars like Paris Hilton and Nicole Richie, and also writing books, designing her own clothing line, and doing a styling show on Bravo, *The Rachel Zoe Project*. L'Wren Scott, also a celebrity stylist, broke away from that business when she launched her own successful dress line. This sounds like a joke, but it's not: If you call a stylist a designer, that's a huge compliment. If you call a designer a stylist? A major dis.

Can *You* Be a Great Stylist?

Of course you can! Career opportunities for stylists have mushroomed over the past ten years. With good training, a good eye, and a few contacts, you can explore the relatively new worlds of celebrity styling, personal styling, and TV or runway styling. Nonetheless, probably the best training ground for stylists is a magazine (see Amanda Ross, page 127), and the most coveted and celebrated of stylist roles remains that of a fashion director at a major fashion magazine. Considering that the magazine business is in the midst of a downturn of historic proportions, you might *rightly* ask, "Who cares about that small insular world?" Or you might be passionate and go for it in magazines. Otherwise, you might train in magazines and take that training somewhere else and shine.

STYLIST///SLASH///DESIGNER

A new "slash" category has emerged from the West Coast where high-profile stylists L'Wren Scott and Rachel Zoe have both launched fashion collections of their own. L'Wren has shown her collection of boudoir-inspired dresses in New York City. Melanie Ward, who worked as Helmut Lang's creative director for thirteen years, started her own capsule collection of loose weaves, called Blouson Noir. L.A.-based stylist Andrea Lieberman has designed her own apparel and jewelry, while Josh Madden, who styles for brands like Vans, Ben Sherman, and Kangol, collects and recycles vintage clothing for his clients.

Conventional Wisdom: Great Stylists Are Born, Not Groomed

"To be a fashion editor [at a magazine], you have to have a vision, and you have to be strong enough to fight for your vision," says *Harper's Bazaar* editor in chief Glenda Bailey. "You also have to be able to collaborate with many other strong personalities who are around you to bring your vision to life. Then you have to have hard work and determination. And you have to have an enthusiasm, and you have to really truly love it because you have to work so hard that if you don't absolutely love it, you don't have a chance.

"I've known so many people who had been Brana's [*Bazaar's* Brana Wolf] assistant or Grace's [*Vogue's* Grace Coddington] assistant, and they didn't turn out to be Brana or Grace. I've never bought in to the idea that people are replaceable. I think if you take individuals like Brana or Melanie [*Bazaar's* Melanie Ward] or Grace, their view is so *theirs* and so unique. You can train with them and learn their work process, but it doesn't mean that you have their eyes.

"I believe in individual talent. If I could clone Brana and Melanie, I would," says Glenda. "You either have that talent or you don't. You can always improve and evolve. It's also subjective—whether you are attracted to a stylist's vision.

"It's the same thing with great writers or designers or photographers. Think about Karl Lagerfeld: Of all the people who have worked with him who have gone off to do their own thing, no one has ever been successful. I so believe in individual talent, and I so respect the creative process. It has nothing to do with age. And, to a certain extent, it has nothing to do with experience, either."

The Family Thing

In some cases, a perfectly logical person will ask why doesn't this or that brilliant photographer work with that amazing, experienced stylist. It's all about a collaborative process. "You either work together, as a family, or you don't," confirms Glenda. "What happens on a set is about family. The photographer has his family around him. If you are not part of that family, there's no way in. It's just not going to happen. They have their own people."

AMANDA ROSS | TV, Film, and Celebrity Stylist

Amanda Ross is the real deal: a traditionally trained fashion editor with an impressive pedigree of mentors. Whether filming a movie or TV commercial or dressing a star for the red carpet, she applies the same superb eye, impeccable organization, and seriousness of purpose. But this wasn't her plan: Amanda had envisioned herself to be a fashion magazine lifer, but circumstances pushed her out of print and into TV and film, where her training and relationships have served her extremely well. If you met Amanda at a party, you'd find her to be well spoken, if shy. Thanks to her chic, superthin Babe Paley look and amazing taste, Amanda is bigger than life.

BACKGROUND

From a family of chic women, Amanda, a twin, grew up in Michigan. Since her family was from New York City, even though they had moved to the Midwest, New York was always a point of reference for Amanda. She graduated from the University of Colorado with a "basic liberal arts education."

STYLE GENE

"My twin sister, Ally, and I are the youngest of a group of cousins. I wouldn't be where I am today without my cousins Katherine, Constance, David, and Jane. They inspired and encouraged me."

Katherine Ross worked fifteen years in the art world before transferring to fashion, where she worked at Prada and LVMH (the holding company that owns Louis Vuitton and Christian Dior, among others). Jane Ross worked at *Vogue* in the mid-1980s, while Constance Ross was a graphic designer and artist at the prestigious design firm Vignelli Associates, also in Manhattan. David Ross is a freelance art director and commercial set designer in Hollywood.

GRANDMOTHER SELMA'S CLOSET

"We all shared a very glamorous grandmother. There were eighty pairs of pumps in my grandmother's closet. And there was a reason for and a difference to each of them.

"She had zips put in her cashmere sweaters so she could escape the hairdressers more quickly. She always wore a pencil skirt, pumps, and great jewelry. She had amazing style and allure. The appreciation of her style has always been with me."

CHILDHOOD DREAM

"Though I grew up in the Midwest, I have family in New York City. I always knew that's where I belonged and where I would live."

FASHION BUG

"I was enamored with fashion. I read *Vogue*. My stepmother (then an artist, now a jewelry designer) wore YSL."

EARLY INFLUENCE

"When we were ten, my stepmom started asking us who we wanted to be when we grew up. No one had talked to us like that before, taken us seriously as young women with bright futures ahead of us. As she was an artist, she let us work with her and encouraged us to create things. She was inspiring and extremely influential."

NYC SUMMER

"The summer after my sophomore year in college, I worked with Jane Feldman at [the then fashion house] Adrienne Vittadini, helping with image and public relations and dealing with the label's outside PR agency, Dente Christina."

FIRST JOB

"Once I was out of college, I interviewed for a job at Condé Nast and moved to New York." While Amanda had first accepted a job at *Mademoiselle* (a Condé Nast title no longer in circulation), soon after (senior editor) Anne Kampmann moved from *Mademoiselle* to *Self*. Anne, who had worked with Amanda's cousin Jane at *Vogue,* reportedly told HR: "I need another Ross girl." Amanda fit the bill.

AMANDA MEETS HER MENTOR

"I moved to *Self* for six years where Anne Kampmann was my boss, my mentor, and like a mother, of sorts. I started to go on shoots. My role expanded. I did have other job offers, but I knew I was where I should be."

WHY BEING AN ASSISTANT FOR SIX YEARS WAS THE BEST TRAINING

"When you begin, the administrative work demands a lot of time and focus. It is through this hard work that your talent comes through. As Liz Tilberis always said, 'Editors should be like sponges.' I think back to those years. Everyone ran into each other in the ninth floor messenger room. All the other assistants, like Kim Meehan and Sasha Iglehart, Inga Fontaine, Amy Astley, would go on to have big careers of their own."

FIRST BIG PROMOTION: "YOU *CAN* DO THIS"

"I was really young. I think they were downsizing the staff. Anne was like, 'I need you to call in all the trench coats for the story,' definitely *not* the work of an assistant. '*You can do this*. You definitely can do it. Now do it.' And I just got it done. That's where it is about instinct and style and good taste.

"In fashion, you operate in a world of people. It's not about acing your SATs or getting accepted at Harvard. You are being measured by something intangible."

VOILÀ!

"My editor would come in and I would say 'It's done.' I was always one step ahead of her. I don't know where I learned that, but that's where I wanted to be. When she said 'trench coat,' I knew what she liked, what the editor in chief liked. I knew how to call in the trench coats they would love and expect to see, but also how to mix it up with some surprises and take things one step further."

FASHION STEP-BY-STEP

Amanda's career followed the classic fashion editor track:

- Editorial assistant (*Mademoiselle, Self*)
- Assistant editor (*Self*)
- Associate editor (*Self*)
- Associate market editor (*Marie Claire*)
- Market editor (*Marie Claire*)
- Senior editor (*Bazaar*)
- Market director (*Bazaar*)
- Freelance fashion stylist and consultant

THE TRADITIONAL TRAINING SYSTEM

"At that time, you were molded by the editors who trained you—whether it was Polly Mellen, Carlyne Cerf de Dudzeele, Grace Coddington, or, in my case, Anne Kampmann. You moved up *if and when* the senior editor you worked for said it was time for you to move up. That's the way it worked. Thank God I had that training. Thank God I was an assistant for that amount of time. That training is so important. Today it doesn't exist anymore."

THE NEW TRAINING SYSTEM

"The mode and speed with which information comes at us today has changed everything. It has created a generation of young people with out-of-proportion expectations seeking instant gratification. People starting out today don't seek out nor understand this training. They think that after one year they should have your job."

REQUIRED READING

"I tell some of the young people who come to work with me in TV and who are interested in the 'other world' of fashion journalism to read these books to get an overview of the fashion system:

- *No Time to Die* by Liz Tilberis
- *In and Out of Vogue* by Grace Mirabella
- *D.V.* by Diana Vreeland"

THE FASHION CLUB

"Today Condé Nast is much more accessible, but twenty years ago you really had to know someone to get in the door. When I started there, senior editors were in their forties and had serious experience. There is a lot to be said for that. It was a club that you felt honored to be part of. You felt honored to be working at Condé Nast."

THE TIPPING POINT

"Working as an assistant under a great editor leads to a wisdom that guides your instincts. You come to trust your good instincts. You become a good problem solver. You begin to understand the bigger picture of a shoot, the story, the magazine, the fashion business."

NEW YORK, LOS ANGELES, LONDON

Amanda married her college boyfriend and decided to move with him to Spain. After three years abroad, she realized she needed to get back to New York. "I'd moved four times with this guy. One day, I just woke up and said, 'I need to go back to New York.' He understood why. He knew what I'd given up. I was missing that high of finishing what I had started."

THE TRAINING, THE TRAINING, THE TRAINING

Amanda had left the New York fashion scene for four and a half years, and then, there she was, single again and back where she'd started her career.

Amanda spent a total of seven years in New York. She began working as the market editor for Glenda Bailey, first at *Marie Claire* and then at *Harper's Bazaar*.

"I just picked up again, as if I'd never left. It was my fashion experience that got me to this point and then took me to the next level. I was able to handle responsibility and to understand the bigger picture."

WORKING FOR A FASHION DIVA

"Glenda always respected me because I was always honest with her and she knew I worked very hard. She knew that I tried everything humanly possible to get what she wanted. At the beginning, it was necessary to prove myself. That is a necessary element to working for her. I give 110 percent to everything I do.

"Creative talent is necessary to be successful as is this understanding of the broader business you are in. But, in the end, you also need to be able to deal with strong personalities."

JET PACK WEST

"Yes! I do move for love!"

Eight years after returning to New York, Amanda got engaged and moved to Los Angeles, where she was named editor at large for *C* magazine, consulted for fashion brands, and styled stories for *Domino* magazine, among others. "But I soon felt paralyzed in Los Angeles. I'd gone to a place and found there was no other place to go. I had just arrived and I was already interested in moving."

BACK TO NYC: FORTY, SINGLE, AND FREAKING OUT

"I moved back to New York because I'd kept my apartment, not because I necessarily thought that's where I would stay. Six months later, I visited London with the idea of moving there."

BIG BREAK

"The day I flew back from London, the producer of *Lipstick Jungle* called. My friend Pippa Holt, an editor at British *Vogue,* had turned down the job and had given them my name. This project just came to me, and I was really grateful. Within twenty-four hours, I had this job. I worked nonstop for a month and then went on to do the second season. This was the first time I worked in TV."

TV FASHION JOURNALISM

Elsa Klensch, the CNN fashion journalist of ten years ago, captured something that no one else has figured out how to duplicate—not on the red carpet, not on the runways. The shocking thing is that no one has replaced her. *The future of TV fashion journalism definitely needs you!!!*

PINCH ME
"It is so rewarding to be in a business for twenty years and to have the opportunity to take what you've learned and apply it to new mediums. Who'd have thought that I'd be styling commercials, TV shows, red carpet?"

FASHION CREDS
"If you are attracted to the fashion business, you must understand that there is a certain amount of training necessary. During this training, you begin to realize where your talents lie. You are drawn to people and projects and they are drawn to you. Then one job leads to another."

LIPSTICK JUNGLE GIG
"I worked with two costume designers, one for each season, who were in charge of the whole show. As I was in charge of the three lead characters, I wasn't required to be on set every day. This allowed me to continue consulting and to build my business. We always styled enough outfits in a fitting so that there were enough looks for that episode. Any extras went into the next episode."

TRY-ONS
During production, Amanda would do three- to four-hour fittings on days when they were not shooting and one-hour fittings on days they were shooting to finalize head-to-toe looks for the actresses. "I would get as much time as I could get with each actress. It's time-consuming to come up with eighteen to twenty-one outfits a week for each of the three women."

WHAT'S COOL ABOUT TV
"TV has a really intimate element that makes it powerful. They are on a screen in your living room. With all the shows connecting to the fashion world in real time (like *Lipstick Jungle* and *Sex and the City* in which characters wear current season, widely available clothing and accessories), the style impact on our world is potentially huge."

NEXT STEPS

Besides consulting with fashion companies and TV work, Amanda has just finished working on her first film, the Nancy Meyers film *It's Complicated,* alongside costume designer Sonia Grande. "What's so exciting is that I now help create an identity for fictional characters. I have a voracious appetite for reading. I love to help create a character. It's kind of incredible how different parts of my life have come together in my work."

TV, COMMERCIALS, RED CARPET, EDITORIAL, BRAND CONSULTING WITH MAJOR FASHION BRANDS

"I LOVE the variety—I love to do all of it. It makes sense, and I need all of it. It's all part of the fashion paradigm."

SUCCESS = MORE THAN GREAT STYLING

"I'm just as confident about my management skills and my business acumen. I was able to run my business for the last two years and, so far, able to do this without an agent. I do all the negotiations. I do all the billing. I pay my health care and do my taxes. I feel great—but the real focus, of course, is the creative work."

LUCK VERSUS HARD WORK VERSUS TALENT

"Luck is a thread through life. We wonder sometimes, 'How does that happen?' But usually I've found if you put your head down, live in the moment, and work hard at whatever it is that you are doing, that good things come to good people. Obviously the talent has to be there too."

PEOPLE SKILLS

"Sometimes I think this is where I'm lucky, and sometimes I feel it's a gift: I really get people. I understand when to take over and when to let someone else take over."

AMANDA'S ADVICE ON HOW TO BE

"Don't be in a hurry. Learn to be in the moment. Be appreciative to those who help you."

MANNERS MATTER

"I was brought up to be kind and respectful. It serves me well in professional relationships."

FUTURE OF FASHION STYLISTS IN TELEVISION

Amanda is confident this is a growing business. "With major talents like Ariane Phillips and Cristina Ehrlich making their mark and some costume designers crossing over to styling, there is a lot of activity. There is going to be a bigger and bigger demand for stylists."

CREATOR   VISUALIZER   CRITIC   SELLER

CRISTINA EHRLICH | Celebrity Stylist

Some stylists get Hollywood and others get Seventh Avenue. Cristina Ehrlich is among the rare talents who understand both, further distinguishing herself with strong ties to Paris fashion houses. As early work with the Olsen sisters attests, Cristina is able to move personalities into higher fashion, bridging the California–New York–Paris divide while image making for her clients on the highest order.

BACKGROUND
Daughter of a Hollywood doctor/photographer father and a showroom model/interior designer mother, Cristina started buying *Vogue* at eight and counts as her favorite picture book one by Helmut Newton. "On a normal day, my mom would be wearing Yves Saint Laurent or Gucci," says Cristina. "They were very visual and had lots of parties. It was a *Less Than Zero* childhood."

Cristina's dream was to be a dancer. Boarding at the Masters School in Dobbs Ferry, New York, after attending Beverly Hills High, proved to be the seminal experience of her youth. "The great part was independent study in my senior year. I created my own program in the city, dancing with Martha Graham and with Alvin Ailey."

BRUSH WITH GREATNESS
"Living in New York, I assisted Irene Albright. She didn't have Imelda's Closet [her store] yet, but she was a regular working stylist."

EARLY STATE OF STYLING
"When I was twenty-seven, the only celebrity stylist was Phillip Bloch."

FINE ARTIST'S EYE
Much of what Cristina brings to her work comes through her own efforts to train her eye: "I would study photographs. I took classes at ICP. I went to photo exhibits. I loved looking at the work of people like Avedon, Irving Penn, and Toulouse-Lautrec. It is something I couldn't get enough of."

COASTAL TUG OF WAR
"I always had a big struggle trying to decide whether to live in Los Angeles or New York."

DOUBLE LIFE

"At the beginning, I was dancing in videos and commercials at same time I was assisting Deborah Watney. I watched how Deborah was working with New York and Paris. Then I started getting styling jobs on my own."

GETTING THERE WASN'T EASY

"I knew I wanted to do something with celebrity dressing and high fashion. I did anything and everything to get there. I did *Playboy* videos. Test shoots. Movie posters. I did any job that I could. I would work sixteen or seventeen hours and got paid $75. And I knew that the jobs I was doing were not the kind of jobs I would eventually want. But I learned about the etiquette of being on set, the art of looking at clothes on a hanger versus on a person, how to do returns, how to be organized. If you don't have someone who gives you a break, you have to just plug along."

STYLING PARTNERSHIP

"In my thirties, I formed a partnership with Estee Stanley. We were two girls who created a company. Our skills complemented each other's, and it just worked. There was a lot I could learn from her and vice versa. The concept was to take on lots of projects and to take care of our girls [celebrity clients]."

The duo lasted seven years. Cristina and Estee recently split up on happy terms because their lives had taken them in different directions.

WHAT I LOVE ABOUT MY JOB

"Working with great fashion houses like Gaultier, Lanvin, Alaia, Chanel, Lanvin, Versace, Oscar de la Renta, Narciso Rodriguez, Thakoon, and others. My job is to get their stuff on my girls: to make it look beautiful and classy."

STAFF

Two regular assistants (paid) and two interns (unpaid).

CRISTINA'S AGENCY

"Margaret Maldonado [LA and NYC] is the best agency for stylists. My agent handles negotiations and money conversations."

HOW IT WORKS

"I have a strong relationship with certain publicists. If that publicist likes my style and my vibe, I'll work with her client. It's a personality thing. These people want to be around you. I am very clear: 'X is not my friend. She's my client.'"

FALSE ILLUSIONS

"A lot of people have this false illusion of what this job is. They think that they will be friends with *the girls* [celebrity clients]?"

HOW DANCE HELPED STYLING

A serious dancer until age twenty-eight, Cristina believes that that training prepared her well for a stylist's life: "Styling draws on the same kind of discipline as dance. You need to know how to listen. You need to understand the food chain."

STYLING IS PART FASHION PUBLICIST

"I deal with big fashion publicists like Bismark Phillips, Karla Otto, and the fashion houses directly. We have the same mission—to get the best clothes on these girls."

For example, "One client has a premiere on Monday. I'm calling in dresses from fifteen to twenty different designers."

JOB = LIFESTYLE

"It's a lifestyle. I'm someone who thought for many years that I might get married, but my work is what I do. I was supposed to leave for Paris today to attend the ready-to-wear shows, but, after the awards show season and 120 days of working nonstop, I decided to send my best assistant. He's twenty-four years old and is going to every show. I can be here going to yoga and doing my acupuncture. That way I don't get burned out."

DRAWING THE LINE

"I am pretty down to earth. I respect the privacy of my clients [A-list actresses and personalities]. My relationship with them is about the service I provide. I'm almost like a doctor: I am there for a specific purpose."

WHY CRISTINA LOVES STYLING

"It's something I found a voice in. The whole thing is a theatrical outlet for me. Very visual. It is a pleasure for me to have this relationship with fashion. I am obsessed with photography and with French films. It all comes together in my work. I think it's an artist's craft."

EXPECTATIONS

"I've paid my dues. You don't just walk into this job and make a ton of money. The truth is I love it so much I would do it for no money."

FASHION CONNECTION

"I have an impeccable relationship with the designers and work hard at these relationships: They go out on a limb for me and I go out on a limb for them. I communicate honestly and directly. There are no games. I return the clothes on time. If I pull two dresses and only one has a chance, the other one goes back."

GLAMOUR MYTH

"I still come home with dirt under my nails. It's a physical business. It's a lot of work. It's NOT glamorous. There was a time that I was flying back and forth from Paris to New York to LA constantly. That's not fun."

WHAT IT REALLY TAKES

"You have to be able to talk to your client and your agency and director. You have to be able to have relationships with the fashion houses. It's people skills. It's also politics. Being nice to and honest with people. And being professional."

GRATEFUL

"My father was so insistent that I go to college—even as a dancer. I was always into it because I was in the city at NYU." (Cristina earned both a bachelor of fine arts and a master of fine arts at NYU and studied dance in London.)

DON'T YOU GET TIRED OF DRESSING PEOPLE?

"I've broken up with boyfriends because of that comment."

THE CONSTANT CHALLENGE

"Making sure it's still fresh and has a pulse."

THE BOTTOM LINE

"I cannot say I have been lucky. I have worked my butt off and will continue to work my butt off."

Photography Team

WHAT: | Photographer, art director, graphic designer, makeup artist, hair stylist.

DEGREE: | None to beauty school, salon apprenticeship, photography school, design school, or liberal arts BA.

TRAITS: | Technical, visual, practical, unflappable.

ESSENTIAL ABILITIES: | To create images that are technically superior, that somehow bear your own signature style, and that tell a story compelling to your client and to your audience.

ROLE: | The photographer is God; the art director is the ringmaster of disparate elements on a shoot (hair, makeup, clothes), plus motivator, driver, seducer, entertainer. Makeup and hair stylist work together to execute the photography.

WORKSPACE: | Street, light box, home studios, large rented studios, runway or location (anywhere you can imagine).

PATH TO POWER: | Apprentice with the best, gradually taking on more responsibility.

MOST COVETED GIGS: | Creating images for *Vogue, W, British Vogue, Italian Vogue,* or campaigns for brands like Calvin Klein, Gucci, Prada, Versace.

MOST COVETED JOBS: | Street photographer (newspaper, Web); still-life photographer (highly technical studio-only work); runway photographer (hardscrabble backstage and end-of-runway situations); studio and location photographer. Hair stylists and makeup artists can represent beauty companies, open their own brands or salons.

DOGGIE JOBS: | None. As long as there's a camera and current season clothes, you're learning.

KEY ALLIANCES: | Editors, designers, advertisers, ad agencies, creative directors, photo editors, celebrities, models, makeup artists, and hair stylists.

LANGUAGES: | There's a tradition of French fashion photographers and a more recent influx of talented English ones.

STARTING COMP: | You work for free.

POTENTIAL COMP: | $ to $$$$.

PERFECT STANDARD

"If you look in your camera and see something you've seen before, don't click the shutter." —legendary *Harper's Bazaar* art director Alexey Brodovitch, advising young photographers.

Photographer

> Here was a young American who seemed unspoiled by European mannerisms or culture. I remember he wore sneakers and no tie. I was struck by his directness and a curious unworldliness, a clarity of purpose, and a freedom of decision. What I call Penn's American instincts made him go for the essentials. —Alex Liberman, longtime Condé Nast creative director, from the introduction to Mr. Penn's book *Passage* (1991), on first meeting Irving Penn in 1941.

Mr. Penn, they called him. Anyone who'd ever worked with him, that is. Irving Penn was among the greatest of American studio photographers. His signature contribution to fashion came in the form of brilliant, powerful, minimal portraits of the most famous people of the twentieth century, Truman Capote, Jackie Kennedy, and Hollywood greats as well as unfamous fishmongers and cleaning women and indigenous peoples, his works always expressing the same majesty and respect for his subjects. His career as a photographer for American *Vogue* lasted an unprecedented sixty years. He wore a suit to his Village studio each morning, changing into a smock for work. He used film, one of the few to never consider adapting to the irrepressible drive to digital. When he died in 2009, at the age of ninety-two, a cacophonous hush fell over the fashion establishment: Clocks were stopped; drums were silenced; hooves muffled. Well, not *exactly*, but they should have been, because the fashion world will never be the same.

Out of respect for Mr. Penn, my creative director pal, Ruba Abu-Nima, left work early that October day, muttering something about how his website should at least have had the sense to shroud itself in black. The next day, in shock that Mr. Penn's passing had attracted virtually no media attention, legendary hair stylist Garren recalled how Mr. Penn, in taking a much younger Garren's portrait, had asked that his subject shave his head

PHOTOGRAPHERS WHOSE WORK YOU SHOULD KNOW

Ansel Adams
Diane Arbus
Henri Cartier-Bresson
William Eggleston
Lee Friedlander
Man Ray
Dorothea Lange
Lee Miller
Lisette Model
Edward Steichen
Alfred Stieglitz
Weegee
Edward Weston
Garry Winogrand

VISUALIZER AGENCIES

Art Department. Represents all categories including photographers (Norma Jean Roy, Max Vadukul, Thomas Schenk), stylists, hair, and makeup. **www.art-dept.com**

Art + Commerce. Top photographers Steven Meisel, Carter Smith, Craig McDean, Ellen Von Unwerth, Solve Sundsbo. Celeb hair stylists like Guido, Orlando Pita, Teddy Charles, Ashley Javier. Makeup like Gucci Westman, Peter Phillips, Diane Kendal. Stylists like Anne Christensen, Bill Mullen, Camilla Nickerson, Brana Wolf. Illustrator Mats Gustafson. And creative directors. You can even apply online for an internship. **www.artandcommerce.com**

Art Partner, NYC, Paris. Represents photographers like Enrique Badulescu, Mario Testino, Mert Alas and Marcus Piggott, David Sims, Mario Sorrenti, and E B ++ and stylists like Lucinda Chambers and Joe McKenna. Internship program. **www.art partner.com**

Bryan Bantry, www.bryanbantry.com. Represents photographer Patrick Demarchelier; hair stylists Didier Malige and Ric Pipino; stylists Adam Glassman and Freddie Leiba, and makeup artist Tina Lipman.

Jed Root, www.jedroot.com. Represents photographers Michael Thompson, Alexei Hay, and Sebastian Kim; stylists Elissa Santisi, Joe Zee, and Inge Fonteyne.

Katy Barker Agency, Inc., www.katybarker.com.

ICONIC FASHION PHOTOGRAPHERS

Richard Avedon

Irwin Blumenfeld

Louise Dahl-Wolfe

Hiro

Martin Munkacsi

Helmut Newton

Irving Penn

Melvin Sokolsky

Lord Snowden

(all the while trimming my own beached-out locks). Laughing now, and essentially hairless, the stylist demurred. No matter, Mr. Penn created a portrait that made Garren look as if he had shaved his head. It hangs in a place of honor in Garren's Fifth Avenue home. Despite everything, my haircut was perfection.

Billy, an assistant on a set I was on recently, after hearing my Norwegian name, mentioned how Mr. Penn tended to hire Scandinavian assistants who would eat smoked fish for breakfast, trivia that made sense only after I remembered that Mr. Penn's wife and muse, Lisa Fonssagrives-Penn, a Swede, considered by many to have been the world's first supermodel, must have thrown back a smoked sardine or two first thing in the day.

Smoked fish, smocks, and shrouds. "Blah, blah, blah," you say. "What does this ancient history have to do with me: tomorrow's Steven Meisel, Mario Testino, Raymond Meier?"

Well, *everything*, if you're smart. Read Mr. Penn's obituary. Look at his images. Buy a book of his photographs. By connecting yourself to the quite short history of fashion photography that Mr. Penn embodies better than anyone, you assure yourself, a young fashion photographer hopeful, a brighter path since it will be enriched with the precise, clean American vision of one of its greatest. Then go shoot your neighborhood skateboard dudes. I promise you they'll look cooler and your image will be more powerful for your time with Mr. Penn.

TIMELINES

Think about it. Fashion was born the first time cavemen put pelt to body. Trust me on this, it's true. Writing was born the first time cavemen put symbol to cave wall—albeit fashion writing came a few years later. By contrast, fashion photography was born in the 1920s with the emergence of Condé Nast—the man, his publications, and two amazing photographers who helped define the field of fashion photography: Alfred Stieglitz (husband of artist Georgia O'Keeffe) and Edward Steichen. If you think about it, Stieglitz and Steichen broke through *only ninety years ago.* So, studying the entire history of fashion photography shouldn't take that long.

DENNIS GOLONKA | Fashion Photographer

His fashion photography career wasn't handed to him on a silver platter. After college in Maryland, Dennis Golonka moved to New York City and put himself through photography classes at the School of Visual Arts. He then slogged for years as an assistant to other photographers before signing on in the art department of a well-known fashion magazine. There, Dennis was able to study up close the work of iconic fashion photographers like Richard Avedon, Hiro, and Louis Dahl-Wolfe.

From his perch in the art department, Dennis was often the first to see photos by contemporary greats like Patrick Demarchelier, Raymond Meier, David Sims, Mario Testino, and Craig McDean, and he watched as their images were edited, massaged, and captioned before finally going to press. During this time, Dennis also built his contacts with editors and managed to get some of his own pictures published in the magazine so that when the moment arrived, years later, to go out on his own, Dennis Golonka was ready to make the leap. Of course it helps that Dennis has an easy smile and a big warm personality, is extremely polite, and puts people at ease in front of his camera. It also helps that Dennis continues to adapt his technique to survive and grow in the tricky fashion landscape. A lot more useful than some stupid silver platter.

BACKGROUND

A Maryland native, Dennis is a lanky, winsome guy who graduated with a BA from Towson University (part of the University of Maryland system), then spent two years studying photography at the School of Visual Arts (SVA), New York City. Dennis is not a famous son and has not dated supermodels. He's a talented, passionate guy who's made it through hard work and never giving up.

STUPIDLY THOUGHT AFTER EARNING SVA DEGREE

"Now I can work as a photographer."

ASSISTING, ASSISTING, ASSISTING

That was the beginning of Dennis' assisting phase. "I sent out tons of résumés and got a call from a still-life photographer and soon became his full-time second assistant. Still-life photography was not for me. Next I assisted Rebecca Blake, a fashion and beauty photographer. I was her third assistant. I was Windexing windows, cleaning bathrooms, and playing gofer. I was learning more about cleaning for a germaphobe than how to be a great photographer."

KNOW YOUR CAMERAS

"I sat at the interview with Steven Meisel's first assistant. By the end of the interview, I thought I had the job. Just as I was leaving, he said, 'Oh yeah, one last question: You know the Pentax 6-by-7, don't you?' I told the truth—that I didn't know it but could easily rent this camera and learn it. I didn't get the job."

BUS OMEN

"I was at the gym one day, when it dawned on me I wasn't getting enough out of assisting photographers anymore, . . . but I was still unable to make a living as a photographer in my own right. I had the idea to go work for a fashion magazine. I rushed home to make a list of publications that may be hiring in the art department. Then I looked up and saw a bus pass on the street that had on its side the relaunch cover of the new *Bazaar, 'enter the era of elegance,'* with Linda Evangelista on the cover. It was like a message to me."

KISMET

"I cold-called the art department, and the girl who answered said I'd need to get my résumé in that day to be considered for the assistant job in the art department."

"I'LL CLEAN TOILETS"

"I sat in the interview with art director Ann Kwong, and I said, 'I am a hard worker. I will do anything you need me to do. If you need me to clean the toilets, I will clean the toilets.' And I got the job, despite the fact that they were thinking to hire a girl."

SEVEN YEARS LATER

Still in his role at the art department at *Bazaar,* Dennis had been shooting pictures for the magazine from the beginning and was gradually allowed to do freelance photography for other publications as well. "And I never had to clean a toilet."

WHY LIZ TILBERIS' *BAZAAR* WAS GREAT FOR FASHION PHOTOGRAPHY

"Most established fashion publications have their contract photographers. *Vogue* has Steven Meisel and Patrick Demarchelier. *Bazaar* today has Peter Lindbergh. But at Liz's *Bazaar,* we gave great young photographers a chance. We used people like David Sims, Carter Smith, Craig McDean, and Mario Sorrenti before anyone else gave them a shot. That was the exception. Today there are fewer major publications willing to give an unknown a chance."

CREATOR   VISUALIZER   CRITIC   SELLER

TIME TO GO FOR IT

When a new editor in chief moved in, Dennis decided it was his time to do the photography thing full on.

NOW *HIRING* ASSISTANTS

"For many freelance fashion photography jobs, it used to be that you could hire two or three assistants in addition to your tech. A tech is the person who deals with the digital portion of the shoot. A good tech can help take a good picture and make it gorgeous. In a slow economy it's more likely to be just one assistant and your tech. I have a regular group of assistants I work with and, occasionally, will rotate someone new in."

NEXT BIG THING

"Videography will be the wave of the future. Fashion photographers who also tap in to this new medium will have interesting careers going forward."

CHASING TASTES?

Despite trends in fashion photography, Dennis advises, "Just do your thing, and eventually it will hit. Luckily for me, I like an upbeat picture, and that's where things are now. These things come in waves. People who shoot dark images are probably not working as much at the moment, but that could all change tomorrow. It's the nature of the business."

SHOWING UP ON THE SET

A guy most happy in jeans and a T-shirt, even Dennis admits: "It's fashion photography, so take pride in the way you look."

FAVORITE IMAGE YOU'VE EVER SHOT

"Last year I did a fashion story for British *Marie Claire*. We photographed the story at the Eden Project in Cornwall, England. In one of the gardens stood a sculpture almost twenty-one feet tall called *The WEEE Man*. It is a huge robotic creature made of scrap electrical and electronic equipment. It represents the average quantity of consumer goods every single one of us throws away over a lifetime. I photographed our model on a ladder shining against the metal of the sculpture."

PHOTOGRAPHERS WHO INSPIRE DENNIS

"Way too many people to list, but a few of my favorites are Steven Meisel, Tim Walker, Jock Sturges, Lars Tunbjork, Richard Avedon, Nan Goldin, and David Sims."

Makeup Artist

These days, no matter where you live, there is a way to become a working makeup artist. Perhaps the easiest start is to get a job behind the counter of one of the many makeup artists' lines of products, like MAC, Bobbi Brown, Francois Nars, or Laura Mercier at major department stores all across the country or, possibly, at some of these companies' stand-alone stores. Once hired as a counter salesperson or "makeup artist," you will be trained in some basic techniques of makeup application. Then, as you work, you will begin to see if you like the process of interacting with a woman and the intimacy of putting makeup on someone's face. You could supplement your store work by offering friends and friends-of-friends free makeup application for special occasions, gradually switching to a fee system if people like what they see and your services catch on. Or you could link up with a popular hair salon, setting up your own chair to do quick or complete makeup application for clients already in the salon. You could ask to see the list of clients with appointments and call individual women ahead to see whether they'd like to schedule makeup with you after their blowouts.

Whomever you get your hands on, be sure to take a digital "before" and "after" photo, which you can use in your portfolio.

Bridal makeup is specialty you can do anywhere. Probably the best way to start is to find the biggest bridal makeup artist in your area and offer to assist that person for free. Once you gain confidence, you can offer to do makeup for the bridal party of a friend, friend-of-friend, or relative. Again, take your own before and after pictures so that you can put them in your book. If you like this work and if it is fun for you, you might want to print up cards and then make an effort to meet bridal consultants in your region as well as leaving cards at bridal shops and catering halls. Another route would be to team up with a hairdresser who does a fair number of weddings. But, even though being a wedding makeup artist is a way of working in the realm of fashion, is it really being *in fashion*?

BOBBI BROWN | Makeup Artist, Naturalist, Empowerer, Founder (1991) Bobbi Brown Cosmetics

You were the kid who had his or her hands in makeup as long as you can remember and have never tired of putting makeup on your sister and her friends. You can't get enough of it. You've read Kevyn Aucoin's book and every last one of Bobbi Brown's books. You even know who Wade Bandy was and that Dick Page and Pat McGrath are both British. Maybe you keep scrapbooks of personalities so that you can analyze different makeup looks in different situations. You know that your first love is makeup but that working behind the MAC counter or doing a bride a month won't cut it for you. That means you are going to have to find a way to live in New York City or Los Angeles, and even then getting started as a studio makeup artist for fashion photography and fashion runway is not easy.

You have to have major persistence. "If a door closes to you, you have to go through the window," advises makeup artist Bobbi Brown, who founded her own beauty company some 20 years ago, which now sells her cosmetics in 55 countries globally. It is also cutthroat, since there are many times more people looking to enter the business than the business can support.

Studio photography is a business based on relationships. When a photographer finds a makeup artist (or two or three) he or she likes to work with and from whom he or she creates great images, there is no incentive for that photographer to try new people.

It is so tough that it defies logic. Assuming you don't know anyone, but to get a job as a makeup artist you need to show pictures of your work as a makeup artist, where are these images to come from? Bobbi suggests starting the way she did, by visiting modeling agencies and offering to do test shoots for free with new models. "They liked me enough that they'd send me on test shoots," says Bobbi. "It's about showing up there and being nice."

Go online and find the names of big photo agencies in these cities and get in touch with them, as well. While Bobbi was pounding the pavement, she sometimes waited tables because the hours could be flexible enough to accommodate a long day in a photo studio. Working at a store or for a company like Bobbi Brown Cosmetics gives great experience but not the flexibility you'd need to pursue a studio career at the same time.

"Everything is about your work," says Bobbi. "You have to show your work. Your job is to get pictures," Bobbi explains. "You're doing it for free to get the pictures for your book. And, probably, after the shoot, you'll have to chase after the photographer to get the picture. Though it's slightly easier today because everything is digital. And don't spend tons of money on printing them.

"After I graduated from college, my father agreed to pay my rent for a year so that I would have the freedom to make this thing work," says Bobbi. "That was an amazing gift.

"For me it was a lot about networking. Every day my job was to sit on my phone and to go out and meet people. I called Bonnie Maller, whose work I'd seen in a magazine and liked. Her machine said to call her agent, Bryan Bantry [an agent who represents photographers, like Patrick Demarchelier, as well as hair and makeup people and models]. So I called Bryan and went to see him. He said to keep in touch and to stop by when I had more work to show. It's hard work. Getting work is your full-time job. I also went to magazines with my portfolio and got to know the editors. That's how I got hired on little jobs. It's really networking. You never know who will recommend you. I was happy to work for free.

"In the end, it was Bryan Bantry who gave me my start. One day a makeup artist was sick and he called me. That was my first shoot."

Eventually, *Glamour* booked Bobbi on a shoot with French photographer Brigitte Lacombe. Bobbi also assisted makeup artist Linda Mason, whose heavily pigmented and densely colored makeup was as far from Bobbi's soon-to-be-famous natural look as you could get, at fashion shows.

"You have to be really open. You can learn from everybody. Linda Mason really helped me understand the beauty of color. Bruce Weber taught me how to take makeup off. [Former *Vogue* beauty editor] Andrea Robinson taught me things on set, as did [photographer] Steven Klein. I've been a student my whole life. I love reading the stories of how other makeup artists got their start. You cannot rest for a second or feel badly if someone says you have no talent. You have to keep going."

Weirdly, another thing working against Bobbi was her all-American-ness. "Unless you are British or French, it's hard to be taken seriously. It's hard for American kids to come into this world and be respected.

"I arrived in New York City from Boston [where Bobbi had graduated from Emerson College]. I was cutting my own hair. I was the biggest dork. I looked at the magazine editors and tried to emulate them. I was always figuring things out." The famously down-to-earth, fifty-something makeup artist then adds: "And, hey, I still am!"

To help change the preconceived notions that the fashion world has of American makeup artists, Bobbi has recently started an education program for young makeup artists. "If we can give young people the tools, and they have a clear vision and goal, they can do it. I tell my students that it's really important to think about what will make you happy. Is your ultimate goal fashion shows in Paris? Or do you want to do brides in Santa Fe? It's important to spell out that goal so that when an opportunity comes, you are clear that you must take it." For the latest on Bobbi's makeup artistry programs, see bobbibrown.com.

"If I can give young people the tools, it'll be that much easier for them."

WHO TO ASSIST? TOP STUDIO AND/OR RUNWAY MAKEUP ARTISTS

Bobbi Brown. The master of all-American natural beauty; founder and creative director of Bobbi Brown.

Linda Cantello. First of the modern generation of makeup artists. British, based in Paris. Launcher of many others' careers.

Gordon Espinet. MAC master; vice president global makeup artistry.

James Kaliardos. American; also with MAC.

Pat McGrath. English spokesperson for Cover Girl and Max Factor; known for working with her hands instead of using brushes. Runway star.

Stephane Marais. Creating the most dewy complexion, this Frenchman brings a painterly quality to bear on the skin.

Laura Mercier. Long-term Steven Meisel collaborator. Founder of her own brand.

Francois Nars. Among the best, this French makeup artist is a glam-master and also the founder of his own brand.

Dick Page. English originator of the minimalism trend of the 1990s. Spokesperson and formulator with Shiseido.

Tom Pecheux. French runway legend, Estée Lauder spokesperson..

Peter Phillips. Creative director for Chanel, Belgian.

Wendy Ro. English, based in NYC and London, fixture at Burberry show.

Charlotte Tilbury. English; spokesperson for Tom Ford beauty.

Gucci Westman. American; global creative director for Revlon.

LAURA MERCIER | Makeup Artist, Creator
of Laura Mercier Cosmetics

Laura Mercier is the last person you'd expect to be a beauty entrepreneur. More of a creature from another century, Laura is instinctual, private, and not always concerned with the practical side of life. So ethereal is her energy, so un-Americanized her French, it is hard to imagine her on an airplane, in a taxi, or even a car, for that matter. Nonetheless, that amazing opportunities just seem to come her way—like the opportunity to work with photographer Steven Meisel for ten years or collaborate with a hard-driven Texan to produce an eponymous beauty line—is accepted by Laura as natural in life. People who know this ultrafeminine French woman well have a hard time imagining her doing personal appearances with "real women" customers in Dallas or Kansas City. Perhaps it is because she is so dramatically out of her element out in Anytown, U.S.A., that she has built such a loyal following there.

UNIQUE CONTRIBUTION TO BEAUTY
Taking the sophisticated and highly technical concept of creating a flawless face via concealer (or "camouflage") and making it accessible to a big audience of appreciative women globally.

AURA
Mysterious, feminine, and private.

LOOK
Flowing long wavy dark hair, huge chocolate eyes, and, of course, flawless skin.

UPBRINGING
Born in Congo, the third of three daughters, Laura was raised in the French region of Provence. After high school, she moved to Paris to attend painting school. She then attended the famed Carita School on Faubourg St. Honoré, focusing on makeup application. Subsequently, Laura was asked to represent the school as makeup artist and instructor, and she soon became the first assistant to Thibault Vabre, a famous French makeup artist.

COMING TO AMERICA
In 1985, Laura was asked to come to the States as part of the launch team for the American *Elle*. "It wasn't for me," Laura says of that time. "I didn't want to come."

BREAKTHROUGH MOMENT

Being called to work for Steven Meisel, which lasted for a feverishly creative and exhausting decade (1988 to 1998).

FLASH FORWARD

"Now it's nineteen years, and I could never go back. I was ready to change my life. It was good for me to come here and start new. I had to start from zero. I wouldn't be where I am today had I stayed in France."

THE REAL LAURA

Hates phoniness. "I am totally antisocial and nonconformist. I don't go to dinner parties. . . . To schmooze is not my forte," she explains in her graceful, undiluted French accent.

WHAT SHE LOVES

To hide in a corner of a lab brewing up the next amazing product. To be sitting in the corner mixing colors or painting a face.

WATCH LAURA WORK

She is an artist. She paints the face, in pointillism style.

EXPLAINING HER SUCCESS

"I believe in not walking on other people's feet. In not wanting things too badly. Something good happens when you think what you'd love in life. I believe in destiny. You can drive your life, change your life."

TODAY

Through her licensing agreement with Janet Gurwitch, Laura has built a line of three hundred products, sold in four hundred stores in seventeen countries.

LOTS OF FACES

Doing thirty-six personal appearances each year with an average of 150 women at each event, Laura touches the faces of some 5,400 women a year, and she has made up 43,200 women in the eight years of Laura Mercier Cosmetics.

REGULAR FACES

Sarah Jessica Parker and Julia Roberts.

"You never know everything. You are never the best. There will always be someone who will go further. Do *your* best. Have *passion* and you will be successful. Take the business for what it can offer you. Do not drown yourself in it. The definition of the fashion business is that it is short term. Quick. Exciting. Exhilarating. The next day there's a new puppy in town and you will go on to something else."

DOWNTIME

Living quietly in Bellport, New York. NOT going to dinner parties.

Hair Stylist

There are hair stylists and there are Hair Stylists. The hard, cold reality is that there are very few Hair Stylists on this planet (you can count them on two hands) who make it in the world of fashion photography and runway. Among them are Orlando Pita, Odile Gilbert, Guido Palau, Sally Hershberger, Jimmy Paul, Julien d'Ys, and Eugene Soulemain. But there is no higher authority on the subject than Garren, a gentleman and probably the most famous and experienced of contemporary hair stylists. Remarkably, for the past thirty-five years, Garren has been American *Vogue*'s top hairdresser, doing more cover images for the magazine than most other hair stylists combined. His career with the magazine spans the careers of iconic fashion photographers Deborah Turbeville, Albert Watson, and Irving Penn, as well as Richard Avedon and Patrick Demarchelier. These days, Garren works predominantly with *Vogue* photographers Steven Meisel, Steven Klein, and David Sims.

THE FASHION WORLD'S TOP HAIR STYLISTS TO ASSIST

Start off assisting any of the names listed here, and you'll be on the right track.

Garren, www.garrennewyork.com.
Sally Hershberger, www.sallyhershberger.com.
Orlando Pita, Orlo Salon (212) 242-3266.
Odile Gilbert, www.atelier68.fr.
Ashley Javier, www.ashleyjavierparlor.com.
Guido Palau, www.julianwatsonagency.com.
Eugene Soulemain, www.streetersnewyork.com.
Julien d'Ys, www.lateliernyc.com.

If you can't face starving in New York, one good way to launch your fashion hair stylist career is to work at a high-profile teaching salon, like Bumble and Bumble, Aveda, Vidal Sassoon, or Toni & Guy. Besides a paycheck, you'll be earning fashion creds, experiences, and, once you've made your mark, maybe even the possibility of transferring to a big-city salon.

PROFILE

GARREN | It Takes a Hair Obsession and a Hair Education

"You have to have it in your blood to be on the set," says Garren. "You have to have grown up obsessed by hair since the time you were young. You have to know your research. You have to know your movie references that date back to people like Mae West, Joan Crawford, and Marlene Dietrich. To understand that Madonna is referencing Marlene Dietrich with her look, rather than originating the look, is critical. . . . You have to have film references from each decade cataloged in your brain and know all your celebrities. You have to understand fashion history from the 1800s on to the present. You have to have a sense of what different looks define which decades and which icons define each decade. Basically all the way back to Roman history."

GETTING IN

The big photographers don't let lots of people into their worlds because they want cohesiveness in the images. They want everyone on the same page. That translates into a regular team of hair stylists and makeup artists linked to a photographer, becoming a collaborative team.

"You don't just wake up one day and decide to be a studio hair stylist. Those people who do that? Their careers are short-lived because when their ideas dry up, they are unable to generate the next thing." Conversely, if you are educated in fashion and film history and are able to draw from significant looks from the past, you have all the references, and the ideas will never stop. "It all goes in cycles," says Garren.

Garren himself grew up in upstate New York, not exactly a hotbed of hair innovation, and says that from the age of thirteen, he was obsessed with hair stylists like Vidal Sassoon and Kenneth and Alexander of Paris, as well as with film and fashion magazines. Similarly, other great studio hair stylists like Guido, Orlando, Jimmy Paul, and Louis D'Angelo (whom Garren trained) immersed themselves in hair history from an early age.

HOW TO GET STARTED

1. You have to move to a big city.
2. Get into a hair salon or at the side of people you admire.
3. Watch and learn, and keep building your references.
4. Once established, you have to find a good agent to keep you going. Do this by meeting the agents of well-respected hair stylists.

KEEPING ONE FOOT IN THE SALON

Garren likes the rhythm of going back and forth between the reality of salon work and the fantasy of fashion photography. "When I'm in the salon, I get to work with all different hair types. When I'm on the set, I work with models' hair, which typically isn't the greatest [thick, full body] hair, so you have to add to it and make it better." Models from the countries in the former Eastern Bloc who are dominant today, Garren notes, typically don't have great hair whereas French and Italian models have amazing hair, attributing the difference to a combination of genes and nutrition.

"At least you have something to fall back on—when you fall out of favor—because everyone falls out of favor," says Garren. Spending too much time in the salon isn't good, either. "People stuck in the salon do *salon hair* [trendy, safe, pretty hair as opposed to outrageous, edgy, or unexpected looks]. You put them on set, they don't know what to do. I enjoy bringing things back to the salon from the set."

Indeed, a well-run salon represents steady income while studio work (particularly editorial) pays little, but its prestige fuels the salon business. In addition to Garren, Orlando and Sally Hershberger each have their own eponymous salons in Manhattan.

HOW IMPORTANT IS RUNWAY TO A HAIR STYLIST'S CAREER?

It's more and more important, says Garren, because of the instant availability of images on the Internet. He cautions against doing only shows with natural hair since that generates little to no buzz and has no news value. "You have to be able to get yourself in the right shows so that you can do extraordinary hair that will help you make a name for yourself."

HAIR STYLISTS' SIX RULES OF THE SET

1. *It's not about you.* Hair stylists who are strung out and need to share everything about their personal lives are destined to have short careers. You shouldn't be there demanding everyone's attention, showing personal pictures or outtakes from other shoots. "People don't need to know about your crazy personal life," advises Garren. "You have to be there for that picture. You have to be present. That is the professionalism of the work."

2. *Know when to step in.* Understanding when to intervene for a touch-up when the model is in front of the camera is critical. You have to implicitly understand when the hair *is* the focal point and when the hair *is not* the focal point, and you need to know how to behave in both instances. You have to know when to step in and when to pull back.

3. *Be discreet.* Chitchat about a photographer's breakdown and model no-show from a previous job will definitely generate momentary interest on your next shoot, but your long-term prospects will be seriously endangered. "I have always been one not to talk about what happens on a set," says Garren. "That has served me well."

4. *Bring good energy.* On a set, it's all chemistry: how you get on with people in the studio; the calmness of your being. "But then you have to follow that up with your craft," says Garren.

5. *Do hairdos in the wind and rain.* You need to be able to work with the elements when working outside. Think of all the possible situations (beach, boat, mountain or building top), and prepare for them.

6. *Don't call in sick.* In studio photography, there is no such thing as a sick day. "The whole team is depending on you. You figure out how to stay healthy for your work," advises Garren. "That's the deal. You stay healthy. You don't even think about calling in sick. It's not an option. So you don't go out late. You get enough rest."

Graphic Designer

The role of a graphic designer is to design type (that is, determine the size of the font, the typeface, the type placement, and how much type goes where) and to combine type (or words or copy) with photographs in a logical, inviting way. Graphic designers can be found working in magazines (designing the magazine pages), at advertising agencies creating print or online campaigns, in freelance situations designing packaging (think of perfume, hang bags), and in advertising agencies creating print or online campaigns.

Misconception. Some people learn a computerized design program and assume they can be a graphic designer. "It's not quite that simple," explains art director and graphic designer Katty Van Itallie. "The program is just a tool."

Education. People go to design school to study graphic design. There, they learn about the legacy of typefaces, the science of color and proportions, and the history of graphic design. How can you be an outlandish and revolutionary graphic designer without first understanding what the rules *are* and *how to break them*?

Good design looks easy, but, in reality, it is complex and has to work on many levels: the architecture, colors, typefaces. Images must all communicate the message effectively and beautifully. How you execute good design depends very much on the assignment, as well as the audience or reader. In magazines, design is a collaboration, and the pages that go to press are a result of that collaboration.

THREE KEY GRAPHIC DESIGN CAREER STEPS

1. Internships are a really good way to get into an ad agency or magazine. Work for free, even for a few days per week. If you work hard and people like you, when an assistant spot opens up, you'll be the most obvious choice.
2. Take graphic design courses, and learn design software like InDesign and Adobe. Illustrator is also handy. Most people now know how to design for the Web.
3. You really only learn by doing it, and you can't get a job without a job. This means, like Katty, you sometimes have to start at trade or small publications that you don't identify with and wouldn't choose to read.

"I learned how to design by hand, and, in the old days, I built pages by hand," says Katty. "Learning computer programs has been liberating in many ways, but in some ways limiting." Katty also emphasizes that the learning process is endless. "I work with someone now that when I watch what she does, I often find myself thinking, 'Why didn't I do that?' Now I'd like to learn how to design movie credits and for the Web. There is so much more to design than just magazines. But magazines have always been my comfort zone."

Katty's formal design training happened at Parsons after she'd completed her four-year liberal arts college degree. She then worked at various jobs for a few years.

In addition to Parsons, the School of Visual Arts (SVA), also in Manhattan, is another good graphic design option.

The graphic design job search. Graphic design work is vast and varied and allows for career and geographic mobility and flexibility: You can work at ad agencies, book publishers, or magazines; you can work inside companies or outside as a freelancer. In fact, you can work pretty much anywhere words and pictures interact. Some graphic designers develop specialties, like logo design or album cover design, while others evolve into art directors (that is, they oversee the conceptualizing of and generation of the images or illustrations as well as designing the final treatments of the images with typography). Knowing the language you are designing in is helpful, but it is not absolutely necessary.

KATHARINE VAN ITALLIE | Magazine Art Director and Graphic Designer

Katty makes designing the cover of a magazine look easy. Real easy. She takes the three-quarters model image and the title of the magazine, along with the endless cover lines the editors insist must appear this month, and, in front of your eyes, she whips up a perfectly balanced, eminently salable, essentially beautiful cover. And while you're still standing there gaping at the marvel on the screen of her computer, she'll spin out a few dazzling variations just so it's superobvious why the first approach was the smartest one.

For Katty Van Itallie, it *is* easy to design magazine covers and just about anything else: ad campaigns, book covers, fashion stories, posters, invitations, CD covers, typography for film. This isn't because Katty is a whiz at Quark and Photoshop (which she is). For Katty, software is only a tool. It is because Katty understands the science of color, the architecture of a rectangle, how the eye absorbs information. Katty paints pictures, and she has studied art history. She could produce the same cover design with only scissors and glue. And, believe it or not, that's pretty much how she designed her first magazine cover.

BACKGROUND
Katty is the youngest of five slender children of Dr. Theodore Van Itallie (founder of St. Luke's, Columbia University Obesity Research Center, teacher, researcher, and renowned Manhattan clinician) and Barbara Cox. She grew up in Englewood, New Jersey. Summers were (and still are) spent in Fenwick, Connecticut, where neighbors like Katharine Hepburn figured larger than life.

BEING THE YOUNGEST OF FIVE?
"It was great. I mean, I was teased and often felt left out of a lot, but I also totally idolized my siblings and thought their friends were supercool. Plus, I was very independent because my parents were pretty relaxed and trusted me entirely. There was nothing to rebel against."

EDUCATION
High school was spent at Dana Hall (all-girls boarding school) in Wellesley, Massachusetts. Then Katty chose to break from family traditions and go west to attend Pitzer College, a small, private liberal arts institution and a member of the Claremont Colleges, in Claremont, California, thirty miles east of Los Angeles. Katty graduated with a major in studio art.

EAST COAST? WEST COAST?
"My mother wanted me to go to Wellesley, but I was desperate to go to California. Academics were not that high a priority for me, but, I believe, school is very much what one makes of it. And there's a lot of opportunity at Pitzer. Plus, it's a really fun place to go to college!"

EARLY RANDOM JOBS
"I had a series of bad jobs that had nothing to do with what I ended up doing—but they were all learning experiences and valuable to any kind of work situation. My first job was working in the publicity department at a record company. One of my tasks was to call a local radio station and request 'Mickey' by one of our artists, Toni Basil. That job didn't last long because the label folded and everyone got fired. Then I got a job airbrushing on T-shirts through stencils. I really liked that job except every night I'd blow my nose and paint would come out."

CAREER REVELATION
"While I was working at a Park Avenue hotel, I got the idea to apply for a job at a magazine. I remember calling my sister Elizabeth, who was the art director at *Self,* to tell her: 'I don't want to copy you, but this seems like fun.' I suddenly saw clearly what I wanted to do."

PARSONS
To get the specific graphic design training Katty needed to work in the art department of a magazine, she went back to attend Parsons New School in the graphic design department. In order to get a loan for these studies, she had to actually be seeking a degree, so she transferred all of her credits from college and got her associate's degree in one year of night school.

FIRST GIG
"While at Parsons, I managed to get a part-time job at *New York* magazine. I worked with Corky Pollan, who did the 'Best Bets' pages. It was a good learning experience. One of my jobs was that I had to Polaroid the merchandise, pack it into bags, and send it to the photographer. And the very nice art director there let me use all his equipment while I was at school."

HOW KATTY GOT THE JOB
"My sister Elizabeth had a friend there who told her that someone else there needed someone part-time."

POSTGRAD JOB

"Macy's—I did my sales associate's training over the Fourth of July. I was a disaster. A customer once asked me where the sheet department was, and I think I screamed 'I don't know!' "

LUCKILY . . .

"I started getting freelance assignments to do mechanicals for [a trade publication called] *Supermarket News.* Then I got enough work so I could quit Macy's."

BOUNCED PAYCHECK

"Then I took a job at this fan magazine called *Faces,* which did one-off issues on stars like Jon Bon Jovi and Madonna. I was mostly doing mechanicals [production], working in a hall with no windows, no nothing. I had to go to the next office, which is where all these porn magazines were, to use the stat room [the room where copies of images and type were made on the photostat machine]. It was definitely a lowbrow job: My paychecks sometimes bounced."

BREAK

"Then I got a call from Marilu Lopez, who was at *Ms.*, and she said she needed a junior designer. Of course she knew my sister. Marilu said the salary was only $13,000. I said 'fantastic.' She hired me over the phone."

ALL HAIL MARILU

"I started as a designer. There was a huge learning curve. Thank God for Marilu—she taught me everything."

MY MAGAZINE

Next Katty was thrilled to get a better-paying design job at *Mademoiselle* (a Condé Nast publication no longer in circulation), a magazine she loved to read.

OTHER TITLES WHERE KATTY HAS WORKED

Glamour, Seventeen, House & Garden, Family Circle, Sports Illustrated, More, Seventeen (again), *Harper's Bazaar* (freelance), *Country Living Specials* (gardening, collecting, holidays), *Departures, Travel+Leisure.*

FASHION MAGAZINES VERSUS SPORTS MAGAZINE VERSUS SHELTER

"Fashion is really fun because you can be playful and adventurous with design and color. It's not so serious. Plus, the combination of images, people, still life, food, and so on, gives

CREATOR   VISUALIZER   CRITIC   SELLER

inspiration and vitality and variety to the pages. *Sports Illustrated* was fun because it was news and felt somewhat urgent even if it's sports news. It felt real. Plus, the photography was amazing. And the people were funny and smart."

FREELANCE VERSUS WORKING ON STAFF

Over her career, Katty has flip-flopped between staff jobs and a succession of freelance assignments. "I worked freelance really only because I couldn't get on staff for whatever reason. The hourly or daily rate of freelance adds up to more than salary usually, but there are no benefits and no paid vacations so it's a bit stressful.

"Plus you are treated differently, and you act differently. You have less emotional investment, and the staff has lower expectations so you can't really contribute as much. You're more of just a hired gun, which can be a relief sometimes but gets a little boring after a while. I prefer to really care about what I'm working on, and I like to feel that my contributions are taken seriously."

WHY GRAPHIC DESIGN IS A COOL CAREER

"I can wear pretty much whatever I want! No more nylons and polyester unless I want to.

"I get to look at beautiful photos and work with them, and the result of what I do is tangible. I can look at a magazine page, cover, whatever, and say, 'I did that.' Plus, the people I work with are always smart and fun and interesting. The casual and creative atmosphere suits my personality."

SOMETHING KATTY HAS NOT DESIGNED

"Ummmm . . . I really can't think of anything. I did ads in the ad department of Hearst Corporate for one miserable week. I have worked on books but have never designed an entire book that was published. I've done newsletters, beauty displays, invitations, business cards, magazines, posters, CD covers."

ADVICE TO PEOPLE STARTING OUT WHO WANT TO BE DESIGNERS

"You don't have to work at a hotel, the way I did. Educate yourself. Explore different careers so that you know your direction earlier than I did. (I didn't even know what graphic design was.) I was also hung up on the fact that I didn't want to be seen to follow what my sister was doing. I felt like I was copying her for years. Now I wish I could do books the way she does!"

ROBBIN RASKIN | Senior Art Director, Neiman Marcus

Thin and striking with long dark hair and pale skin, Robbin personifies *fashionista* as she teeters along in her chic high shoes, narrow trousers, and a tight-fitting blazer or her latest favorite minidress. As a ten-year-old, she made stop action films with her father's camera; she studied film at college, then stepped into a ten-year magazine career in New York. "I need to feel a strong fashion design element in whatever I am doing," Robbin explains of the link between fashion magazines and her second career as art director at Neiman Marcus, the hub of Dallas fashion. Robbin is the rare talent who's found a way to stay in fashion *and* go home again.

BACKGROUND

Born and raised in Dallas, Robbin attended the St. Alcuin's Montessori School for her primary years, finishing at the Greenhill School. She studied film at the Tisch School of New York University. Robbin is married to furniture designer Michael Solis, and they live in Dallas with their two sons, Gus and Roman.

TRAINING

"I was a film major. That's how you learn about fashion."

FILMS INFORMING ROBBIN'S VISION

"*The Eyes of Laura Mars* ('How can you understand YSL if you haven't seen it?'); *The Women; Bonnie and Clyde; Swing Time; The Big Sleep;* and any Astaire-Rogers films."

CATHARSIS

As a teen, "I saw this Cindy Sherman exhibit at the Dallas Museum of Art that really moved me. I had tears in my eyes it was so beautiful. I said 'I love photography. I'm done here. I'm moving to New York City.' And I did."

FIRST FASHION JOBS

Fashion magazines: *Seventeen* working for Sasha Charnin Morrison and *Harper's Bazaar* working for Melanie Ward.

HOW IT HELPED HER

"It's like the exact training of ballet when you are a little girl. When you follow the rules and you are creative, you're on the right path."

CREATOR VISUALIZER CRITIC SELLER

WHERE FASHION MAGAZINE EDITORIAL TRAINING CAN TAKE YOU

"Anyplace where they do advertising in house and you can be involved to do the visuals."

SURPRISES AND STANDARDS

"I never would have thought that there'd be opportunities for what I wanted to do in Dallas and in retail. You want to be where you can do it beautifully. And I am."

LIFE WORKING FOR NEIMAN MARCUS

"My boss is really incredible: We want to make HER look good. Make her ideas our ideas and make her ideas look better.

"I'm emotionally involved, since every minute we're creating something new. I'm doing story after story—an evening gown story, then dresses, then jewelry. I'm in charge of budgets. It's all-involving. I love it."

WHAT YOU DIDN'T LEARN IN MAGAZINES

"Budgetary stuff. If I'd had to manage $50,000 for one day, it might have helped me."

WHAT YOU DO NOW

"I'm a senior art director. We break the books into stories—just like a magazine. Our book has a theme and stories supporting the theme. I make it real fashion. So I might get fifteen pages. I have to come up with a concept, hire a photographer, makeup artist, and hair stylist. After the shoot, I paginate the images, putting looks in order and in story form."

PACE OF WORK

"I photo art direct every two to three weeks and do a total of eight books per year for women plus two men's books. I also do trends, which is really fun. I end up getting really into that. For example, September and March are the higher-priced designer or trend books. October and April are not designer. December is always a holiday or party theme. I do fine jewelry for that book."

THE RULES

"Oh yeah. It's very editorial, but you have to know the rules. If it's seated, it has to be full body. The issue of cropping is important: You can't crop into the clothes unless it's just a plain black pant. You can't crop into a dress. You have to show the hemline. You have to show the clothes. That's the point."

CAREER CHANGER

STARTED AS: FASHION EDITOR, MAGAZINES
SWITCHED TO: ART DIRECTOR, RETAIL

To return to Dallas from New York, Robbin knew she needed to reinvent herself. She also knew that Neiman Marcus, the Dallas fashion institution, was her best bet for employment. Her experience organizing and styling editorial fashion photo shoots at magazines translated into an art director's job at the retail giant: Robbin now oversees retail fashion photo shoots for the store's myriad catalogs, mailers, and advertising. Regrets? Robbin wishes she'd had more budgetary responsibility in magazines and training in computer design.

HOW YOU FOLLOW THE RULES AND STAY CREATIVE
"That's really hard. But I now know when it has to be a spread and the models have to be standing. I know what Prada likes. I know what most of the designers like to see.

"You have to be with good photographers who understand what Neiman's is. You take it as far as you can go—then you have a backup just in case you've gone too far."

WHAT ROBBIN LEARNED FROM MELANIE WARD
"She gets everyone to see things her way. She is really good. She has a quiet way—but she gets her way."

HOW TO GET PEOPLE ON A SET TO SEE THINGS OUR WAY
Robbin tries to have really high energy and keep things positive. "Someone asks, 'What do you think about the makeup?' I think to myself, 'What's the one thing I can say something positive about?' Then I say, 'I like the blush but do you think, maybe, we could try a glossier lip?' You find the one thing that you love and build from there."

STICK TO YOUR FASHION TRIBE
"We were doing a jewelry shoot in Dallas with a Dallas photographer. I had seen the makeup artist's book and had her references, but I had never worked with the makeup person before. I walked in and she was bleaching the girls' eyebrows. The theme was Goddess, but she had

her own idea of Goddess. A bleached eyebrow is a major decision. She fought me the whole day. I went into the bathroom and cried. I hated the pictures, but the buyers and everyone else loved them."

MORE THAN A VISUAL STANDARD
"Neiman's has a voice—a very distinct, witty voice. The writing here is every bit as strong as the pictures."

DON'T DIS DALLAS
"There's an incredibly rich, world-class architecture and art scene that cultivates the eye: the DMA in Dallas, the Modern Art Museum of Fort Worth, the Kimbell Art Museum, and the Amon Carter Museum."

THINGS ROBBIN WISHES SHE'D LEARNED
Computer skills with software like Adobe's InDesign and PhotoShop. "It's just normal in this world to know those things. I studied film, not graphic design, so I don't know the graphic designer software that's so good for grabbing images and making presentations. This is something I don't have."

Model

WHAT: | Model.

DEGREE: | None.

TRAITS: | Emotional maturity, inner calm, watchfulness, patience; is a good traveler.

ESSENTIAL ABILITIES: | Gaze wide-eyed into the camera and communicate a wide range of emotions; walk the runway.

WORKSPACE: | Last address your booker texted you.

PATH TO POWER: | Get seen by a good agency; get shot by a renowned photographer.

MOST COVETED GIGS: | Solo *Vogue* cover; Calvin Klein; Chanel ad campaign; first, last, or wedding gown runway turn at Haute Couture show.

DOGGIE JOBS: | While they pay well, don't put cheesy lingerie ads or Sears catalog pix in your book.

DRAWBACKS: | Unless you are among the world's top fifty models, you are made to feel like an easily replaceable commodity.

MODERN SUCCESS STORIES: | Kate Moss, Christy Turlington, Cindy Crawford.

MISCONCEPTIONS: | That you can model part time to put yourself through college. (If you have the option, go to college instead.) There's nothing part time about modeling. And if you start at age eighteen or twenty, it's too late.

KEY ALLIANCES: | Agencies, bookers, and photographers and their hair and makeup teams.

LIFESTYLE CHALLENGES: | Given setting and emphasis on skinny, it's hard to eat healthy; hard not to give in to cigarettes or other worse habits; hard not to grow up too fast; hard to maintain normal relationships with abnormal travel and hours.

CHANCES OF MAKING IT: | 1 in 1 million.

LANGUAGES: | You'll need basic English to survive in NYC; beginner French for Paris; Italian for Milan.

STARTING COMP: | You'll probably have to pay to have your first pictures made.

POTENTIAL COMP: | $$$$$.

Modeling

In a perfect world, this is how you'd become the next great supermodel: You're sixteen, flying back from spring break in South Beach (your best friend Caitlin organized everything). This totally legit guy approaches you at the Miami airport, gives you his card, and says you should call and set up an appointment to visit him in the city when you get back to Connecticut. The weird thing is that Caitlin is considered the *pretty* one, the *popular* one, *prom queen, cheerleader* material. You're the hot girl's best friend—NOT in the same league. You are tall and gawky. Superpale, even after four days in Florida. Boys tease you that you should be on the Romanian basketball team. (They all know you were adopted as a baby from some skanky orphanage in there.) Stunned, Caitlin pretends to be happy for you.

You peek at his card. "FORD MODELS"!

You are so calling him next Monday.

Skipping school, you take the train into the city on your own. If there's a real possibility of this thing happening, you know it would be better **not** to have a quietly jealous friend, nagging mom, or clunky boyfriend in tow.

You arrive at the address on Fifth Avenue and Eighteenth Street a little early, so you dip into Starbucks for a coffee. Inside your tote, you have a few simple, clean headshots taken by a friend who's into photography. You've automatically intuited that it would be uncool to bring in overproduced, highly retouched, heavily made up, tacky pictures of yourself. Or goofy yearbook pictures taken outside on a log.

You are signed by the Ford agency on the spot. (Well, technically you'll need to get your parents to sign as well.) The next day, you are supposed to go to a photographer's studio in Tribeca to have more test shots done. Within days, your agent prepares your portfolio and sends you a series of "go-sees."

To save time and money, you buy a $20 MetroCard, grab a subway map, and learn how to zip around the city, visiting six to ten ad agencies, magazines, and commercial clients each day.

WOW! You hear back from your booker that you've been booked for your first shoot with Steven Meisel (the *Vogue* and Italian *Vogue* photographer) for something for the Italian edition. Things go fast forward from here. You find someone to share an apartment with in the city. Get your passport, and it's LA one day and Laos the next.

After appearing in Italian *Vogue* and spending three years in the exclusive *Vogue* model rotation, you get your first U.S. *Vogue* cover! You've made it! You are a SUPERMODEL!

You spend the next five years pulling in as much as $50,000 a day for commercial clients. You do advertising campaigns for the likes of Chanel, Calvin Klein, Victoria's Secret, and David Yurman.

You hook up with a just-as-rich rock star, have a baby, keep working, and live happily ever after.

Oh, and Caitlin? She hasn't spoken to you since Miami.

In Our Real, Imperfect World . . .

There are lots of disreputable people and agencies out there willing to tell you that you're going to make it big, when, in fact, you will end up *paying them* for photography sessions, a portfolio, and so on. "Right now, there's an oversaturation of agencies, and almost *any* girl can get signed," explains my friend Kirsten Kenney, head of the model division of the Bryan Bantry Agency. Kirsten previously booked models for major magazines like *Harper's Bazaar* and *Allure.* "Whether that girl will make any money is another matter."

But how do you figure that out without getting sucked in by the wrong people promising superstardom? Go to top agencies. If they all say no? It's no.

Do You Have "It"?

"You either have it or you don't," says Kirsten.

"It" means being photogenic: Even if it is not obvious to you or those around you, the face you were born with has to photograph beautifully; you must be able to express yourself through the lens of a camera; and, thanks to your genes, the planes of your face are perfect and the surface of your skin is flawless. And something magic comes through in the image of you.

What Are Your Chances?

Before meeting potential models, most agencies determine whom they will meet based on the headshots the candidates have e-mailed to them. Ford, however,

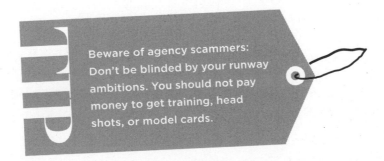

Beware of agency scammers: Don't be blinded by your runway ambitions. You should not pay money to get training, head shots, or model cards.

does an "open call" in New York City every Wednesday from 3 to 4 p.m. (see www.fordmodels.com).

Highly selective in her prescreening, Kirsten signs one out of one hundred young women she meets (that's only 1 percent, pals!). But here's the amazing part: A top agent like Kirsten can expect that about 60 percent of the women she does sign will be successful and make money for themselves and for the agency. (Kirsten defines a successful model's salary at $250,000 a year or higher.)

Model Myths

You'll be "discovered" at the mall. Unlikely. While Kate Moss *was* discovered by an agent at an airport, it doesn't happen often. Girls who live in big cities should visit the big agencies there. Girls who live in the middle of nowhere can either travel to the big-city agencies or try to "bubble up" into the system through modeling contests.

TV REALITY VERSUS MODEL REALITY

Besides being fun to watch and addictive, shows like Tyra Banks' *America's Next Top Model* (ANTM) and Tyson Beckford's *Make Me a Supermodel* (MMAS) offer a live glimpse inside the brutally tough world of modeling.

Sadly, these shows do not produce supermodels. To date, not one actual supermodel or even bordering-on-supermodel has walked off the sets of these shows onto the pages of *Vogue* or the runways of Paris. The lucky ones are able to transform their TV-land training, acclaim, and attention into the lucrative career of a working commercial model.

Why? Because still photography (not reality television) is still the best testing ground for models; because many of the model contestants are often too old to be starting their careers (over eighteen); and also because the shows do not take into account the subtle shifts in tastes of those few, powerful fashionistas who actually decide these things, people like photographers Steven Meisel, Italian *Vogue* editor in chief Franca Sozzani and Chanel designer Karl Lagerfeld. Now if *this group* were the judges . . .

You need to be at least five feet, ten inches tall to model. Negatory. To walk *runway,* you do need to be five feet ten or five feet eleven inches, but for studio photography, you just need to have long legs and be long-waisted. It's a question of proportions. Kate Moss stands only five feet eight inches tall, but she has exquisite proportions.

You can "earn your way through college by modeling." Not. If you start with an agency in earnest and your go-sees start turning to bookings, you'll need to be available full time. To model seriously, you'll need to give up everything else for one to three years.

MODEL SCOOP: TOP AGENCIES AND WHAT THEY'RE LOOKING FOR

Of the four top modeling agencies—Ford, DNA, IMG, Women—Ford has historically been the most parent-palatable and "apple-pie-American seeming." And even though the founding Ford family is no longer involved, image-wise, it still has its imprint.

Wherever you end up, Ford's website—www.fordmodels.com—is a better model primer than any book I've ever seen.

Click on the "become a model" tab at the bottom of the home page. Here you'll have three choices: "apply now," "Supermodel of the World Contest," or "open call information."

The power of Ford is that it has locations in Toronto, Miami, San Francisco, Los Angeles, Milwaukee (as in *Wisconsin?!*), Chicago, and New York as well as a subsidiary office in Arizona. Your best path in is to get yourself to an open call at the most convenient of these locations. Its instructions—"Please bring clean, clear snapshots (no makeup)"—are clear. But, even better, if you click on the Supermodel of the World contest and scroll down, where there's the opportunity to apply online, it's here that they show great examples of the four different digital photos they are looking for:

1. Straight-on, full-length portrait in tight-fitting clothes
2. Straight-on, waist-up portrait (just wear the *same* clothes, OK?)
3. Straight-on, shoulder-up portrait
4. Profile, waist-up or shoulder-up, portrait

Notice in the examples how natural the girl looks in these pictures. Her hair is clean and pulled away from her face. No perms. No blowouts. Her face is devoid of foundation, blush, lipstick, eyeliner. This is the definition of "clean." She's wearing a cool T-shirt and jeans. Nothing forced or fashion-y.

Study these pictures. Work with someone you trust (he or she doesn't have to be a photographer) and get the photos you need. If there's no way you can get to any of Ford's urban offices, send in exactly what they're asking for.

You shouldn't even THINK about being a model if you:
- Hate sitting around
- Can't leave the house without tons of makeup
- Hate cities
- Hate traveling
- Hate people playing with your hair or doing your makeup
- Are not comfortable with people who don't speak English
- Are religious to the extent that it would affect the clothes you are comfortable wearing and the days you would be able to work
- Intend to fit modeling in with your high school or college class schedule

What to Wear on a Model Go-See

Flats, sneakers, or low boots. "Heels are my number one pet peeve," says Kirsten Kenney of Bryan Bantry. "Don't do that. You may need to bring heels to a runway casting to show them how you walk, but not at an agency or magazine appointment."

Dress as simply as possible. Wear your best-fitting jeans and a white tank top. Your hair should be straight, clean, and pulled back. *Not* blown out. And don't do a perm or color your hair the night before.

"My biggest nemesis is the aunt who tells her niece that she should be a model, and then this girl with mall hair and too-pink lips shows up," says Kirsten.

Wear moisturizer (it can be tinted if it's superlight and if it matches your skin tone perfectly), nude lip gloss, and the slightest single swipe of brown or brown-black mascara.

What to Say When You Visit an Agency

Nothing! The less you talk the better.

Don't gush. "This has always been my dream."

Don't elaborate. "I love horses and tennis."

Don't personalize. "I knew I would be booked for this shoot!."

The cold, hard truth? All an agency cares about is if you take a good picture and if you'll make them a lot of money.

How to Act on a Job

A good personality helps. Show in a quiet way that you are mature and can act in a professional manner. Indeed, in this world of glamour and image and fawned-over beauty, the big irony is that the more grounded you are, the more successful you will be.

Go to bed early the night before a shoot. Don't show up hung-over. Be on time. Be an active participant in the process without being opinionated. It's a matter of learning your place in the process. *No one really cares about your opinion on how you look.* You need to know your best side and your body angles. Be calm. Be ready to work. Don't complain. Don't be grumpy. Don't make crazy requests (for special food, car services, free clothes, and so on). Remember that the maximum amount of time you'll be in front of the camera for a full-day shoot will be two hours.

The Stories That Don't Get Told

There was an underage model who showed up for a Michael Thompson beauty shoot for *Bazaar* still high from the night before. She came in and passed out on the sofa. At lunchtime, she was still sleeping, and the stylist tried to wake her up and get her to eat something. She wanted a Big Mac and a Coke. After that, it was 3 p.m. and she was ready for hair and makeup. And the pictures? Sublimely beautiful. Precisely why this model got away with her outrageous behavior.

The Worst Thing You Can Do to Your Booker

Not showing up for an appointment with a photographer would be bad. Not showing up for an appointment with *Vogue* photographers Mert Alas and Marcus Piggott is model suicide. Think about it: What are the chances you'll have this opportunity again? How hard is your booker going to work for you if you don't do your part?

How to Be a Model Agent

You have to know the history of photographers. You have to love photography. You have to feel comfortable in the agency craziness and, ultimately, get pleasure from linking the right models to the right projects. You have to be able to visualize models in the various scenarios that present themselves. Probably most important, you have to have an eye for who will shoot well.

It's a combination of a sales job—selling the models to photographers and casting agents—and a babysitting job. "On a bad day, it's like being a mother to bad children," says Kirsten Kenney, who works with agency Bryan Bantry. "The girls tend to have the attitude 'What can *you* do for *me*?' But the reality is that we both have to do 50 percent of the job. I will create the introduction and get her in the door. She needs to physically show up and get the job."

The Consummate Professional

Which model stands out in the minds of stylists, photographers, agents, and editors as the consummate professional? Christy Turlington. Because she never complains. She understands her role in the process, which is to step onto the set and make the best pictures possible. She possesses an inner calm. She keeps the perfect professional distance—always kind and friendly—but understands that this is a job and the people on the set aren't going to be her new best friends.

3

CRITIC

WHAT: | Writers, editors (magazines, newspapers, websites, television programs).

DEGREES: | Liberal arts BA and/or journalism BS; your major isn't important.

TRAITS: | Opinionated, organized, verbal, driven.

ESSENTIAL ABILITIES: | To write and speak clearly and engagingly.

ROLE: | To package fashion news to a wider audience, providing guidance, fantasy, entertainment, relevancy, and context.

WORKSPACE: | From bullpen or closet to gray cubicle or corner office.

PATH TO POWER: | Work for or be published in one of the key brands (listed below).

MOST COVETED JOBS: | Editor in chief, fashion editor, accessories editor, producer.

DOGGIE JOBS: | Assistant to anyone (but you must put in time), credit or closet editor.

KEY BRANDS: | *Vogue, W, Harper's Bazaar, Elle, WWD, Project Runway.*

KEY PERSONALITIES: | See mastheads and list of credits of the key brands listed above.

MODERN SUCCESS STORIES: | Anna Wintour, Carine Roitfeld, Glenda Bailey, Grace Coddington, Kim France.

MISCONCEPTION: | That the in-house staff writes the big stories.

LANGUAGES: | French and Italian useful in dealing with Paris and Milan fashion houses; English accent a plus.

STARTING COMP: | Half a dollar sign.

POTENTIAL COMP: | $$$.

PERKS: | Car and driver; preseason, highly discounted (even free) clothing, accessories, jewelry, shoes; invitations to film and theater premieres and sporting events; travel to Paris and Milan for fashion shows; high-level access to personalities and celebrities from worlds of film, music, politics, sports, media, art, design, and photography.

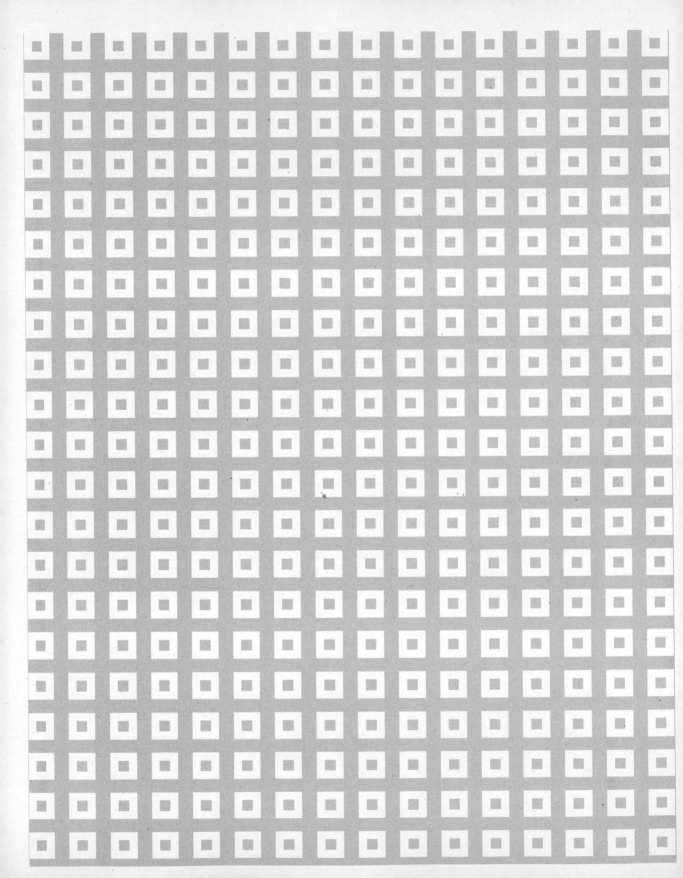

Call me biased, but I think fashion magazines are the greatest postcollege playground in America. Most practically, magazines are an excellent platform from which to launch amazingly divergent careers—whatever you choose to do next, no one *ever* looks down on a glamorous editorial experience. I know people who started at magazines and later became TV producers, novelists, makeup artists, celebrity stylists, accessories designers, clothing designers, TV journalists, Hollywood screenwriters, retailers, department store executives, moguls, ad sales stars, and public relations people.

The biggest surprise might be that magazines are excellent training grounds for both academic snobs, as I was, and those of you with altruistic dreams of making the world a greener, cleaner, safer, or more equitable place. Magazines are also a huge amount of F-U-N—a near perfect postacademic state of arrested development. This is an environment where irreverence is essential and sarcasm sacrosanct; where boredom isn't an option; where colorful and unconventional personalities thrive; where each day is different: One day, it's a sitcom, the next a docudrama. Either way, you feel as if you are at the center of the universe. This is a world with direct access to major personalities, musicians, authors, actors, artists, politicians, dancers, designers; to news and events and openings that define our culture right now. One day you're struggling over credits for a weekend knitwear story; that same night you're on a last-minute flight to Paris delivering a Couture Chanel gown back to the House so that Nicole Kidman can wear it in the next day's filming of a new Chanel No. 5 commercial; then, boom, you're on your knees on a cement floor tying Madonna's shoes on a photo set in Los Angeles. "More water, Madonna?"

Plus, given that you've survived four years of college, you're already in the groove. Creative businesses like book publishing, television production, advertising, and magazines are intense and fun in the same way college can be. Closings are like finals; deadlines like midterms; story meetings like seminars or self-study courses. Daily interactions are often sophomoric—not unlike those in a sorority or fraternity—but this mostly female environment welcomes (actually *requires*) gay men. The pace is supersonic. Interaction is crackling with intensity. Your commitment must be complete. Since you spend more time with your officemates than with friends or family, it can be hard to remember that it's a j-o-b. For most of us who have thrived in these worlds, it takes over our lives.

As in college—where months of labor and learning are expressed and then purged via a term paper, project, or final exam—in the creative business world, you get the regular massive satisfaction of seeing your efforts published and distributed or packaged and sold to hundreds of thousands or millions of readers or viewers or consumers every month. Compared to the fast-paced, adaptive world of creative business, it would be suffocating for most people like me to work for a packaged-goods company where it takes *years* to make any impact on the look or feel of a product and, even then, the feedback and matrices of success are rarely objective.

If fashion magazines strike you as superficial and unworthy, consider this: If deep in your heart, you are an altruist and dream of devoting all of your energies to saving endangered dolphins, building girls' schools in India, or funding clean

CRITICS' COMMON CAREER PATH

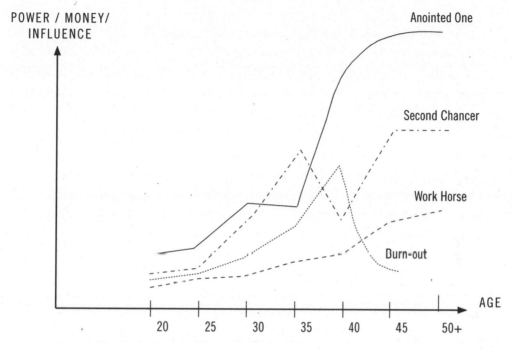

POWER / MONEY/ INFLUENCE

Anointed One

Second Chancer

Work Horse

Burn-out

AGE

20   25   30   35   40   45   50+

As you can see, there are different ways to get to the top as a fashion critic. Of course, we'd all like to be Anointed Ones, but, alas, this happens only rarely. It's safest to be a Work Horse, but even this doesn't offer job security. No one wants to be a Burn Out, but how one manages this process on one's way to a fresh start as a Second Chancer (or not) determines true fashionista greatness.

water sources in Nigeria, an editorial setting would sharpen your skills and open your eyes to the reality of what motivates people far better than some sappy, inbred, not-for-profit organization. Magazines arm you with glamour creds, providing you with connections to major personalities and companies always on the prowl for the next "cause." You'll get on a most basic level something most mid-career do-gooders never grasp: how to make your cause sexy. Because, perhaps sadly, even in philanthropy, sex(y) sells. That today's most effective U.N. goodwill ambassador is Angelina Jolie says it all.

What's tricky for newcomers is that each magazine, TV show, ad, and agency has its own distinct internal language, dos and don'ts, habits, and customs and border controls. There are hazing rituals, the most common relating to staying very late on a Friday night or mandatory attendance in the office on Thanksgiving

Day for a taping or a "close." It's standard initiation when at week two the managing director comes by your desk and demands that you clean up your area *and* your look. You naively express a desire to write and soon find yourself with 225-word captions to finish by the next morning while all the experienced assistants boisterously exit for cocktails. Get past the early social rites and you'll begin to enjoy the incredibly appealing freedom of speech and access that is inherent to creative businesses. Every shoe company, exercise method, bra brand, nail strengthener, and hand cream manufacturer wants access to YOU and to your magazine or to your blog, website, TV or radio show, because *if you pay attention to their products, better yet, photograph their items, you could change their destiny.* Help them make it. This is touching and a tremendous responsibility, and, if not properly managed, it can turn into a major annoyance. But think of the plus side: When you have hundreds of companies and their PR spokespeople after you to write about them, you naturally harden into a cynic, a judge, an editor, and an arbiter of style and substance. *Isn't that what you set out to be?*

Alas, consider yourself forewarned: This is not a world of great stability. Nor is it a world for great riches. Other than the top five to six names on an editorial masthead (see the listings of editorial mastheads at MediaBistro.com), the pay is paltry. Rich perks and the high "glam" factor keep the magazine machine firing with beautiful, well-educated "talent."

Seeking freedom, money, or more time for their families, countless magazine people (like me) have dropped out of the daily swirl of fashion publications to write or style freelance for those same magazines and a slightly wider group of competitors. Others shift into PR or retail sales. Unlike so many women who had lucrative careers as bankers or lawyers and are unable to use their experience in the context of a more flexible schedule after they've had children, I have always felt fortunate to have skills that could be translatable into myriad fronts: corporate brand consulting (beauty, fashion, high tech), copywriting for ad agencies, and developing PR strategies, as well as writing for magazines and authoring books.

Let's look back in history to find some interesting examples of editors leaving the "bubble" of fashion magazines and entering cool, creative, much higher compensating, second careers:

- Now here's a role model. The arch and quotable **Dorothy Parker** managed to sell some poetry to *Vogue* (1917) and converted the relationship into a full-time job with Condé Nast himself, moving to the boss's *Vanity Fair*

(1920), before moving to Hollywood and becoming a screenwriter. While she continued to write reviews for *The New Yorker,* Dorothy wrote *A Star Is Born* and won the Oscar for Best Original Story. She became politicized, standing up against Nazism and Fascism, and was blacklisted for declaring herself a Communist during the McCarthy era. She worked as a frontlines reporter during the Spanish Civil War, collaborated on plays, and helped found the Screen Writers' Guild.

- The daughter and sister of literary talent, the brilliant self-effacing **Nora Ephron** blows me away. Upon graduating from Wellesley, she started her career as a reporter for the *New York Post.* She then worked at Hearst's *Cosmopolitan* in the late 1960s (where she is credited for answering the phone "what fresh hell is this?"), then writing a column with a woman's point of view for Hearst's *Esquire.* She went on to become an award-winning author (*Heartburn,* a novel, and *I Feel Bad about My Neck,* an essay collection) and screenwriter (*Heartburn, Silkwood, When Harry Met Sally, Sleepless in Seattle*), often collaborating with her sister Delia. She is a totally cool lady—I know because I spent a whole day in her apartment with her once while shooting her for the cover of *New York Woman* magazine. Nora has the amazing talent of finding humor and bigger meaning in everyday catastrophes.

- The perfectionist **Carol Phillips,** *Vogue* managing editor in the late 1960s, went on to help found Clinique, now the $3 billion global beauty brand at Estée Lauder, Inc.

- The elegant and groovy **Mary Randolph Carter** left Condé Nast Publications, where she was a fashion editor, to join Polo Ralph Lauren, where she's had a long career as a muse, art director, and stylist.

- **Andrea Quinn Robinson** left off shooting beauty stories at *Vogue* to run beauty companies like the Polo Ralph Lauren beauty brand for L'Oréal, its licensor.

- **Shirley Lord** went from being the *Vogue* beauty diva to writing a succession of successful romance novels.

- And, in the interest of full disclosure, I should mention that I, too, have sprung from the confines of fashion magazines. I am now working at Bobbi Brown Cosmetics overseeing creative, PR, communicating her practical teaching approach to beauty, and product development. My fave thing about the job? Bobbi's sincerity and the cool kids I get to work with every day.

EDITORIAL JOB LISTINGS: A TRANSLATOR

Checking the names and titles of the people who work at magazines couldn't be easier. You need to find the magazine's *masthead*—that is, the list of jobs at the magazine. It usually falls within the first thirty pages of a publication and can be found on a left-hand page. The *editorial masthead* lists the *editors*—that is, people who create the editorial content of the publication—with their titles. The *publishing masthead* lists all the names and titles of the people who sell the advertising and market the magazine, supporting the advertisers with special access and events. You might see the same title, say, "jewelry director," on both of these mastheads. The editorial jewelry job is to cover trends in the jewelry marketplace, help conceptualize stories based on those trends, and integrate jewelry into other aspects of the magazine. The publishing jewelry person is responsible for bringing in (selling) and keeping jewelry advertising pages. A fashion magazine's jobs are listed below in descending order of importance. Basically, the lower your name in the masthead and the smaller the typeface, the more unimportant your job. *How clear is that?*

EDITORIAL JOBS

Editor in chief. The top editorial talent at a publication who determines its vision, tone, and content and, ultimately, which photographers, writers, and editors work there. Famous examples include Anna Wintour (*Vogue*), the late Liz Tilberis (*Harper's Bazaar*), and, fictitiously, Miranda Priestly (*The Devil Wears Prada*).
  Requirement: **You are the glamorous embodiment of the publication.**

Deputy editor, executive editor, managing editor. These are the number 2 editors, to whom all decisions are deferred when the top cat is away. While there is no science to these titles, an *executive editor* tends to come from the features side of the business and focuses more on the word content, whereas a *deputy editor* brings along production experience (making deadlines and smoothing the connection between the art department and the printer), and a *managing editor* is more the gatekeeper, focusing on the hiring and firing of editors and assuming other administrative or corporate duties. Sometimes two or possibly three of these positions all exist at a single title in various orders of importance. Maintaining good communications with the business or publishing side and an ability to manage the crucial pacing of the magazine (the ordering of an issue's editorial and advertising pages in the most logical, visually pleasing way for the reader and nonconflicted way for the advertisers) are among the key functions.
  Requirement: **You know who's boss.**

Fashion director. This most-senior fashion editor reports to the editor in chief and is responsible for conceptualizing, creating, and producing all fashion pages. Often fashion directors are also the most-senior sittings editors.

>   *Requirement:* **You're good in Paris and Milan, and your ideas are brilliant.**

Fashion editor. Reporting to the fashion director, the fashion editor oversees (which includes sifting through and amalgamating their work) the various market editors.

>   *Requirement:* **You have been trained by a great fashion director.**

Sittings editor. The person responsible for the fashion photography of the publication and for budgeting, booking, and interacting with the photographers, models, and stylists. Reports to the fashion director but is in direct contact with the editor in chief.

>   *Requirement:* **An operator, you have been trained by a great sittings director.**

Market editor. For the variously titled market editors (accessories editors, sportswear editors, denim editors, swimwear editors, fur editors, and so on), watching a runway show is an exercise in memorization. In addition to almost daily conversations with key runway brands' PR staffs and regular visits to their showrooms, smart market editors comb downtown shops and foreign publications looking for the next cool designer or trend in the category. *Assistant market editor* is a higher rank (representing one to five or more years of experience), and it is the next step up from assistant to the market editor.

>   *Requirement:* **A good understanding of how a fashion department functions; a good grasp of brands and personalities who populate your particular area; you've done time as a fashion intern and/or assistant.**

Beauty director. Equal parts ambassador to the beauty marketplace (Estée Lauder, Chanel, L'Oréal, Cover Girl, and so on) and inside (in-house) story generator, a beauty director is a most coveted position that reports to the editor in chief.

>   *Requirement:* **Writing, editing skills, and fresh ideas as well as being able to competently represent the magazine to the advertising community.**

Beauty editor. A well-organized, efficient editor who manages to attend two-hour advertiser lunches and then pop by a shoot to grab quotes from the hair and makeup people—after which, she still makes the deadline.

>   *Requirement:* **Know how to make your publication and the beauty director look good.**

ASSISTANT-LAND: WHERE TO START

Beauty assistant. A fun, booty-filled job for someone who is superorganized and manages a tight beauty closet.

continued on next page

CREATOR VISUALIZER CRITIC SELLER

Editorial assistant. First job that can be wonderful or horrid depending on your attitude and the person to whom you are now cojoined—your BOSS. Who'll look up to you? Interns who arrive after you did.

Assistant editor. Not to be confused with the above, this is your first step up in the world! A PROMOTION! Perhaps in name (not $$) only, when you become an assistant editor, you've earned a stripe. Well, maybe half a stripe.

Art department assistant. Great start if you aim to be a photo editor or a graphic designer.

Production assistant. Fine start if your wish is to be in production.

Fact checker. Great job to learn everything that matters to your publication. Like taking a graduate-level reporting class in J school. Don't do this for more than one year unless you are in a rock band at night.

Copy editor. A great skill to have, but often a dead-end job. Don't do this for more than a year unless you want copyediting to be your calling. An easily freelance-able skill.

Research assistant. A good start if you want to be a fashion writer. A good way to get a "sign-off" (not a proper byline, but your name is tagged at the end of an extended caption). At Time Inc., this is an excellent first posting.

Assistant to the managing editor. Great job for getting the lay of the land, knowing who's who and what's what. Not as demanding as being an assistant to the editor in chief, and probably more administrative.

Assistant to the features editor. Perfect for the English majors among you. Besides cappuccino runs for features meetings that you are technically invited to attend and booking lunches for your editor at DB Bistro, you may actually get to read (unsolicited) submissions, thumb through reviewers' copies of new releases from all the publishing houses, and meet writers whose work you've admired. I know you are still idealistic, but one word of advice: Don't bring up printing your favorite poetry or fiction unless you're at *The New Yorker*. Even there, I'd wait a few years.

Assistant to the lifestyle editor. *Lifestyle* is usually code for cooking, home decorating, and architecture *lite*. If "shelter" magazines (that is, about the home) are your thing, this is the job you want.

Assistant to the fashion editor. If you want to be a stylist (see Visualizer, Stylist, on page 122), this is the best training. Organization is key. Being flexible and happy to travel on a moment's notice. A roll-with-the-punches kind of personality. Love to pack (and repack) trunks lovingly for photo shoots? Have the ability to work slave hours compensated with some fun location trips, late dinners with models and photographers?

Assistant to the market editor. If you want to learn the business of fashion, this is a nice seat to occupy. When you are not filing expense reports or lugging garment bags around town, you may have the opportunity to visit designer showrooms and to attend some standing-room-only (SRO) fashion shows.

Assistant to the accessories editor. Because accessories is a higher-margin business for most brands and it is the most-status category for women, this is among the most coveted starter spots in fashion

THE EDITOR IN CHIEF POSSE

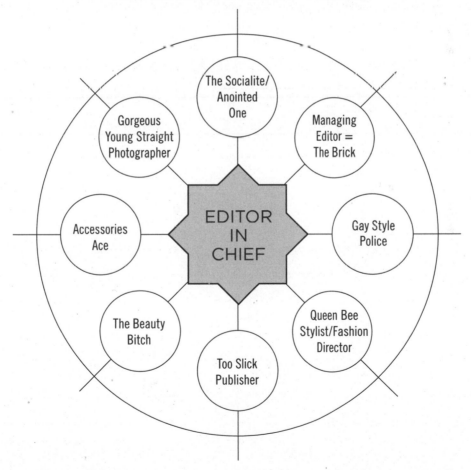

While the personalities supporting an editor in chief must function as a team, their competing interests are rarely far from the surface.

FASHION PUBLICATIONS AS SPRINGBOARDS TO COOL CAREERS

"Your Last Day Is Friday"

Getting fired is commonplace and more of a rite of passage than a shame or an embarrassment. The conversation we need to have is how to take control of your own situation—when to walk and how to be a survivor, not a victim. In magazines, the average editor in chief lasts less than three years, and when your editor is ousted, you'll be expected to try out for the job you thought you already had. Within a year, much of the staff has changed out. Assistants call their parents crying. The wise know to leave in the weeks and months before anything happens. In advertising, ad agency heads and creative directors typically last longer. While it sounds brutal, it's true that as a copywriter, you are only as good as your last great ad-line. If you wrote that line more than six months ago, that's *not* good. A creative business education offers learning opportunities so huge that you could launch a brand, agency, publication, or a website with the know-how you gain. Or once you've lived the madness, as my life shows, you're likely at some point to be "revived" and swept back into the fold.

WHERE YOU CAN GO FROM HERE: FROM EDITORIAL TO REAL LIFE	MAGAZINE BEGINNINGS	SUBSEQUENT CONQUESTS
Jennifer Jackson Alfano	*Vogue, Bazaar,* fashion writer, editor	Jennifer Alfano, handbags, designer/founder
Fabien Baron	*New York Woman, GQ, Bazaar,* graphic designer, art director, creative director	Baron & Baron, founder ad agency; graphic and editorial director, industrial designer; photographer; *Interview*
Luella Bartley	British *Vogue, Face, Dazed & Confused,* fashion journalist	Luella Bartley, fashion designer
Beth Blake	*Vanity Fair,* stylist	Thread (bridal collection), Thread Social (dress collection), designer/founder
Michel Botbol	*W, Bazaar* fashion editor, creative director	Polo Ralph Lauren, creative director
Aimee Cho	*Vogue,* fashion writer	Gryphon, founder/designer

WHERE YOU CAN GO FROM HERE: FROM EDITORIAL TO REAL LIFE	MAGAZINE BEGINNINGS	SUBSEQUENT CONQUESTS
Francesco Clark	*Bazaar,* fashion assistant	Clark's Botanicals, founder/CEO
Nicole Colovos	*Bazaar,* fashion assistant	Habitual, then Helmut Lang designer, with husband Michael Colovos
Lucy Wallace Eustice	*Mirabella, Bazaar, Elle* accessories editor	M Z Wallace, designer/founder (with Monica Zwirner)
Alex Gonzalez and Raul Martinez	Graphic designers, art directors at titles like American *Vogue,* German *Vogue, GQ, Mirabella*	AR New York, founders
Thakoon Panichgul	*Bazaar,* fashion assistant	Thakoon, founder/designer
Amanda Ross	*Self, Marie Claire, Bazaar,* fashion editor	*Lipstick Jungle,* fashion stylist, film, TV, celebrity stylist
Richard Sinnott	*Bazaar,* accessories editor	Accessories designer, Michael Kors
Kate Spade	*Mademoiselle,* accessories editor	Kate Spade, founder/designer (acquired by Jones New York)
Mary Alice Stephenson	*Bazaar,* fashion editor	On-air fashion TV personality, celebrity stylist
Vera Wang	*Vogue,* senior fashion editor	Ralph Lauren, design director, then Vera Wang, designer/founder
Lauren Weisberger	*Vogue,* assistant to the editor in chief	*The Devil Wears Prada,* author

CREATOR   VISUALIZER   CRITIC   SELLER

The Interview

Q. What should I wear to my interview?
A. We suggest that you wear professional attire appropriate for a first interview. —from www.CondéNast.com.

Gee thanks. That's hugely helpful. The right answer is wear something so that you will fit in, which changes in nuance every millisecond. In fact, there is no answer to this question. But if you feel comfortable and pretty, you'll project confidence and competence. That's a very good place to start.

Fashion interns I've talked to about interview outfits make things very clear: If you are interviewing for an internship, wear dark trousers, a shirt, and a cute jacket or trench coat, and high heels or boots. The look shouldn't be head-to-toe matching but, rather, items pieced together in an original way. Shop for your outfit at H&M, Zara, or J. Crew as well as vintage stores. If you have one nice designer piece, say, a Marc Jacobs jacket or an old Coco bag, throw it on with the same ease you wear the H&M. If you have completed your internship and are interviewing for an assistant-level position, most interns say it's time to wear a skirt. To snap things up a bit.

"There was this gorgeous girl who came into the *Glamour* offices interviewing for a fashion job," says Serena, an intern from Florida. "She was wearing head-to-toe Dior. The fashion editors basically rejected her the second she walked through the glass door. Like she 'doesn't get it' or she has 'no natural style.' The outfit cost thousands of dollars but didn't show any creativity."

There are interviews and there are *interviews*. If you are meeting someone in the human resources department, this is likely to be a general "screening" interview: No specific job is at stake. In this situation, you must articulate what you really want to do at the company without pigeonholing yourself too narrowly. You need to seem open to all possibilities. If you are asked to see someone inside the company—a business manager or managing director, for example—there may or may not be an opening. It would be appropriate when you are there to ask if you are being considered for an opening and, if so, what it is. If the interviewer is not forthcoming with this information, don't push. Someone is probably about to be fired or give his or her resignation, and the powers that be want to be prepared with potential candidates all lined up.

If your interview is the result of your sending in your résumé for a specific opening, then actively following up, congratulations: You've made it into the pool of ten or fewer candidates being considered for the job. Remember, however, that among those other nine people are the art director's first cousin, the star intern from two years ago, and the son of the president's next-door neighbor. I say this not to discourage you, but to toughen you up to the reality. Your foot is in the door. You have an interview. Even if you don't snatch this job, if they like you, you'll be considered for other positions.

How do you usually perform in stressful situations? Like taking the SAT? Serving at match point in a tennis game with lots of friends watching? Speaking in front of a class? If these things don't faze you, you're lucky. That's rare. If you crumble under scrutiny as do most humans, remember that you wouldn't be asked in if they didn't want to see you. Admit to the interviewer that you are supernervous; he or see will instantly want to put you at ease. Some of my favorite hires of all time were the worst possible interviews. Yale graduate Rebecca Onion sat in front of my desk with her head hanging, avoiding eye contact, and mumbling because her hand was covering her mouth. All cardinal sins. Yet I saw beyond those things to her gentle, wise personality and wonderful writing voice and ear. She got the job as my assistant over all the spiffed out, perky girls because I felt Rebecca's potential. I'm usually suspicious of people who are too charming or smooth because I'm not convinced that they seriously and sincerely will do the work.

Colleagues report that Cathie Black, CEO of Hearst Magazines, likes it when candidates practically "jump over the desk" to get a job. Her preference may originate in her sales or business background. That level of hunger, however, might put off people who grow up on the creative side of the business. This is a lesson in itself. More often than not, the top bosses come from sales, marketing, and/or administrative backgrounds, so it's important that you, a creative type, learn to speak their language and, most important, know where the money comes from.

Staying a Step Ahead

Is it vulturistic to swarm when something is about to blow up? Yes. But there's a proper, calculated, and smart way to swarm. I think it's good basic business smarts to know who's up and who's down. When the papers started gossiping about Liz Tilberis possibly coming over from British *Vogue* to run *Harper's Bazaar,*

I was all over it. At this point in my career, I knew I was never going to be a Great Anointed One at Condé Nast. If I wanted to do my swan dive into serious fashion, I needed to find my place and ride with it. This was my moment. I decided I would work for this woman. This was it.

Internships from God

May 15th IM to Posse:
"Going 2 Teen Vogue 4 July!!!! Kat + me both @ 4 Times Sq. Italy in Aug. Must shop 4 amazing work clothes!"

The images in a bright worthy young fashionista-to-be's head and the reality of a magazine office rarely overlap. Nevertheless, the best first step in is to work for free, which, for me, was about as far away from the epicenter of fashion cool as you can get.

Cruising the funky music bungalows on my way to Heard Library one day, I discovered that CBS records had a division in Nashville, Tennessee, where I was in exile attending Vanderbilt University, awaiting graduation and my chance to break from my parents' grip and finally go to New York City. I flew to New York the day after graduation, and despite the fact that my summer sublet was teeming with cockroaches (so many that you could hear them clattering over the counter in the kitchenette), that my Amelia Earhart fabric luggage and Lilly Pulitzer sundresses seemed all wrong, and that within weeks I was mugged at knifepoint in an elevator, I've never looked back.

During my senior year, I had worked a couple of afternoons each week in the publicity department at CBS Records for two ladies who were neither very helpful nor very friendly. I Xeroxed stacks of badly written press releases about country artists I cared little about (I was more of a Ramones/Blondie girl, myself) except for the totally cool and talented Rosanne Cash, whom I got to interview so that I could update her bio. I had revered her dad, Johnny, but I had been intimidated by him since I was a young girl watching June Carter and him on TV. The "prison" thing was just too scary. Hearing Rosanne's voice on the phone for my first-ever interview was thrilling. I knew I'd found my thing!

C- B - S

Those three gleaming letters on my résumé impressed everyone who interviewed me for years to come. Did they know I was doing donkeywork and no one even spoke to me or barely knew my name??? No. Didn't matter. I had been there, and that's all that mattered to them. It's almost bizarre to consider how much that helped me. It's true that magazines, publishing houses, ad agencies, and TV shows need interns, tons of interns, but the "education" aspect of the experience is dubious. Will you have a desk? Doubtful. Will you have a phone? Not for personal calls and only to be answered in a clearly scripted manner. Anyhow, you'll have your cell. Will you have a chair? Not one that's yours alone. Computer? Shared.

Imagine what you, Ms. or Mr. All Important Intern, will be doing all day. Sitting in meetings with Anna Wintour listening to the senior editors debate the merits of the fall Chanel couture collection? No. Meeting the models and photographers and writers who bring the magazine to life? Unlikely. Writing, even the smallest captions, from time to time? Highly unlikely. Submitting your brilliant ideas to the powers that be? You can try, but they had better be original; otherwise you are wasting their time. Weighing in on photographs and layouts of future stories in the art department? Not unless you are asked, and the person *really* seems to want to know what you think.

Fashion magazine interns' key purpose is to ease the workload of assistants working there. Even though corporations profess to have sensitivity trained the staff overseeing interns, the reality is this: Your immediate "boss," so to speak, is a girl who might be a year or two older than you and is so stressed with her new-found responsibility and intelligence that she can't help but make you feel like a fashion moron from another planet. Your summer job responsibilities typically include stuff she doesn't have time for, or the inclination to do—that is, the bottom of the to-do list that she keeps postponing:

- Fetching the right caffeinated beverage for her boss.
- Fetching the right breakfast for her boss.
- Fetching the right lunch for her boss.
- Serving lunch in the right way.
- Packing clothes and sending them back to the designers after photography shoots in the small, dark, dirty, smelly fashion closet.

- Cleaning out and organizing the beauty closet.
- Fetching prescriptions (not your own), Aleve, the right size and strength, and so on, at Duane Reade.
- Fetching or picking up clothes (not your own, most likely samples) at the dry cleaners' or seamstresses' shop.
- Restocking the sitting editors' (the ones who style the photo shoot) kit, which contains things like thread, body stockings, tape for bottoms of new shoes, clamps to cinch too-large clothes, chicken cutlet bra fillers, black marker, white marker, double-sided tape, pins, photography release forms, pens.
- Answering the telephones exactly the way you've heard the other assistants do it, in a professional and timely manner. Then magically sensing when to interrupt your boss with personal or professional calls. (Ask another assistant for the short list of "put-through" callers.)
- Writing or e-mailing phone messages in a clear, timely, thoughtful way when you are stuck at the phone so that the assistant doesn't need to decode them.
- Running to an art store *without being asked* to buy the sketch books, pens, and pencils that are preferred by the Boss and are not available as general issue from the storage closet. (Just any blue Bic is NOT the Pilot navy fountain pen she prefers!)
- Updating contact lists (and this is a truly monotonous, truly essential task that could suck up your entire internship) by calling all related businesses and checking names, spellings, titles, e-mails, and cell phone and office numbers of all people associated with your business.
- Opening the mail, endless stacks of press releases from the Cotton Council, the Diamond Council, the Halitosis Association, and Nine West, as well as every book publisher, movie studio, and trade group on the face of the earth.
- Filing stacks of press releases into a system that you've yet to devise, a task undertaken with the understanding that NO ONE will ever thank you.

Of all the listed duties, one seemingly monotonous intern function stands apart. One of the tedious tasks offers true education, opens doors of power and knowledge, and is a job that practically no one else will want to do. You should volunteer to do so as enthusiastically and perkily as possible and perform your services tirelessly and without complaint.

Yes, even the FILING. An outdated concept, it might seem, but it's not. Filing gives you access to key names, key companies. Who does the public relations for whom? By reading the endless stream of launch announcements and "breaking news," you will learn by osmosis who matters and who doesn't. What is important and what isn't. How to speak the language. You will begin to see what fraction of 1 percent of information that is sent into the office is actually noticed by or important to your office.

"Don't be afraid of filing!" asserts former West Coast *Women's Wear Daily* intern Kim-Van Deng. "It's the most important job in the office. You get to read every piece of paper. You get to see what is kept and what is put in the garbage. When I was at WWD, I reinvented the filing system, and because of that, I was controlling of all the information because, AHA! only I understood the system. So I very quickly made myself indispensable."

Okay, so ring ring. You answer the phone because everyone else is out or on deadline. It's Suzy Smith on the phone. You already know her name from one of the press releases you filed from the endless stack. You chat briefly with her to learn about a cool event that's coming up to showcase a new fiber. And, guess what, you'll end up attending the event, and probably writing about it. Instead of simply taking a message, you make a job for yourself. That's how you put your knowledge to work for you so that you can move on up from the steel filing cabinets.

"Once I got the filing system down cold, then it was a matter of maintenance filing," Kim, now a freelance writer and beauty consultant, continues. "I came every day to the office, scheduled my classes around it, even though I wasn't expected that often. When I first got there, there were two thousand pieces of information to file. When it became maintenance filing, one day there'd be ten pieces of mail to file, the next day, twenty. It would take me only five minutes, so then I'd become a nudge: 'Is there something I can do for you?' 'Something I can help you with?' 'Maureen, don't you want me to go with you on the photo shoot so that I can steam the clothes for you?' At some point they would let me out of the trailer, because I had steamed everything in sight. Then I would stand there quietly watching the shoot, not saying a word. Finally one day the French photographer, Pierre, said: 'Hey, KEEEM, what do you think of my shoot?' I said, 'Don't you think it would be better to take the picture in front of that palm tree?' He said: 'Oh, Keeem, it's so cliché. Not everything in California must be next to a palm tree, you know, darling.'"

So, guess which picture the New York bureau ran? The picture next to the palm tree. "Next time I'm steaming clothes in the trailer, Pierre comes to find me: 'Keem!!! Where should I do the next picture?'"

Kim would volunteer for other assignments. "The staff was older and busy with their adult lives. I was the kid," she says. "I'd see an invitation on an editor's desk for a film opening that night and say to her: 'Wouldn't you rather go home to see your baby? I'll go see Tom Cruise on the red carpet or Brad Pitt at his premiere.' I became the red carpet girl, and I was still in school. Still an intern."

The Intern Keeper

As part of her job as deputy fashion director at *Glamour,* Sasha Iglehart helps her staff vet intern candidates and decide which interns to hire. "Sometimes you meet great intern candidates, and other times they seem to have a totally different sense of entitlement than we did when we started out," says Sasha.

"I make it very clear that their responsibilities are exactly what I did myself when I was an intern. That it is part of the training. Every fashion editor in the department has done these same tasks—like making photocopies and putting together storyboards, rolling in racks, and returning clothes—earlier in their careers. If you want to see what a Chanel jacket looks like up close, that will probably happen. If you want to go on a shoot with Angelina Jolie, that is probably *not* going to happen.

"OK. *Sometimes* you might be asked to drop off clothes for a cover shoot. But, in general, fashion department interns are responsible for the essential task of keeping all samples organized, which contributes to the overall smooth functioning of the entire fashion department. Interns need to be organized. They need to have a place for everything. I don't say this to deter anyone in his or her fashion career. It's just one of the necessary tools they need to begin to appreciate the bigger picture. And they should get satisfaction out of what they contributed in putting out the final product. Seeing how things visually come together is one of the biggest satisfactions for me."

HOW TO BE GREAT IN THE FASHION DEPARTMENT

"Great interns are relentless," says Sasha. "They go the extra mile to get the sample. They stay that extra hour to help everyone on the trip get to the plane on time. They are team players. They are thorough."

The Tactile Thing (If You Don't Have It, You Shouldn't Be There)

Almost as an afterthought, Sasha mentions the physical handling of clothes as a tactile experience that, for her, is pleasurable and satisfying. I've watched the "touch" of great fashion editors (like *Bazaar*'s Melanie Ward's touching, folding, and organizing the Agnès B. baby clothes I'd bought in Paris ten weeks before the birth of my first child), and it speaks volumes about their appreciation for the art and craft of fashion.

I've interviewed interns who speak about the difference between the majority of their colleagues who just want to cut out for the day and the relative few among them who really get into the craftsmanship of the clothes, taking their time to pack things with tissue and care. Who would you think is having more fun?

So if you wish to enter into this realm and intern in a fashion closet or for a designer, the manner in which you take off or hang your coat, the care with which you fold a sweater or pack a gown sends a message about your appropriateness for the role. If you don't have a passion for these subtleties, then it really might feel like donkey's work. And if it *feels* like donkey's work, well, then it *is* donkey's work.

WHERE TO INTERN

OBVIOUS INTERNSHIP TARGETS

Magazines. Like *Elle, W, Vogue, Harper's Bazaar, Marie Claire, Glamour.*

Network TV. Shows like the nightly news, morning news, late-night shows.

Cable. MTV, VH1, HBO.

Ad agencies. While the big ones like BBDO Worldwide and Chiat\Day (TBWA\Chiat\Day) would be instantly recognizable on your résumé, you'll probably get closer to the word at independent fashion agencies like AR New York and Baron & Baron. (See page 247.)

Newspapers. In a perfect world, you'd find your way to T, the fashion magazine of the *New York Times*. But even the style or society pages of a local paper would offer good experience.

Book publishing. Focus on the more visual imprints like Assouline, Rizzoli, or Clarkson Potter.

Public relations agencies. Like KCD, a cool PR fashion agency, and LaForce + Stevens, a PR agency specializing in fashion, retail, and beauty shops.

NOT-SO-OBVIOUS TARGETS

Women's Wear Daily. The trade newspaper for fashion business. Or any number of the various Fairchild titles.

Photography studios. Like Industria (Manhattan); Smash Box (LA); and Seventh on Sixth, the organization that puts on the twice-yearly NYC fashion shows, which is run by IMG.

Booking agencies (who represent photographers, stylists, and hair and makeup artists). Like Art + Commerce; Bryan Bantry.

Trade publications.

Trade organizations. Like the Italian Trade Federation, Fashion Group, Council of Fashion Designers of America (CFDA), or Cosmetics Executive Women (CEW).

Don't Be Afraid to Ask

Sometimes, in the creative workplace there are words, labels, and habits that no longer make sense but continue to be used. For example, "blues" is a term that once aptly described blue-tinted proofs from the printer. Today "blues" is used to describe a completely non-color-specific, electronic, late-stage version of the edited copy. "Why is this called 'blues'?" is a great question that not many manically busy people would have the energy or time to answer.

The only stupid question from an intern is the one not asked. Or the one asked at the obviously wrong moment—when the air is so thick with missed deadlines and bad energy that anyone with a lick of sense would know you should save it for a brighter day.

Today I was reading about an "Editorial" opening at a magazine. This reminded me of an office tradition that I had so disliked that I had abandoned it. Apparently, *horrors*, my personal most logical stance hasn't convinced the rest of the world to follow suit. According to this condescending, nose-thumbing-at-fashionista concept, the fashion department and the beauty department stand on their own, as does the art department. "Editorial" was used to describe only the brilliant well-educated features and articles staffers, who actually were too smart to have a clue as to what the fashion and beauty editors were up to on the editorial side of the magazine.

I believe that anyone working on the editorial, nonsales (or publishing) side of a magazine—whether in fashion, beauty, features, art department, or health—should be considered editorial. But since my idea has not prevailed, asking what is considered "editorial" would be a good question. Even for me.

The Test

Entry-level jobs. These don't usually involve editing tests. For decades, Condé Nast asked every potential assistant to take a timed typing test. The company finally came to its senses and dropped the rite a few years ago.

Writing, copy editing, and research jobs. These will involve completing some sort of test, probably something you can take home to do. The skills involved here are very specific and best learned on the job or in journalism school. Careful critical reading of the publication you are applying to is essential to hone your skills to fit the individual word style of the place.

Fashion department jobs. These do not come with tests. If the job is assisting an editor on a shoot, you might offer to come along for a day on a tryout basis. Fashion features and health and beauty department jobs, as well as general editorial jobs, might require a written critique of a recent issue or section of a recent issue plus a list of headlines and story ideas for pages you might be working on.

How to Critique a Piece of Work

The big difference between recreational critiques (sitting around with your friends talking about what you love and don't) and professional ones is that professionals are expected to know how to make things smarter, more original, more compelling, more perfectly tailored for that publication. Things to think about:

1. Who is the intended target audience of this publication, ad, newspaper, or book? How old is the average reader? How much money does she earn? Does she live in a city or small town? Does she work? Have kids?
2. What is the stated mission of the publication, brand, or book?
3. Is the audience reached, and is the mission communicated?
4. How does this creative work compare with others in its sphere?
5. How, keeping the above in mind, could it be made better?

Say you've been asked to critique a story as part of your consideration for a job. What to do? First, read it once to get the feel. Then, read it again *critically*. Make a list of what works in the story and what doesn't. Be fair and balanced since a potential employer wants to see both sides of your thinking. For each of your negative items, offer a solution that would correct the problem. You hate the headline? Hate the lead-in text? Write new ones. Make them better. Show your ideas for your top three headline choices and display copy.

Go the extra step whenever possible. Show that you can think through problems and get to solutions. **Bosses love problem solvers.** I've sometimes written

FISHNET FIASCO

I am not proud of my behavior. Not in the least. But things like this would just happen. More out of boredom, I'd prefer to think, than malice.

One day in Liz Tilberis' office, all the senior editors were gathered around to think through a big fall fashion issue. The smart ones who arrived early to the meeting plopped their skinny butts casually on the large white denim–covered sofa. The later arrivals were forced to sit erect on blisteringly cold metal chairs. This particular spring morning, I was seated cozily on the cushy sofa next to Richard Sinnott, an accessories editor and an especially naughty, brilliantly funny guy.

Because the metal chair was cold, the hair on one of the features editors' legs went erect, popping out of the confines of her fishnet stockings. From our view on the sofa, it was like a thigh-sized Black Forest that space aliens had mowed into perfect diamond shapes. Richard and I occupied ourselves for much of the meeting sketching the Black Forest leg hair in our notebooks. Naughty. Immature. So much fun. And, in the end, the only thing I actually remember from the meeting.

This, by way of advice. You don't want to walk around at a fashion magazine, designer's studio, or cool new store with Black Forest diamonds on your legs. Stick to trousers until you are cleaned up for what are the most revealing of all stocking choices: fishnets. No matter what your size it's wise to find small-scale fishnets (that is, smaller diamonds). They rip less easily, make you look skinnier, and they are infinitely more chic. Bare, tan, skinny legs are always good. Opaque black tights, plain or with texture, are better than sheer. Footless tights with ballet slippers if you are under thirty, regardless of how fit you are. Sheer nude shades look stupid.

Post-it notes on layouts to make suggestions about things I would have changed or to applaud what I liked. It's perfectly fine to hand in a critique like this as long as your handwriting is *totally legible* and your grammar and spelling are impeccable. Ask someone good at this—a friend or family member—to check for mistakes before you hand it in.

Interview Notes

Why *Not* to Obsess Too Much About Your Clothes

Above all else, confidence is what's important. How small-town, Yale-educated Emily Dougherty got the job with me at *Harper's Bazaar* was the sheer confidence with which she wore her ruby crystal-covered slippers. Self-assurance. Love it. **Expensive clothes never impress fashionistas. Head-to-toe designer clothes do not impress fashionistas.** Good styling does. Personality does. High self-esteem does. Quirky shoes or a vintage bag do. Got the point?

The HR Take on Things

When Eliot Kaplan, Hearst talent scout, scans your résumé, what matters most to him? "The internships you've done outrank where you went to college," says Kaplan. "But that's becoming harder as good internships are rare.

"I like to hear about someone's working through school," adds Kaplan. "I always ask, 'Did you work at the school paper?' If the answer is no, I want to know why."

Kaplan's attitude might well reflect a fatigue with spoiled Y-generation applicants—too long coddled by parents, privileged enough to take on a series of prestigious unpaid internships, but having no proven experience or capacity to work hard.

At Condé Nast's HR offices, the trick is to be focused and clear. Name the two titles you'd like to work for and, as specifically as possible, in what capacity. Know the titles. Know the mastheads. Recognize the names from the individual mastheads. (Visit www.mastheads.org.) Hopefully you already have the name of an inside connection that you can drop at your HR interview.

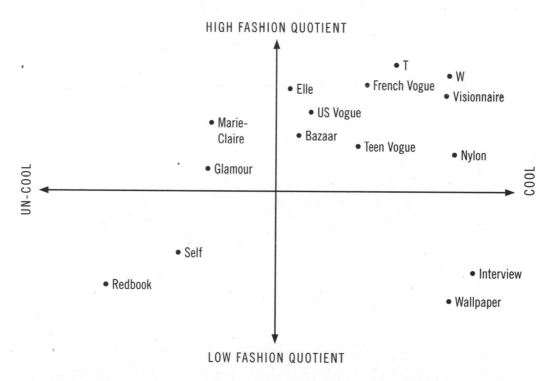

FASHIONISTA MAGAZINE MATRIX

HIGH FASHION QUOTIENT

- T
- Elle
- French Vogue
- W
- Visionnaire
- US Vogue
- Marie-Claire
- Bazaar
- Teen Vogue
- Nylon
- Glamour

UN-COOL ← → COOL

- Self
- Redbook
- Interview
- Wallpaper

LOW FASHION QUOTIENT

Where a future fashionista wants to be? Anywhere on this chart. Where you'd want to be in five years? In the upper right corner. Please note that a publication's positioning on this grid is subject to constant shifts, boosts, and slides.

CREATOR   VISUALIZER   CRITIC   SELLER

CHOOSE YOUR FASHIONISTA PLAYGROUND:
CONDÉ NAST VERSUS HEARST

Here's a good rivalry. Though either company is a great place to work, they couldn't be more different on almost every level. Look at their two founding families. Hearst is a WASP, newspaper family, old money, with some family craziness. William Randolph Hearst, upon whom the lead character of the film *Citizen Kane* is based, left his wife and family behind in Manhattan to live a Hollywood fantasy. The base of the original Hearst building remains much as he built it in 1928. The six-story Art Deco building was supposedly erected as a theater at which his beloved mistress, Hollywood actress Marion Davies, could perform. Hearst's wife and mother of his five sons, Millicent, saw to it that the couple never stepped foot in New York and that the "theater" was converted to house the home offices of the newspaper giant.

Condé Nast was Catholic, the son of a French mother and American father. He was born in New York City but was raised in St. Louis and had longtime ties to photography and the arts. While the Hearst Corporation remains in the hands of its founding family, Condé Nast has in its modern times been owned by the reclusive, hard-working Newhouse clan, a Jewish family from New York City.

Look at their list of publications. Look at their two towers. Stand in their lobbies and look at the people who work at each place. The auras couldn't be more different. Then, at least in your best fashionista fantasy, choose where you'd most want to be, and then make it happen.

	CONDÉ NAST	HEARST
Famous Founder	Condé Montrose Nast, a successful advertising sales executive at *Collier's*, bought *Vogue* magazine and added *Vanity Fair*, *House & Garden*, and *Glamour* to form a fashion group of titles.	William Randolph Hearst, newspaper baron extraordinaire, as portrayed by Orson Welles in *Citizen Kane*.
Running Things Now	Various members of the low-key, workaholic Newhouse family; S.I. Newhouse famously comes to work and takes meetings at 4 a.m.	Extended Hearst family enjoys dividends, but hired guns run the mother ship.
Manhattan Headquarters	Glam building in brash center of universe at 4 Times Square.	Green Building designed by Sir Norman Foster constructed on base of original Hearst Headquarters (8th Avenue and 57th Street).
Flagship Brands	*Vogue, The New Yorker, Vanity Fair, GQ.*	*Esquire, Cosmo, Good Housekeeping, Harper's Bazaar, Town & Country.*

	CONDÉ NAST	HEARST
Fashion Brands	*Vogue, Teen Vogue, Allure, W, Glamour, Lucky, GQ.*	*Harper's Bazaar, Marie Claire.*
Internships	Centralized, well organized; see website.	Practices vary title by title; scattershot.
First Job Advantages	Higher visibility.	Higher starting salaries.
How Your Career Would Unfold	Career tracking (words or pictures, you choose).	Broad experience; hard work pays off in the end.
Website	www.Condenast.com: all about "passion" and "talent"; images of turned-on readers hugging favorite magazines suddenly missing.	www.hearst.com: self-congratulatory focus on new green building with Tom Brokaw voiceover.
New Magazine Launch Style	Splashy and bold. Big commitments are made to editorial, with time and space built in to tweak the formula.	Tentative, low overhead, low risk; evenness and predictability appreciated in personality and newsstand sales. Launch editors are often hired on a freelance basis.
Magazine Closing Style	Slow and torturous. Sometimes the buzz is so loud about a magazine's imminent closure that you forget whether it has closed or not.	Swift and crushing.
Slogan	"Talent is our passion at Condé Nast Publications."	"You're only as good as your last cover at Hearst."
Lobby	Miniwaterfall; a few big magazine covers standing around lobby of shared building.	Stunning. Runway-like escalator triplet cutting diagonally across Niagara-sized recycled waterfall, climbing three stories to atrium lobby.

	CONDÉ NAST	HEARST
Brushing Shoulders with	Badly suited Skadden Arps lawyers, who occupy a chunk of the building.	Fellow employees from the Good Housekeeping Institute who oversee testing of vacuum cleaners, irons, and clothes dryers.
Lunchroom	Dizzying, dark, and gimmicky, a Frank Gehry–designed scene stealer.	Spectacular, light-flooded, altar to healthy eating.
Lunch Specials	Kobe beef hamburgers, sans bun.	Made-to-order sushi and/or sashimi.
Fashionistas in Residence	Anna Wintour, Grace Coddington, Paul Cavaco, Tonne Goodman, Elissa Santisi, Hamish Bowles.	Glenda Bailey, Brana Wolf, Melanie Ward.
Fashionista Ghosts in Residence	Diana Vreeland.	Liz Tilberis, Carmel Snow.
International Magazine Presence	Spottily developed.	Extensively developed.
Recent "Hot" Magazine Franchise	*Lucky,* the fashion shopping title.	*O, The Oprah Magazine.*
When Your Boss Is Fired	Chances are good you will be "absorbed" somewhere else.	Don't stick around to find out.
New Media Savvy	New Web-only titles in research and launch stages; content-driven approach.	New Media is said to be an important new group at the company, though, curiously, it isn't housed in the tower.

Getting and Keeping a Cool Job

In Search of the Cool Place to Work

Town & Country regularly receives industry recognition. Recent honors include being nominated for National Magazine Awards . . . and being named to *Adweek's* list of the "Hottest Magazines of the Year" in 1996.
—From the Hearst website

What is wrong with this picture? It looks bad for *Town & Country.* Very bad. Why? Because the august title has nothing more interesting, timely, or compelling to write about itself than a mention in *Adweek fourteen years* prior? That's close to two centuries ago in magazines. So anyone reading this listing on www.hearst.com should sense something is up. Or will be up. My guess is that first, the powers that be will change publishers (again!) to make sure the business side of things is *not* the problem. Then, inevitably, the big bosses will begin whispering about a new search for the right creative person who will make *Town & Country* pertinent to readers and a viable media outlet for advertisers for the next ten years. At the very least, to keep the thing alive. Or if they had balls to dare to imagine a perfect world, empower someone to reinvent the magazine so that it had a resonant cultural, social pulse. So that people would *talk* about it. So that it would reflect, introduce, and *bring on* change. So that it could be controversial, opinionated, alive! Stay tuned.

Putting Yourself Where Things Are on the Upswing

Every business has clear trend or growth cycles. In magazines, there are giant cycles that reflect society's changing tastes and übertrends. The U.S. edition of the French *ELLE* was launched in the 1980s bringing clean white backdrops, Euro-excessive styling, and multiethnic models. It was exciting, liberating, and hugely successful. Every other publication noticed and adapted. Anyone who didn't looked old very quickly. Then in the 1990s, *InStyle,* once a column in *People* magazine, sprung out on its own and a celebrity-centric nation quickly embraced a celebrity-driven publication to dramatically positive results. More recently, *Lucky* homed in on our consumer-driven obsession and emerged as the "category redefiner" with its focus on the hunt, getting the exact right stuff that's on the page. Off-shoot *Domino* (which, alas, shuttered) was the most fun, young, stylish take on home out there (a cool "shelter" magazine). I loved looking at it. Whatever your source, getting in touch with macrocycles in books, design, architecture, home, food, and film helps you get a grip on the marketplace.

So, where are the coolest places to work right now in magazines? From a visual standpoint, *W* magazine is doing the most innovative work. Its oversized format is a great forum for photographers, and stories run much longer (up to twenty pages sometimes) than they would in conventional magazines (where center-of-the-book fashion stories are a tight four, six, or eight pages generally). For writing and editing, *Vogue* is excellent with a consistently clear mission. *New York* magazine under Adam Moss is exciting to read and watch. The *New York Times* fashion magazine supplement, *T*, delivers smart words and clever images.

Insiders know what's next by means of gut, instinct, and gossip. You can develop your own predictive abilities by keeping your eyes open, reading the trade papers, *Women's Wear Daily,* and *Ad Age* to familiarize yourself with the players and the buzz. You should also read the business section of a good daily newspaper like the *Wall Street Journal, New York Times,* the *Washington Post, Los Angeles Times,* or *USA Today* to know what's happening to companies on a corporate level and at companies that are among a publication's biggest advertisers.

Getting on the Right Track: Your Path to Power

I sit on the edge of the white plastic bubble chair in front of the enormous white "modern" desk of longtime *Seventeen* editor in chief and one-time nun Midge

Richardson. For someone deep into her fifties, Midge has an athletic body, tastefully blond-streaked hair, and a coquettish manner and way of dress. I calmly try to articulate my professional desire as beauty editor to go to some of the magazine's photography shoots. Seeing the hair and makeup process would surely help me write about what was happening, I reason. This is the basic reporting necessary to make the copy surrounding the pictures clear and useful for the readers. (Like *real journalism,* I think to myself, but wisely edit this insolent phrase.) Since the concept behind the photo shoot is mine anyhow, wouldn't it be useful for me to be there to make sense of it in words?

I assure Midge that I will fulfill all other duties of my position so that the hours spent at the shoot won't in any way affect my performance. Midge knows I am the biggest nerd, always at my desk at 7:30 a.m., hours before most of the staff drags themselves in; I'm a good solid producer!

I await her response. Midge stretches her face into her big phony smile that signals bad news. She ends the meeting by explaining that I have attended a good college and that I possess writing and editing skills and therefore do not belong on the set of a photo shoot. The people rightfully populating the set are "street kids," uneducated, not our "kind."

"Leave it to them, Annemarie. That's their job! You don't belong there. Run along now." Being a non-Catholic, I had *never* made the sign of the cross. Yet, so powerful was her aura that I believe I actually crossed myself at this moment while doing a little half curtsey as I rushed out of the room. Fast-forward fifteen years. After a dizzying series of post-*Seventeen* magazine and nonmagazine jobs, I actually occupy Midge's office for a few months before the magazine is shuttled to new offices on Broadway, in what would be the start of my short and ill-fated reign as *Seventeen* editor in chief.

Though I didn't realize it at the time, I learned that what Midge had explained to me way back then was actually the old Condé Nast theory of creative management: that there are people talented in creating pictures, and they should stay away from the words, and that there are those talented in writing, assigning, and editing words, and they should have nothing to do with the pictures. Success at Condé Nast meant knowing which role you were best suited to play and then proving yourself in it. I checked in recently with Condé Nast hiring types and learned that this division between pictures and words is still alive and well. So when you appear at 4 Times Square for your interview, know which way you want to go.

Internet Fashion: The Future of Fashion Journalism?

What does the Internet bring to fashion? Instantaneousness and democracy. The fact that each of us—regardless of our ability to snag a seat at the show or eventually purchase the clothes—may now watch collections within hours of their runway showing is perhaps the most radical change in the documentation of fashion of modern times. The question of how this immediacy and openness affect the status quo is awkwardly obvious: Headlines these days declare doomsday stuff like *The Death of Glamour Glossies*. While it's true that some fashion magazines have been shuttered due to the recent economic downturn (and even the most revered titles are historically slim, which means, *hello*, down in advertising income), I am here to promise you that fashion magazines will never, *ever* go away. At the advent of television in the 1950s, media watchers predicted the death of print journalism—magazines and newspapers—which, in hindsight, was ridiculous. Doom-and-gloomers are doing the same today.

The intimacy and wonder one feels when flipping fashion magazine pages filled with beautiful dresses, creative fashion photography, and gripping, pertinent stories assure this medium's future. But the harsh reality is that there will likely be fewer and less powerful fashion publications. So, if you are just starting your life in fashion journalism, I *beseech* you to open your eyes to the online fashion world that desperately needs your new energy, vision, and creativity much more than the moldy old print world does. Plus you'll be guaranteed to express yourself week one, whereas at a magazine it could take years (decades?) before you are able to see your ideas come to life on the pages. Really.

One guy friend, a twenty-something blogger, said it best: "I like writing long form, but things aren't moving in that direction right now. With the Internet, you reach a broader spectrum, and you get the message out faster. It's like being at a fashion/style news desk." He likens his job to that of a fashion journalist at a newspaper, which sounds exciting in an old-fashioned, low-tech sense. So, even as the print world shrinks, perhaps irreversibly, there is no limit to the number of fashion publications on the Internet.

SARAH CRISTOBAL | Senior Fashion Editor of StyleList.com, an AOL Site

Downtown, funny, connected, wry, Sarah Cristobal has a groovster style all her own, mixes up labels—like Chanel satin ballet flats worn with thick tights and a girly boho dress—to suit her distinct look. Her experience covering the international fashion and party scene at StyleList.com as well as working on the prototype of *Vogue*'s style.com, then bringing to life the Web pages for *Harper's Bazaar,* puts twenty-something Sarah in rare company. A member of a small group of savvy online journalists, Sarah now works at the largest stand-alone fashion and beauty site on the Web.

WHY SARAH LOVES DOING ONLINE FASHION
"You get to work in real time. You can be immediately relevant to your audience. You can come up with cool concepts using interactive technology. Editorially speaking, it's like working at a newspaper where you're rushing to break news, but with the Internet features can be produced faster and you can see how well it tracks right away through comments and page views."

WHAT IT TAKES TO DO IT
"It's a different skill set than what you are taught in J school (at least when I was there). Learning the technical aspects was akin to learning a different language. It's helpful to have the insight behind how everything works. If you're not well versed, take a computer science class. Learn about HTML and XML. Familiarize yourself with Facebook, Twitter, Tumblr, and all of those social networking sites which have become so important for media outlets that want to reach a broader audience. Maybe even get your hands dirty and start your own blog. It's so easy to do these days."

THE RACE TO POST
"I think knowing PhotoShop is useful so you can crop your own images and put them up yourself. With a small team, if you have to put your request into an overloaded photo editor, then wait for her to help, chances are that someone will beat you to the story. It's a race to be first and relevant. You want the page views. You want the credibility."

"WRITING IS LIKE THE ICING ON THE CAKE"
"Once you master the back-end stuff, then there's the fun part that is the actual fashion journalism. Know the designers, and know their collections and their histories. You have to be quick on your feet and fast."

"I DIDN'T GRADUATE FROM COLLEGE"

Sarah was working toward a double degree in journalism and Spanish at the University of Massachusetts, and she had completed more than half of the degree requirements.

"I was saving money to spend a semester in Spain and fell short, so I moved to New York instead. Made sense at the time, even though NYC is not cheap! I guess I wanted to get on with things and live my life so I packed up and went. I had grown up near where I went to college. It was and still is a lovely area, but I knew that I was ready to move on."

BIG BREAK

"When I left school, I immediately got an internship at *Blackbook* magazine—this cool downtown fashion and art quarterly. I was lucky that the editor in chief gave me a shot. This lovely man named Al (to whom I am forever indebted) used to bring *Blackbook* into the restaurant where I worked in Northampton, Massachusetts, and the whole staff used to drool over it. When I decided to move to New York, he gave me the editor's phone number because he was one of his best friends. I've been really lucky. I've had nice people giving me breaks along the way."

"I WORE A *SUIT* TO MY INTERVIEW WITH THE EDITOR IN CHIEF"

"We met at the funkiest coffee shop/art studio in Soho. I was so young and green, and I thought, 'Oh God, I have an interview with the editor in chief, and I need to look professional.' Mind you, I was not going on an interview to be an insurance salesman! Anyhow, I got the unpaid internship and worked there two or three days a week for ten months. I made coffee runs. I delivered magazines. I got to write a little. I was in heaven."

NEXT STEP

Sarah then went to work as an editorial assistant for Bob Guccione's *Gear* magazine. "I assisted the editor in chief and got to write. It was a total laddie mag but I learned a lot and still keep in touch with the friends I made there. I ended up staying for three years."

STYLE.COM

"Then I went to Style.com, kind of as a utility player. I started doing returns for the fashion closet, then subbed in as managing editor (ahem, short-lived!), then shifted over to the fashion department as a junior market editor.

"Back then filing stories was akin to a magazine process. Everything was written in a Word document, then it would go through channels to the editor in chief. After the copy editor formatted it and signed off, the story was cut-and-pasted into the content management system (CMS). Now everything is written directly into the blog platform."

FASHION MARKET EDITOR

"At one point I was working directly with Candy Pratts Price [the former executive fashion director of Style.com] as a junior market editor, sourcing product for her shopping and trend stories. She's a legend in the business, and I learned a lot from her. Not just about fashion but also about being accountable for your actions. If you said that you were going to have something ready for a meeting, you had better have it ready. You couldn't be laissez-faire around Candy. After doing that for six months, I moved to Barcelona for a change of scene. I had some friends there and I speak Spanish."

BARCELONA BEAT

"I lived there just shy of six months and worked as a freelance writer and editor for Dresslab.com— a BCN-based fashion and design website, and I also did some travel writing for the [now defunct] *Spain* magazine."

STYLE.COM, PART DEUX

"I returned from Barcelona totally broke and was lucky enough to land at Style.com again as the associate editor. I was the social reporter for three years. I covered glamorous parties, went to the Oscars and the Golden Globes, to Istanbul with Zac Posen. It was quite the whirlwind, and great exposure."

NEXT STOP: *HARPERSBAZAAR*.COM

"When I got to *Bazaar,* I was responsible for getting the magazine content online as well as coming up with original content in the form of a blog, videos, etc. That equated to having a good handle on the back-end practices to make sure the content is search-engine friendly (SEO data). Also getting the content out there was essential via *Bazaar*-branded pages on Facebook and other social networking sites. I also worked with the PR team to "break" stories at specific times. Tracking the success of the site and anything that was trending was measured by using analytical data platforms like comScore and Omniture. In addition, I also wrote features for the mag itself, which was great."

STYLELIST.COM

"There's a nice hodgepodge of backgrounds, not just fashion magazine people, but women who've worked in television, newspapers, wire services. There's definitely a sense of everyone working toward a common goal. It's a great place to be."

Since Sarah started in March 2009, "It's got a huge built-in audience and we're making it relevant in the fashion/blog community. It's getting there. We've gained a lot of traction recently."

FASHION MAGAZINES VERSUS FASHION WEBSITES
"Working in magazines is great, but I love the Web. It feels a bit freer and more interpretive."

HOW DID SARAH FIGURE OUT THE TECHNICAL STUFF?
"Repetition. Making mistakes. A lot of late nights of trying to figure what goes where and how. Each site has different strategies, and so it's been great to learn everywhere I went."

WHAT MOST PEOPLE DON'T GET
"There is an editorial schedule to working on the Web. I think there is a misconception that you can just throw any story up at any time. While we make room for daily updates, that is only one component of the site.

"Every site is different and has its own lexicon. It's really involved and there's a lot of minutia, even more so than magazines. The process isn't necessarily as thorough as print and sometimes mistakes are made, but, fortunately, you can go in quickly to fix errors and republish the piece instead of issuing a retraction."

JOURNALISM 101
"In the blogsphere grammar and prose can go out the window, and it kind of drives me crazy. If you can submit clean copy and have your facts straight, you'll get a lot of work. Some writers are lazy and not very good, and that creates more work for the editor, which is not favorable."

LOOKING BACK
"I've written tons of articles; it's important to keep developing yourself as a writer whether it is print or online. It's a humbling experience to have an editor tear through your copy. It's happened to me countless times, and you pretty much want to crawl into a ball under your desk, but you can't be precious about it. It's the only way to learn and get better."

IF YOU WANT TO BE A WEB EDITOR
"Know who your competition is, and, even more important, know who your audience is. Stay true to them. Be informed. Read a lot—including *Women's Wear Daily* every morning. Be credible, not a couch-potato critic who offers up unfounded opinions. Be ready to work in a reactionary environment. It's like being at a news desk. StyleList is a fashion/beauty/pop culture news desk."

WHERE THE $$$ IS
"Most advertisers are clamoring for the online buy these days, which translates to lots of opportunity on the Web."

THE SATISFACTION OF INSTANT INTERCHANGE

"Sometimes you'll work hard on something and it won't yield the results you were hoping for. Other times a story will take off like wildfire across the Web. It is instant and pretty subjective."

STYLELIST NUMBERS

"Last month (April 2010) we averaged 5.7 million unique visitors and about 45 million page views. We're the largest stand-alone fashion and beauty site on the Web!"

PEOPLE WANT THEIR VOICES HEARD

"Look at Cathy Horyn's *New York Times* fashion blog. Some of her commenters will write the equivalent of comparative literature essays in response to her posts, and she will reference them. It's a very democratic way of connecting with your audience and gives everyone a voice."

ONLINE OUTREACH = COMMUNITY

"It's nice to work at a place that runs the gamut from affordable, real-women fashion to high-end pieces. Fashion and style shouldn't be alienating. It's a creative mode of expression and is always up for self-interpretation.

"Online fashion feels a bit more flexible than magazines and less exclusionary. Especially if you consider how all of the sale sites like Gilt and Outnet have taken off. It's interesting to see how things have shifted. And it's just gaining momentum."

The Next Big Job: How to Prove You're the Absolute Best Person

Here, we're talking promotions or stepped-up responsibility. There are two ways this can materialize: more money and/or a new title. It always looks good on your résumé if you start with one title and then earn a promotion, so in this respect the title is more important than the money.

Creative jobs are the most sought after positions around, requiring that you show more commitment, passion, and tenacity than anyone else in the running. If you hear that someone is leaving in your office and it's a job you'd like, go for it with the same seriousness of an outside search.

It's grueling, but chances are this will be the only time you sweat it out this painfully. Once you earn the job and spend a couple of years proving yourself, you'll soon start receiving cryptic messages from masthead-reading managing editors or head hunters looking to fill an even better slot.

Normal Tryouts

If you're really in the running for a position, the boss may ask you to do a tryout. This is a good sign, and you should take the assignment seriously. You may be asked to do any or all of the following:

- Write a list of ten story ideas.
- Rewrite an ad or story.
- Critique an ad or an issue of a magazine.
- Take an editing test.
- Lay out a page or ad (if you are a graphic designer).

Be prepared to spend an entire weekend working on this, which is a drag, but that's the deal. Don't hand over your assignment unless you've written it, put it away, then rewritten and polished it. Make it look as exciting and readable as possible. Run it by friends whose opinions you trust. Get it in on time. No excuses!

Real Tryouts

Often, what it really takes to get the job is a whole different level of commitment, verve, and tenacity. Atoosa Rubenstein worked for free as an intern for years at *Sassy* magazine before she was made a staffer. From a staff job at *Cosmopolitan* magazine, Atoosa was the founding editor of *CosmoGirl.* She later took over *Seventeen* and is now out on her own building an empire.

Before winning the title of beauty editor at *Harper's Bazaar,* and without even asking if I'd get paid for it, I agreed to write a 2,500-word story for Liz Tilberis on the opening of the minimalist Mecca, the gleaming new Barneys New York store on Madison Avenue. What did that have to do with landing the beauty position? Everything. It was a test. Did I write acceptably well? Could I turn on a dime and produce good text over a weekend? Would the staff accept me? Was I "cool"? To build consensus with her staff and create the illusion that they could weigh in on my hire, Liz passed around the draft of my story to key members of her team asking if they thought I "had it." Next, Liz sent me to collaborate with the new fashion stylist, the amazing Elissa Santisi, and the genius Swiss photographer Raymond Meier to come up with an image for the story: a Barneys hanger with an exotic bird on it. Not an idea I ever would have dreamt up in a million years. I learned a monumental lesson here: Don't get in the way of genius, especially if it makes you look even better. Next came collaboration with the art department, formatting the story and writing a headline that looked good with the photograph. Fact checkers and copy editors descended on me to assure complete accuracy and good sense. Sound intense? It was. But that's how I got my dream job with Liz Tilberis.

Catfight: Meow! Why It's Good to Have an Enemy

This is about a face-off of nearly equal powerhouses. In boxing, it was George Foreman versus Muhammad Ali. In late-night television, it was Jay Leno versus David Letterman. In baseball, the Yankees versus the Red Sox. In art, Picasso versus Matisse, Michelangelo versus da Vinci.

It's the fly buzzing around your head. A rival is someone who shows you how well or how horribly you are doing. The absolute bane of your existence, she always puts you on edge. You can sense her presence in a room long before you see her. Your fur stands on end and your ears cock for every encounter.

But this is not all bad. Let's look at the bright side: Without a rival, would you become complacent, plump, unkempt, bored? No matter how much grief she causes you, a rival keeps you on your toes. Alive. Awake. Inspired.

No one is immune from competitive forces; nor would you wish to be. Creatively American *Vogue* must admire and envy the young energy and original design of French *Vogue*. From an advertising or sales perspective, French *Vogue* is but a shaky scaffolding to American *Vogue*'s gleaming skyscraper of success.

The Face-off

The much-reported Anna Wintour–Liz Tilberis rivalry taught me a lot. The competition between these two English women (or perceived competition) made each of them bigger somehow and more clearly defined. The daughter of a newspaperman, Anna started as the lingerie editor for *Harper's & Queen* in London; the daughter of an eye surgeon, Liz began as the lingerie editor for British *Vogue*. Anna is stick thin; by comparison, normal-ish Liz seemed elephantine. To all outward appearances, which is all we're talking about anyhow, Anna was brisk and efficient, translating in the cartoon world of comparison to bitch; Liz publicly acted sweet and kind, which, trust me, was good propaganda.

Who was the first to phone *Bazaar* after Liz died? Anna Wintour's office. Anna was devoting her editor's letter to Liz and needed some backup information. Was Anna operating on the often-quoted notion "Keep your friends close and your enemies closer"? No, I think Anna understood the usefulness of the rivalry, but ultimately she showed amazing humanity and newsroom grit by eulogizing Liz so automatically and graciously.

I conducted my own mini Liz-Anna rivalry, though perhaps only in my own mind. I, the blonde, Midwestern, young, smart, and iconoclastic beauty editor of *Harper's Bazaar* accepted the job while Shirley Lord, *Vogue*'s long-standing beauty royalty and dirty book writer, was still occupying her throne there. I looked forward to the comparisons. My hands-on, journalistic approach—showing up backstage at every fashion show to interview the hair stylist and makeup artists—made her company-driven coverage, hair-sprayed coifs, and moldy skirt suits seem old-school. After I'd had only a few months on my new beat, Shirley was gracefully retired, and Amy Astley, who'd worked briefly and inauspiciously under Shirley, was shuttled into the role. Instantly, pretty, fresh Amy from Michigan, who'd previously worn a short brownish bob, clunky shoes, and Pilgrim skirts, was transformed. Whambangmakeovermam! She showed up blond—blonder than *moi*—wore sexy Manolo sandals, and the exact same spring navy Gucci double-breasted suit as, you got it, me! Soon, to my horror, Mrs. Evelyn Lauder and a young publicity girl both called me "Amy" at a beauty event. Warming up at the bar at my regular 6 p.m. Lotte Berk class, I glanced up to see who was that person performing a marginally deeper grande plié than my own? You got it, Amy Astley. This was beginning to feel personal. Maybe I was being systematically cloned, and soon all beauty editors from all publications would be identical. Voilà, the Ultimate New Model Beauty Editor! Looking back, I realize I should have been kind, instead of competitive, and embraced her. BBBs, we both could have learned from the friendship and had some good laughs in the process. As it was, the very idea of a *Vogue* clone motivated me to work harder to get more original and exclusive stories.

I'm happy to report that Amy and I eventually buried the lipstick, so to speak. Soon after Amy was named editor in chief of *Teen Vogue,* again, weirdly following my path to be editor in chief of two other teen magazines, I—recently thrown out on my derrière from a parallel role—phoned to congratulate her. She picked up right off. It was cathartic for me to hear her voice and to clear the air. My sources inform me that Amy is a fun, fair, excellent person and that much of the *soi-disant* rivalry was something I had invented. Now I cheer on this star at every opportunity, celebrating her every success. After all, Amy is a nice Midwestern girl like me, with a great work ethic and a hot magazine to call her own. *Brava!*

A Fashion Editor's Orientation

It's a Hypervisual World

What you wear and how you look matters a great deal. It is material for everyone to notice, for sure, comment on if they feel comfortable enough even to your face, and tease you, especially if they love you. **You are what you wear.** Develop thick skin on this one, baby. Best to stick to a simple uniform (see pages 214 and 294). The hallway is the runway and *you are on it*!!!!

Your Own Inspiration Board

While it is generally a collage of incongruous items that informs others about your taste, an inspiration board should actually inspire you. Fashion designers create inspiration boards each season. The theme might be an old movie, a city, a color, a voyage, a rock star, a punk rock star, Coco Chanel from her Deauville days, Frida Kahlo, Edie Sedgwick, and on and on and on. Somehow an entire collection—ninety runway looks—emerges. *Your* inspiration board, be it a mini cork bulletin board or a chunk of your cubicle wall, should make you happy. Otherwise, redo it immediately. Or keep it blank. Some obvious starters:

- A black-and-white photo of Audrey Hepburn
- A favorite vintage fashion photo from Avedon, such as one from his elephant, circus series, or one of Melvin Sokolsky's plastic bubbles over the Seine
- A cool invitation
- A postcard from somewhere unexpected
- A matchbox that's graphic or cool
- A handwritten card from someone you admire
- A bit of ribbon from Lanvin or Hermès
- Photographs and illustrations of all your favorite current season and classic shoes

Or bring alive:

- A favorite author, like Virginia Woolf, or a director, like Sofia Coppola
- One must-have thing like spring coats, perfume bottles, or the ballet
- One amazing color, such as fuchsia, robin's egg blue, that energizes you

Whatever you do, don't make your board home economics or Martha Stewart cute. That means no perfect fabric background or ribbons stretching diagonally across to create perfect diamond shapes. This board should be a work in progress. Artist messy and real.

Why Fashionistas Wear Black

There are loads of fashionistas who wear color. Mix things up. Even throw in a print now and then. Spectator shoes. A strong red lip. Or a crisp red suit. They don't wear head to toe of one designer. Watching a top-level fashionista play with her own look every day is an education all in itself. Besides being a total pleasure. Here, I'm thinking in particular of my friend Elissa Santisi, who on a molecular level understands the essence of American style. She plays with its elements, mixing things up in a modern, original way. But despite her presence and a few others in her orbit, there remains an overriding shroud of black.

In the midst of a deeply black minimal phase when the entire fashion world turned out *en noir,* we at *Bazaar* heard from good sources at *Vogue* that Anna had issued orders for her staff to stop wearing black. That seemed to me at the time unreasonable, dictatorial, and harsh. It was, in fact, prescient. Anna knew that black would run its course as do all good fashion trends. Of course she was right. Before long, even the darkest of designers, like Helmut Lang, Jil Sander, and Tom Ford, were showing fuchsia, chalky Delft blue, and daffodil. Head-to-toe black was officially out.

Yet many, many top arbiters of style stick with black. Why? It removes them from the day-to-day conflict of what is the right thing to wear. Like a judge's black robes visually separating him or her from a courtroom of messy lay folk, a fashionista's black look sets her above the fray. Black clothes aren't as likely to scream out what label is sewn in the back or which collection or season they came from. Fashionistas who practically live on the set of a photo shoot and travel all over the world to make pictures choose black out of practicality, in part. It's also understandable for those surrounded all day long by racks of garments and closets of accessories to choose to remain personally neutral. Those who've lived through the Japanese fashion revolution of the late 1970s and early 1980s seem especially reluctant to leave their noncolor. Blackists might argue that by eliminating all color, they are free to explore the nuances of shape, texture, layering, fabrications, and other such sublimely subtle details on a more granular level. Whatever. Too much black is depressing. I prefer the girl, like Elissa, who inspires everyone with her look.

Vocabulary

Every place of work has its own language, both technical and colloquial. At some magazines where I worked, for example, the type after the headline was called a *blurb*, while at others, it was called the *deck* or the *sell*, while at still others, it was generically referred to as *display type*. At *Seventeen*, you were a *dork* for doing something stupid. At *Bazaar*, you were a *cow*. You need to listen and adapt to the local dialect quickly.

What's being judged every time you open your mouth? Everything. Your intelligence, your ability to do the job, your experience. There are some general rules that apply to all situations. It's always better to say nothing than to be a know-it-all. The best advice:

Be terrifically smart or just be quiet.

FASHION FEVER

Fashion fever is triggered by the realization that you can actually exist one season ahead of everyone else. You can wear and carry samples of clothes and bags that won't be produced for another several months. You can be ahead of the pack. A fashion leader. No one can buy or possess what you have.

The euphoria that results from this exalted status clouds judgment. The girl who would never dream of shoplifting a bag at Bergdorf Goodman (why would she when she need only pull out her dad's black Amex?) covets a tiny gold, quilted Chanel bag that, she naively reasons, no one would *ever* miss from the overflowing closet. She is so deluded in her thinking that she actually *wears* the bag to work the next day.

Further complicating the usual black and white of right and wrong is the common practice among lots of senior editors of taking stuff they fancy. They, due to years laboring in the business and earning major credits (which translate into bigger sales) for all major fashion houses, have earned the right to "borrow" with impunity. Junior editors might feel bitter over this sense of entitlement, especially when senior editors make sometimes as much as ten times more money than starving assistants.

You say to yourself: How could anyone be so stupid? First of all, where would you *ever* wear something you'd stolen from the closet? They must have wanted to be caught.

It comes down to losing one's head. Getting caught up in the fashion fever. Caring too much about *the stuff.* Wise to the debilitating effects of fashion fever, editors are wary of hiring people whose love of the materialistic might surpass their true love of fashion.

Fashionista Lexicon

Heaven: An adjective to describe nice clothes, pictures, locations, events

Sick: An adjective to describe good, and somehow edgy, clothes, pictures, locations, events

Fab: Fabulous

Genius: Common overstatement; rarely used for true genius

Cool: A person, concept, place, or thing that is accepted, "in"

Not cool: Opposite of above

Senior: A serious effort worthy of attention

Junior: Not up to standards

Other good words: *new, derivative, modern, brilliant, original, honest, complete, sensual, concise, muse, inspiration, faddish, old,* and *edgy.*

Nonfashionista Words
Neat, gee, gee whiz, rock'n, different, copy, knock-off, chill'n, stupid, dude, and *ugly*
You get the idea.

Be Literate
How did my love of William Wordsworth pop up at *Harper's Bazaar* circa 1998? Drawing from Wordsworth's words, I was able to help elevate a story on summer female Olympians, shot beautifully by Wayne Maser, to a higher level. Reading great works—those of Shakespeare, Faulkner, Blake, Yeats—at some point in your life can only help you bring more to your own creativity.

If you are a stylist, being literate means knowing the proper names for a coat: Is it a reefer, a trench, a wrap, a bomber, or military? For sleeves (raglan, inset), collars, pants options (Capri, gaucho, short), and on. A stylist should know all relevant brand names past and present.

If you are a designer in the art department, *literacy* superficially means experience with the right software. On a deeper level, it refers to photographic and design references past and present, and these will ultimately matter more profoundly than anything else.

Be a Better Wordsmith (Even If You Are *Not* a Writer)
How you dress communicates your style. How you speak and write tells others about your brain. Even if you are the assistant to the footwear editor, you will be presenting ideas and speaking in meetings as well as writing and answering e-mails. The manner in which you communicate matters: Do you express yourself in a stiff, corporate way? Are you too casual, slangy, and friendly? Follow a few of the rules below, and *I promise* more people will listen to you and be receptive to what you are saying.

1. Always be alliterative. Repeated initial consonant letters make things more memorable and look better on the screen or on paper. Sometimes alliterated headlines or words can seem daft, like "Better Body." Usually, though, they help make the message memorable. Once you start thinking this way, noticing how headlines or titles are crafted, the film or music references that they play off, you'll be one step closer to communicating in the creative "code." Headlines sometimes enter my brain while I'm trying to sleep, when I first wake up, or while I'm in the shower. I *know* when it's good. Some of my favorites include: "Makeup for Mortals," "Beauty Bitch," and "Give Me Glam." Writing and brainstorming headlines or cover lines in a group is one of my all-time favorite ways to spend time.

I loved how Sally Koslow, a senior editor of *Woman's Day* who helped hire me there, and later editor in chief of *McCall's* and *Lifetime* magazines and now a successful novelist, could speak in rapid-fire headlines. Whenever anyone had a vague concept for a story, she'd reverbalize it as a dazzling cover or headline. She inspired me. Scared me. I wanted to be that fast and verbal. Even if you are making pictures, you need to *sell* your concepts—that is, you need to find novel, exciting ways to describe your vision.

2. Get-it-right grammar. Don't get me started on my grammar pet peeves. I'll just cover a few of the biggest offenders. No matter WHO you are or WHAT your job, you are hereby FORBIDDEN from making these mistakes. Sorry, bubs, but this is the hard, cold truth: There is a great grammar conspiracy. Even though you THINK this stuff doesn't matter, the managing classes will, consciously or not, judge you negatively if you don't speak or write decently:

Quick trick: See an apostrophe? That means TWO WORDS have been combined!!!

Its / It's
Its = possessive = The coat is fuchsia: Its color is cool.
It's = contraction of two words (IT IS!!!) = It is a fuchsia-colored coat.

Your / You're
Your = possessive = Your cat has leopard spots.
You're = contraction of two words (YOU ARE!!!!) = You are so lucky to have a leopard-spotted cat.

Their / They're
Their = possessive = Their mom gets a discount at Gucci.
They're = contraction of two words (THEY ARE!!!) = They are so lucky that their mom gets a discount at Gucci.

NEVER SAY "between you and I"
ALWAYS SAY "between you and me"

The best short read on this subject? The classic and charming *Elements of Style* by Strunk and White (1918). Afraid of looking like a grammar nerd? While your friends are listening to their favorite rap mixes, you can soak up the latest Grammar Girl's "Quick and Dirty Tips" podcasts:

3. *Spelling matters.* One fashion HR executive told me that if a candidate misspells the name of a top brand he or she supposedly wants to work for, that he or she will not be given access to jobs inside that brand. The following are actual spelling mistakes made by college-level fashion students looking to intern at the following "dream" brands:

"Perada" for *Prada*
"Cenneth Cole" for *Kenneth Cole*
"Donna Carin" for *Donna Karan*

Similarly, Marc Jacobs is not "Mark"; Karl Lagerfeld is not "Carl." When in doubt, Google the company name. This isn't the place to make a stupid mistake.

SELLER 4

WHAT IS IT: | Retail (working for stores, buying from showrooms, selling to real people), wholesale (working for the brand selling to stores), ad sales, public relations.

DEGREE: | None necessary. Useful, however, might be studies in psychology, business, economics (undergraduate), an MBA (for higher-level corporate marketing, finance, acquisitions posts). After your first job, probably no one will ever ask again.

TRAITS: | High energy, enthusiasm, focus, thick skin, results oriented.

ESSENTIAL ABILITIES: | Fearlessness; finding motivation in the word *no*.

ROLE: | To be the Vision of what you're selling: great posture, sleek, well groomed, fit, fashionable.

WORKSPACE: | From Starbucks to dingy cubicle to gleaming corporate office.

PATH TO POWER: | Start in the lowest job in a low-profile operation to learn the lingo; then, even if you need to take a salary and/or title cut, sign on in a junior position for your dream company.

ALTERNATE PATH TO POWER: | Align yourself with a dazzling design talent as the business and marketing brain, then build an empire together; for example, Barry Schwartz (Calvin Klein), Robert Duffy (Marc Jacobs), Domenico De Sole (Tom Ford).

MOST COVETED BUSINESS JOBS: | CEO of fashion label, divisional merchandise manager, fashion director of specialty store, publisher of an online fashion magazine, CEO of an ad agency.

DOGGIE JOB: | A dead or dying category (print, bridge, better) where your boss has no sense of humor.

KEY BRANDS: | All fashion labels, all fashion magazines, all stores.

KEY PERSONALITIES: | Michael Gould (Bloomingdale's), the Nordstrom brothers, Robert Duffy (Marc Jacobs), Patrizio Bertelli (Prada), Bernard Arnault (LVMH), François Pinault (Printemps).

KEY ALLIANCES: | Anyone you've ever worked for.

MODERN SUCCESS STORIES: | Jeffrey Kalinsky, whose Atlanta-based Jeffrey store—Jeffrey Atlanta—took off in New York's meat-packing district—Jeffrey New York—just as that neighborhood was becoming the next big shopping destination. The folks at Nordstrom, identifying with his outsider intelligence, invested with him.

MISCONCEPTION: | That the business end isn't creative.

LANGUAGES: | Time, space, money, margins, SKU (Stock Keeping Unit), ROI (Return On Investment).

STARTING COMP: | Basic with performance bonuses built in.

POTENTIAL COMP: | $ to $$$$$.

PERKS: | Quick mobility. You can move up from Bloomingdale's sales associate to assistant buyer to Dolce & Gabbana showroom manager to regional sales associate, etc.

Without Pierre Bergé, there'd have been no Yves Saint Laurent.

Without Francesca Versace, Donatella Versace, and Santo Versace, there'd have been no Gianni Versace.

Without Giancarlo Giammetti, there'd be no Valentino.

Without Robert Duffy, there'd be no Marc Jacobs.

Without Domenico De Sole, there'd be no Tom Ford.

Without Barry Schwartz, there'd be no Calvin Klein.

Without Susan Posen, there'd be no Zac Posen.

Without Bud Konheim, there'd be no Nicole Miller.

Without Judy Kors, there'd be no Michael Kors.

Without Paul and Linda McCartney, there'd be no Stella McCartney.

Without Patrizio Bertelli, we'd never have heard of Miuccia Prada.

This chapter is about how *you* can be the next Robert Duffy, Domenico De Sole, Susan Posen, or Patrizio Bertelli. Getting there doesn't involve earning a degree and being supersmart or supercool. It's about putting yourself in the right milieu to work in the singularly thrilling, demanding, daunting, fun, cool world of fashion and grabbing on to the most talented person you find. This is the business side of fashion that requires a highly functioning left side of the brain. The fashion *business* brain is logical, rational, analytical, and objective. He or she thinks in a sequential way, breaking down a large objective, like creating a stunning collection for fall, into smaller, less daunting steps. He or she is consistently able to make things happen. Most important, this person, this alter ego of the designer, must know the designer well enough to think the way he or she thinks in order to communicate well with the designer. Which means that this person is probably something of a saint as well as being a renaissance person.

"At least I knew that when you add 3 plus 3, it will equal 6," says Giancarlo Giammetti, modestly explaining his slightly more evolved abilities to run a business than his partner of forty-five years, Valentino Garavani, in the 2009 Matt Tyrnaurer film *Valentino: The Last Emperor.*

Let's talk about *your* brain. I'm making the giant assumption that you, like Giancarlo Giammetti, are a left-brain thinker who sees things in a logical, sequential way whereas your friend, the Creator, has brilliant visions but isn't necessarily able to complete the steps to bring the vision to life.

Seeing the Valentino film brought to my mind the sometimes sophomoric dynamic I've witnessed between Marc Jacobs and Robert Duffy, who met as teenagers working at the Upper West Side, then-edgy clothing store Charivari and who, throughout their careers, have sat at desks pushed together and facing one another. Duffy likes to complain about Marc's absent-mindedly swiping papers stamped "Confidential" or "Audit" and sketching on the back, then forgetting them somewhere in the design studio to be unearthed seasons later. Or for leaving bits of salad on Robert's spreadsheets. Thanks to Robert's abilities and to a total trust between the two, Jacobs is able to exist in a kind of fashion bubble.

Without Harvard-MBA-former-Gucci-finance-whiz Domenico De Sole at his side, Tom Ford may not have left Gucci to have his stint at Yves Saint Laurent before founding his own fashion house.

In some cases, as with Michael Kors and Zac Posen, there is Mom. Michael's mom Judy has worked for her son's company since its beginnings. Zac's mother, corporate lawyer, and company CEO Susan Posen has created the structure and alliances in which her son's design talent has thrived. Gianni Versace learned the dressmaking trade from his own mother, Francesca, at whose side he worked as a child. In turn, his older brother, Santo, and younger sister, Donatella, worked at his side, until his tragic death, and they continue to run the house of Versace.

Then, there's the odd case of the catalytic impact one personality has on another. Without Patrizio Bertelli, her pushy, driven Tuscan husband of decades, Miuccia Prada may never have taken the reins of her grandfather's luggage business and found a way to create simple, utilitarian bags and jackets that would explode the brand overnight into a global fashion powerhouse. After all, Miuccia had studied political science as a student and enjoyed living her life in the counterculture. She had no training in fashion, sketching, or designing.

DESIGNER LABELS' RELATIVE COOL

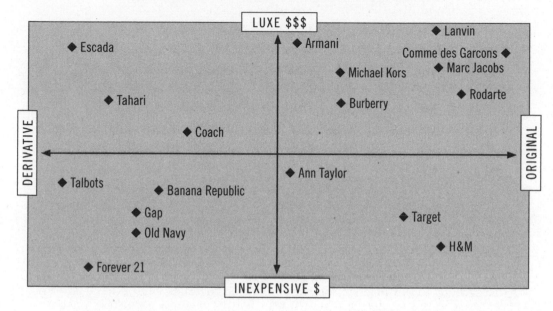

Of course this is much bigger than just selling. This is taking the germ of an idea and bringing it to life. Yes, this involves business smarts. But there's a tremendous amount of creativity involved with keeping things running smoothly so that Marc, Tom, and Miuccia can focus their energies on what they do best.

The most obvious lesson is to link yourself with the biggest star in your orbit. Which is what Giancarlo Giammetti clearly did on that summer's night in Rome fifty years ago, when he met a young Valentino at a café on Corso Veneto.

On the flipside, you can look at amazingly talented designers who have never found their business alter ego. I'm thinking here of the exquisitely talented Cuban-American Narciso Rodriguez or the young star Chinese-American Peter Som. Neither has had a built-in business partner, which has made making it in fashion (already a painfully difficult proposition) even more acutely challenging.

Then there are the other exceptions—those who've succeeded beyond most measures of success without a strong CEO at their side. While Karl Lagerfeld has had the structure and DNA of Chanel upon which to rely for inspiration, he is essentially a one-man fashion phenomenon. And, of course, there's the man behind Polo Ralph Lauren, one of the most successful fashion labels of our time, who seems to have both sides of his brain firing at all times. The success of Ralph Lauren is probably bigger even than his own Hollywood fantasy.

Anatomy of a Partnership: Nicole Miller + Bud Konheim

WHY IT WORKS (TWENTY-SIX YEARS AND GOING STRONG)

- Nicole is a serious designer who knows how to find newness that is original; Bud is a Seventh Avenue legacy who knows how to run a fashion company and showcase the talent of a serious designer.
- Nicole and Bud share a serious work ethic.
- Nicole and Bud agree on the basic premise of the company. Bud says, "We are a design company, not a commodity company. The beauty of design, and the appeal of design, is that it's individual and it's different. You can't take one design and make zillions of it because then it's not individual anymore. It dilutes its specialness."

Bud adds:

- "Everybody in our place has a work ethic that matches what Nicole and I do. And that doesn't mean we don't relax and have a good time. We do. Nicole goes off to St. Bart's for two weeks, and I go off to Florida. But when it's work, it's work.
- "Nicole is mature and emotionally stable.
- "Nicole attends sales meetings and can handle hearing about the negative reality of the marketplace from the sales force.
- "Nicole is no diva. When she hears bad news, she doesn't scream or throw things. Nothing. She puts her nose to the grindstone and starts revamping what isn't working.
- "We've had the same vision for growth. We chose not to be a giant, but to remain a midsized company. That way, we can remain a design house."

Stellar Sellers: Getting Past No

Selling is a serious art. At its essence, you have to get past the barriers the person you are selling to has built up in his or her mind about your product or brand. You have to find a way to understand what that person's personal prejudice is and then find a way to move past it.

"I find that the key to selling is that a real salesperson hears the word *no*

WHO DOES WHAT (MOST OF THE TIME)

FASHION SUCCESS STORY: BREAKDOWN OF RESPONSIBILITIES	SELLER/CHIEF EXECUTIVE OFFICER (CEO): LEFT-BRAIN THINKER	DESIGNER/CHIEF CREATIVE OFFICER (CCO): RIGHT-BRAIN THINKER
Runway Show	Creating budget, schedule, PR (ensuring key retailers and editors attend event), deciding venue	Finding inspiration; making samples; fitting clothes; working with the stylist on the look of the show; overseeing model selection, hair, and makeup
Retail Store	Does the square footage analysis to make sure sales can support location and design spending; hires and trains staff	Conceptualizes how to translate clothes into a breakthrough and original shopping destination; IDs the next cool neighborhood
HR	Talent nurturer and keeper	Talent magnet
HQ	Keeps back office running like clockwork	Fills showroom with excitement, cool people, cool music, unexpected inspirations.
Global	Plots out an aggressive but doable global expansion plan; creates appropriate structures to sell in Europe and Asia	Travels, visiting to get the vibe and energy of new markets; finds like-minded, eccentric creative people to connect with in individual markets
Image	Hands-on with nontraditional media plan and buy: viral, interruptive, guerilla messaging	Art directs the ad shoot with BFF female star and mega fashion photographer; the shoot itself the subject of gossip and news

as a challenge whereas normal people hear the word *no* as rejection," says Bud Konheim of Nicole Miller. "To a salesperson, *no* is not an answer; it's the beginning of the conversation.

"Great salespeople are very difficult to find, but they do share one distinguishing characteristic: their ability to face that struggle, to figure out what are the other person's prejudices causing him or her to be negative and then to get past *no*.

"Most of the salespeople I know have had a personal history of challenges. These are people who grew up with no real privileges. They had to fight for everything. Nothing came easily to them. They had to hear *no* from their parents again and again and again, and they were smart enough to find ways to turn it into *yes*. That's salesmanship."

Profiles in Courage: Two Seventh Avenue Sales Stars (and How They Win)

Star Number 1*

A second-generation garment center guy who lives in the suburbs. He's an average guy with no huge intellectual curiosity. What makes him a great salesperson? He is highly competitive.

To use a sports analogy, his bosses liken him to a great fullback: "When you give him the football and tell him to run it to the end zone, does he complain that the field is too crowded? No. He just does it. Winning is what it's all about."

Star Number 2*

A Midwestern Asian-American woman who came up through the retail shops, first near Chicago. Then, after spending one week in the New York City store, she is named the manager.

"She is aggressive," explains her boss. "She is a killer. She doesn't hear the word *no*. She has no idea what it means. Plus she is really good at feeding the retail information back to the designer. Also, she's good at wearing the clothes, embodying the label to the industry."

*Names have been withheld to protect their employers from losing them to the competition.

Did Your Parents Say *No* a Lot?
You Might Have a Future in Sales!

Q: How do we know if it'll sell?
A: We *don't* know.

"We put a small number of each dress out there and watch to see how it does," explains Bud Konheim. "It's a test. We see how it does. What you can't do (and this is my fifty-fourth year in the business) is push fashion, and you can't push style. What you have to do is allow it to develop.

"When you try to sell more, increase volume, make guarantees and deals with the retailers, you lower the price, [the result is that] you end up diminishing your product and your brand, saturating the market. None of those things work."

ANSWER THESE QUESTIONS

Would *you* make a great fashion salesperson? (Clue: More *yesses* mean *yes*.)

- Do you like meeting new people daily?
- Is it easy for you to speak with strangers?
- Are you naturally competitive?
- When you hear the word *no*, do you consider it a personal challenge to find a way to convert the answer to *yes*?
- In your work life, have you often and naturally gravitated to sales roles (lemonade stand, Gap store, Starbucks)?
- Do you possess an impeccable work ethic? That is, if the job is officially from 9 a.m. to 6 p.m., you automatically make sure you are there from 8:30 a.m. until 7 p.m. most days. In sales, you are expected to be available during business hours whereas creative types keep their own, usually later and more erratic, hours.
- When confronted, are you able to fire back a logical, nonaggressive verbal response?
- Do you feel a natural affinity for certain brands and products? Are you able to express and embody that passion?
- You've never been asked to play Sleepy or Dopey in a casting of *Snow White and the Seven Dwarfs*?

How a Salesperson Makes His or Her Mark

It's hard to hire a designer, but a designer has to have talent and taste, and there are benchmarks to measure those things (what fabrics he or she chooses, what he or she wears, his or her sketches and references). When you get to sales, every salesperson will tell you about all the accounts that he or she sells to and rattle them off—"Saks, Neiman's, Nordstrom"—but the truth is that it's his or her current company who sells to those stores, not that person himself or herself. When they're having a great year, selling a lot of clothes, most salespeople come in and ask for a raise, says Konheim. "When they're having a bad year, they say 'Who can sell this shit?'"

In the end, a salesperson's success is defined by his or her relationships with retailers. Building trust with buyers takes time, patience, and, normally, thick skin. But if you start with one assistant buyer at a time, you'll find that as you climb up the ladder in sales, your contacts will be rising similarly in the retail ranks. The first phone calls a potential new boss will make when checking you out? Your biggest *and smallest* retail accounts.

COOL, UNCOOL, TOO COOL?

There's an old girls' network—a sorority really—that's all about cool. Are you in the club, or are you out of the club? Are you cool? Or, TOO cool? The irony is that what's cool and what's successful are often inversely proportionate. What's cool is small and clicquey. As soon as it's recognized, it's on to the next, undiscovered thing.

How to Find Your Place in Fashion

FIVE LESSONS FROM BUD

1. *Forget camp.* "The most important thing is to spend your summers working at something from the time you are four years old. Forget about going to sleep-away camp. Take your summers and work at something. Little by little, you'll rule out what you shouldn't be doing."

2. *Try out different jobs.* "At fifteen, I was the equipment manager at day camp. Not my calling. Next I got a job as a soda jerk. The first customer came up and asked for a coffee, and I responded, 'Don't you know how to say please?'

   "Then, after I was suspended from school for being too social during my sophomore year at Dartmouth, I went to work on Wall Street because my parents told me that from then on out I'd be paying for my own education. After six months at Neuberger Lowe, I said, 'This is stupid. I'm watching the ticker tape of what other guys are out there doing. And I'm not adding anything.' If it had been just about making money, I'd have stayed there, but that wasn't it. I wanted to be one of those guys out there making the ticker tick."

3. *Find something that intrigues you.* "During the last two weeks of that summer, I asked my father to let me work in his clothing factory as a gofer. They had a hot-selling item, and I got interested intellectually about the idea of what makes a hot-selling item. I wanted to understand how it was, with all the stuff out there in the stores, that on the same day in Sandusky, Ohio, one dress style sells out. The thing was really an intriguing puzzle to me. And watching the ticker of the stock market seemed like a stupid thing to do. Fashion is really an artistic thing you can get off on. And you get an instant vote—if people like it, they will buy it."

4. *Feel passion. See the big picture.* "Seventh Avenue has no rules. There is no résumé required for being here. No entry level; no credentials necessary. It's just an amazing business."

5. *Toughen up.* "There is no such thing as an established player on Seventh Avenue. You are vulnerable every day. Reputation matters a little, but not that much. There's a saying: 'You're only as good as your last dress.' You can have the most rip roaring season with lines out the door and stuff selling. And the next season? It's a ghost land. Success on Seventh Avenue is measured in how well you can bounce back."

LAURA M. GOTTLIEB | Vice President of International Sales, Vince

"Budding Fashionista" wasn't among Laura Gottlieb's numerous high school honors. Academic achiever, yes; all-star athlete, check; superlikely to succeed, yup. Growing up in Westchester County, New York, Laura considered herself a total tomboy, always into sports as an essential element to the fast track to success. At Emory University, the driven young woman focused on the most competitive fields she could find, first as a premed student, then switching to finance. Wall Street sounded like her kind of fun. It was soon after her first big breaks in finance that something weird began to happen: Her closet began to suffer from acute schizophrenia. Front and center were Laura's neat button-down shirts and fitted suits, perfect as a Brooks Brothers catalog, but off to the side was a growing collection of edgy, alternative pieces from decidedly nonmainstream designers like Martin Margiela. The happy ending to Laura's confused clothing story is that she listened to her closet, and to her heart, and found her future in fashion. *Executive Fashionista* is what they'd call her now.

BACKGROUND
Laura grew up in Chappaqua, north of New York City, and attended the competitive Horace Greeley High School there, where she played varsity tennis and lacrosse. The oldest of three siblings with supportive parents, Laura was diligent in academics and involved in community service while enjoying a healthy social life. "Although it was a fairly homogenous community, I was able to break out of the mold."

EXPOSURES
"My mother grew up in Manhattan, and to broaden our suburban horizons, brought us into the city to see shows, museums, try new foods, and expose us to other lifestyles. In high school, a train ride into the city with friends to explore Greenwich/East Village, visiting haunts like Antique Boutique, Pat Fields, Unique, and Andis Cheepies, was the ultimate experience."

BUDDING FASHIONISTA?
"Not at all. I was a total tomboy, always into sports."

CHILDHOOD DREAM
"I always thought I should be involved with psychiatry and/or psychology."

PSYCHIATRY TO SALES?
"What I do is so relationship oriented. There is a psychology behind sales. So I am intrigued by that human element that I was attracted to even in my youth. There's still me in there."

WHY EMORY?

"What I loved about Emory was that it was culturally diverse with people from all types of backgrounds from all over the world. It was also *near* a city [Atlanta] without being *in* a city, and it has a beautiful and warm setting."

SHIFTING EXPECTATIONS

"I first attempted the premed track, but I realized at the beginning of my sophomore year that it wasn't for me. I found myself signing up for finance classes."

CRACKING THE BANKS

"I decided to be a finance major because investment banking was hot at the time and competitive to get into. I knew I could handle the intensity."

EARLY FASHION FEELERS

While at Emory, Laura explored the possibility of working in the finance departments at fashion brands like Tommy Hilfiger, Donna Karan, and Ralph Lauren. "But there's no finance career track inside these companies. They told me, 'Once you have finance experience, get back to us.'"

FIRST JOB: ERNST & YOUNG

"I did cross-training in different industries like retail, energy, and manufacturing within the investment banking group, and I worked with a partner who specialized in financing deals in the health care sector."

NEXT STOP: MERRILL LYNCH

When that partner left for Merrill Lynch, she asked Laura to join her team there. "It was flattering to have the opportunity to be mentored by a woman on Wall Street. I'd also accomplished my goal of attaining a job in investment banking with a bulge-bracket [largest and most prestigious U.S. banks] firm."

LAURA'S STOCK-IN-TRADE

Never overpromise. *Always* overdeliver.

FRUSTRATED FASHIONISTA?

"There was something about banking that was not doing it for me. It was suits, five days a week. Meanwhile, I was dressing funky on the weekend. People assumed this was a backlash to my job, but I began to understand that fashion was a creative outlet that I needed *in* my job. Yet I didn't know how to accomplish that."

IN SEARCH OF A FASHION FIT

"I had interviews at places like Gucci where I'd have had to start at the bottom, in the sample closet. They knew that without the challenge of more analytical work, I wouldn't stay long. At other companies I'd hear: 'You're bright. You're stylish. Get some showroom experience and get back to us.'"

FIRST FASHION JOB

"[Being an assistant fashion buyer at The Limited] was grunt work—crunching numbers and doing financial analyses. But I'm great at this. To this day, people come to me with Excel questions. All my analytical skills have served me well. I'm grateful for my banking training."

UPPING THE GLAMOUR ANTE

"Since I wanted something more up market, after a year, I found a job in sales for Lejaby [Warnaco's French lingerie brand]. I loved the product."

WHY NOT RETAIL?

"I never wanted to work at a department store. I left finance because I wanted to be in an inspired environment. I wanted to be surrounded in the workplace by the lifestyle a single brand exudes."

STILL NOT A FIT

The Warnaco environment proved too corporate for Laura. "It was time to move on into a more fashion forward company." On the plus side, "Lejaby got me some luxury experience and relevant sales experience since I opened the brand at Bergdorf Goodman and Marshall Field."

WELCOME TO ELIE'S WORLD

"A girlfriend at Elie Tahari told me there was an opening on the retail side. I interviewed and got the position." Laura would spend the next four years at Elie Tahari, being cross-trained from retail to wholesale, domestic to international, working with consultants from around the world, and building a valuable network of relationships.

DECISION TIME: BUYER OR SELLER?

"I started at Elie on the buying side, helping to open the SoHo, Las Vegas, and Chicago stores. Then, the sales director asked me to join the wholesale side." This shift would totally change Laura's path.

EIGHT RULES FOR SALES

1. Make the right impression when you walk in the door. Exude confidence and positive energy.
2. Don't resign from a company just before or during a sales campaign. "It's bad ethics. You cannot be seen to compromise your brand like this."
3. Keep a good working relationship with everyone you've worked with. It's a relationship business, and it's a small world.
4. Mix up how you wear the brand at work so you don't look as though you just stepped out of the look book.
5. Be discreet. Never discuss internal trade details, plans, or events with external resources.
6. Be correct. Double-check your work and e-mails. Spelling someone's name wrong in a casual e-mail is not OK.
7. Work is work. Never forget that it is a business and that social elements are secondary.
8. Never be unprepared or late for a meeting whether it's your boss, staff, or customer.

WHAT'S THE BEST WAY TO GET INTO FASHION (WHOLESALE) SALES?
Relentless follow-up.

AND THE WINNER IS . . . SALES!

Laura made the move, initially focusing on building the domestic specialty store business. Then, when Elie signed its first distribution agreement in Japan, Laura was asked to be the liaison there. The opportunity to visit Tokyo and Osaka thrilled Laura.

JAPAN, DONE; UNITED KINGDOM, NEXT?

"One day, the head of sales threw the business cards of the Selfridges and Harvey Nic buyers on my desk and said, 'See what you can do.' I brought in the buying agent from Harvey Nichols who loved the brand but had just accepted a position at Selfridges. We ended up doing a 'dual exclusive launch' with Harvey Nichols and Selfridges—a double coup."

OUTSIDE SUPPORT

The company hired a consultant to assist in negotiating the more complex international deals. "I worked closely with one consultant for two years. He taught me about international markets. We grew the international business together, and he is still a mentor and a friend."

FREQUENT FLYER

Laura went to Milan every season as well as making visits to Moscow, St. Petersburg, the United Arab Emirates, Qatar, Dubai, Paris, London, Germany, Tokyo, and Hong Kong. "No one had even *been* to certain stores in certain markets. I developed working relationships in all these places that continue to this day."

FREEDOM/STRUCTURE BALANCE

"I realized at Elie that I love being an entrepreneur within a financially backed structure. I love doing the foraging and feeling ownership over my own business within a business."

DIRECTOR OF INTERNATIONAL SALES, ELIE TAHARI

"I got incredible cross-training—retail and wholesale, domestic and international. During my last five months, I was asked to oversee the Saks Fifth Avenue account, which was the largest piece of the domestic volume. I was overseeing international, the most significant area of growth, and Saks, the most significant account domestically. My career had blossomed."

THE ALLURE OF LUXURY

One of the consultants Laura had worked with had signed on to be part of the relaunch of Halston. "He waved the carrot in front of me, saying 'It's *Luxury*! It's *Fabulous*! Come be a part of this!' I'd always thought the Halston brand had an amazing heritage. To be a part of fashion history was alluring to me. I was offered the position of director of sales, overseeing the global wholesale part of the business. I jumped at it."

SAYING GOOD-BYE TO ELIE

"They were like a family to me. It was a business that I had cultivated. I was broken up when I walked out of there. I have a place in my heart for Elie Tahari, the man and the company. It was an amazing experience."

ELIE TAHARI ACCOMPLISHMENT

Laura opened at least twenty-five countries and some eighty points of distribution.

HALSTON DIRECTOR OF GLOBAL SALES

Laura started at Halston just after she closed Elie's fall sales campaign in Milan, which was the best time, in her view, to make a break. "I literally accepted the opportunity right after I got off the plane from Milan."

CAREER CHANGER

STARTED AS: INVESTMENT BANKING ANALYST
SWITCHED TO: ASSISTANT FASHION BUYER

After three years on Wall Street, Laura Gottlieb decided to go with her heart and find a job in fashion. That meant taking a pay cut from her Merrill Lynch salary, but Laura was determined not to make less than her first year in finance so that she could remain independent from her parents. Luxury brands weren't a fit because her finance experience wasn't senior enough. When she interviewed at The Limited, "I made the argument with them that it would be easier to teach the fashion cycle to an analytical person than to teach the financials to an FIT grad. It must have worked because I got the job."

She's never looked back: "I always knew that being happy in my career was bigger than just working for a paycheck. I was always encouraged to do what I loved. That if you follow your passion, the money would follow."

LAURA'S NICHE
International expansion of domestic brands.

HALSTON HOP
Even though her stay at Halston lasted only one year, Laura is thankful for the experience of helping to set up the infrastructure of a new organization.

WHEN THE ECONOMY TURNED SOUR
With U.S. stores buying less, everyone began looking to expand international distribution: Laura's "niche" was now the hot category.

HOW VINCE LURED LAURA
"First, it was very flattering to be sought out [Vince hired a headhunter to find Laura and had previously tried to hire Laura when she worked for Elie, but Elie personally asked Vince to back off]. I also felt an immediate connection with the CEO. There were other people there who'd worked at Elie. The CEO knew exactly what kind of training I'd had. I had already earned my badges. Working at Elie as long as I did said something to him about my work ethic."

IT'S A MATCH

"When I went back to Vince, on my request, for a second interview, the CEO told me that he knew I was 'the one' because of the confident way I walked into the room and took off my jacket. He said that my ease made him comfortable as well. And he liked my energy."

LAURA'S LOOK

On that interview: a Margiela sweater, belt, and leggings.

In general: "You have to be fashion. You can't show up in a suit. Do I wear Vince? Yes. I am proud to represent the brand, but I wear it in my way. I mix it up. Some people want a brand to look like it does in the look book. I love vintage. I have a lot of eclectic pieces. I'm a downtown girl. I want people to see that Vince can be funky or classic. That you can insert your own personality into it."

VINCE SNAPSHOT

Vince is a hip, accessible brand. Well established in the United States, it is sold at four hundred outlets, including major department stores and specialty stores. In department store speak, Vince is considered contemporary because it is youthful, casual, and less expensive than designer labels.

LAURA'S VINCE CHALLENGES

- Creating a structure for its European business
- Blowing out international distribution
- Overseeing international PR

THE AMERICAN PACE

"I like working for an American brand and taking it international. Especially if you are a New Yorker, you are used to working fast and hard."

DOES LAURA HAVE A LIFE?

"At times, it's been compromised. As soon as I start dating someone, I end up disappearing to Milan for three weeks. It's a challenge to have a home life when I am never at home."

HAVING IT ALL?

"Yes, I can. I'm young, and life has much to offer. I'm ready for the next challenge or opportunity, personal or business. I'll embrace it because I don't like to do anything halfway."

Brand Life: PR, Advertising, Retail, and Retail Management

"If you are young and beautiful, go into PR," advises my friend Roberto Pesaro, who held, among other posts, the chief operating officer job at Giorgio Armani North America for many years. By "PR" Pesaro means "public relations," but this could be variously called "communications" or "imaging." It is absolutely *the most exciting* side of the fashion business and among the most important. If you have the PR gift, you might just want to develop it. Here are some eye-opening reasons why:

- A top PR person helps set the agenda, as well as the voice and the niche, of a designer.
- A top PR person *is* the inner circle and gets as much face time with a designer as the CEO.
- A top PR person can make as much money (in a top multinational brand, we're talking $1 million or more) as the CEO.
- A top PR person has independent relationships with top fashonistas, editors in chief, newspaper journalists, publishers, and stylists, as well as some of the top celebrities who come to events and runway shows, and who wear the clothes.
- A top PR person helps orchestrate the relationships between the designer and the personalities who wear the label.
- A top PR person is the gatekeeper to all external relationships and associations with the brand.
- A top PR person attends important red carpet events with the designer and is wined and dined (or does the wining and dining) at the coolest restaurants and clubs.

Sounds lovely, but, trust me, there's nothing easy about PR. As with many fashionista roles we've discussed, you're on constant call and, at least in the first decade or so of your career, it's tough to have a private life.

Do you have thick skin? Are you able to separate your professional role from your personal self-worth? Do you look relaxed and confident, even when you are being grilled? Are you a natural "spin doctor," working out on the spot how seemingly bad news can, in fact, be flipped into a major opportunity? You are the first person the designer calls when he's screaming, mad, and putridly upset. You are also the first person the CEO calls when she's spitting angry upset. *Everything* regarding the press coverage and the image of your brand—and others—is your fault. As the expert in this arena, you are called upon to explain why *other* brands get attention, why celebrities would wear *other* designers' clothes, why *your brand* doesn't get more, more, more attention all, all, all of the time.

In short, designers get crazy jealous of stories done on other designers. They never get enough attention, and they are never happy about it. Think of the worst behaved child you've ever witnessed screaming for ice cream. Bingo!

How to Get into PR: Education

In a perfect world, your education would be a BA degree from a liberal arts college. To get into PR, you have to be literate, and you have to be able to write and communicate and speak and think in concise bullets and sound bites. But that's not the only priority. You need to be culturally in tune. You need to understand the world. You need to understand and be able to interpret references to artists, personalities, and works as vastly divergent as Mondrian, Warhol, Whitman, Cher, Chanel, Dalí, Eames, Kate Moss, Catherine the Great, Kate Hepburn, Guy Bourdin, Van der Rohe, Mme. Grès, Blondie, Anna Karenina, and Vargas without rushing off to do a Google search.

Here's my point of view: Majoring in communications or PR is a huge waste of time and money. Instead, why not study something you have a passion for or are curious about: like film, French, art history, Italian, or ancient or European history? If you study English lit, as I did, you spend your time reading novels and poetry and walking around campus with stacks of beautiful books starting with Shakespeare on the bottom, Romantic poetry, Faulkner, Walker Percy. It's one of the best things America has to offer the world: a good liberal arts education.

What you gain in terms of historic context and disciplining your mind will far outweigh any practical skills you would acquire in the communications department. Trust me, you'll learn everything you need to learn through one or two core PR classes, during internships or your first six months on the job, and probably most of it isn't on the curriculum at most schools.

The PR Personality: Do You Have It?
More yesses = more PR success

Do people remember you after meeting you only once?

Are you great at remembering people's names and faces?

Do you have a high glamour quotient?

Do you have a high stamina for work?

Are you socially confident?

Are you comfortable *not* being Number 1, but working for him or her?

Do you thrive in an unpredictable work environment where there is no such thing as a *normal* workday?

Does your mind remain calm, unfazed, and organized, even when under pressure and amid chaos?

Can you keep your head and stay verbal under pressure?

Do you love the buzz of multitasking under tight deadlines?

Do you put people at ease and make every situation feel like a party?

Do you create good spin? Can you transform potentially negative questions and situations into favorable outcomes?

Do you look for inspiration in unconventional places?

Do you innately understand the business back story (that is, "where the bread gets buttered")?

First-Job Options (Even If a Second Career)

Start in fashion editorial and make the jump whenever you want.

Start in advertising and make the jump whenever it makes sense.

Start in retail and make the jump whenever.

Start working for an accessories company and make the jump later.

Start at Sotheby's or Christie's in events or PR and make the jump to fashion after a year or two.

Join a small fashion public relations agency.

Intern part time or start as an assistant in the PR department inside at a fashion brand.

The Best Way to Jump-Start Your PR Career

Team up with a young designer-friend so that you can found and build the brand together.

GOOD PRESS: TOP FASHION PR FIRMS

- *BPCM (previously Bismarck Phillips).* Bismarck Phillips Communications and Media is the most uptown minded of this group of agencies. Fashion clients of the ten-year-old company include Catherine Malandrino, Alberta Ferretti, and Céline.
  Offices in New York, LA, London, and Paris
  www.bpcm.com

- *Bureau Betak.* Headed by Alexandre de Betak. Clients include Donna Karan and TSE Cashmere.
  199 Lafayette Street, New York City
  (212) 274-0669

- *KCD Inc.* Originally named for its illustrious founders (*Vogue* editor and fashion visionary Kezia Keeble, stylist and humanist Paul Cavaco, and *New York Times* writer and intellect John Duka), this agency was the first to combine into one shop styling, advertising, and public relations. Now run by protégés of the founders, Ed Filipowski (PR side) and Julie Mannion (production), it retains its integrity, high standards, and ability to edit brilliantly for the editors. Its original client, Versace, is still with the firm, as well as a rich mix of some of the world's most influential and exciting designers, like Marc Jacobs, Zac Posen, and Anna Sui, and Europeans Yves Saint Laurent and Chloé, among others.
  www.kcdworldwide.com (access only with a pass code)
  450 West Fifteenth Street, No. 604, New York City
  (212) 590-5100

- *Karla Otto, Inc.* Clients include Pucci, Marni, Lucien Pellat Finet, Hussein Chalayan Rochas Victor, and Rolf. Offices in New York, Milan, and London.
  Via dell'Annunciata 2, 20122 Milan
  Telephone 39-02-6556981; fax: 89010179
  E-mail mail@KarlaOtto.com
  545 West Twenty-fifth Street, New York City
  Telephone (212) 255-8588

- *Kevin Krier & Associates.* Long-term production and PR agency with clients like Halston, Hugo Boss, and Ellen Tracy.
  84 Wooster, Manhattan
  Telephone (212) 431-0550

- *PR Consulting.* Company founded and run by the intense Pierre Rougier. Clients include Narciso Rodriguez, Balenciaga, Proenza Schouler, Pierre Hardy, Dries Van Noten, and L'Wren Scott. Offices on Bond Street, in Manhattan, and in Paris.
  www.prconsulting.net

- *Staff USA Inc.* Representing (often in both sales and PR) supercool clients like Dsquared, Martin Margiella, and Sophia Kokosalaki.
  220 West Nineteenth Street, New York City
  Telephone (646) 613-8457

Can You Handle It?

PR gets blamed for everything, including when:

The coffee is cold.
The ceiling falls down on editors' heads at your fashion show.
The strawberries aren't fresh.
The flowers had too many colors.
We should've done *Charlie Rose*.
Madonna didn't show up.
Because Madonna didn't show up, Gwyneth didn't show up either.
You don't win a CFDA award.
Kate Winslet doesn't wear our dress at the Oscars.
Vogue did only one spread on your fall collection.
Vogue spent only twenty minutes previewing the collection.
Anna doesn't show.
Style.com didn't review the show.

Art and Commerce

In life, we understand the natural divide that separates generations—those who understand the new digital world, for example, versus those who don't. In school and in life, we learn about the natural tensions that exist between big institutions, like church and state.

In fashion, there is a fundamental tension between the *art* of fashion—which celebrates creativity, experimentation with new materials, breaking new ground on every front, and even redefining the most basic notions of clothing's form and

TOP FASHION HEADHUNTERS

- Floriane de Saint-Pierre (Paris, Milan), www.fspsa.com
- Karen Harvey (NYC, London), www.karenharveyconsulting.com
- Heads!, executive consultancy (Munich, Frankfort, Zurich), www.headsgroup.com
- Maxine Martens (NYC), www.maxinemartens.com
- Herbert Mines (NYC), www.herbertmines.com

function—and *commerce*—the business of making money, selling clothes, and paying your vendors and employees. Whatever your role at a fashion brand, make it your goal to better understand the *other* side. If you are in finance or accounting or sales, say, try to embrace the alien design side of things, where creating newness endlessly is the mission. If you are on the creative side, open your mind to the dog-eat-dog world of selling to stores. Make a friend in finance. Ask what he or she is doing all day. Bring him or her a cappuccino one morning. It is these kinds of surprising relationships that make life a lot more fun. And, in the end, it is the people who get both the art and commerce of fashion who become its leaders.

Q&A with Former Armani COO Roberto Pesaro

Q. On the business side, what are the qualities that separate top business talent in fashion from top talent in other industries? A. "In fashion, there is a unique equilibrium: You must be able to recognize and respect the fact that, in the balance of creativity and business, *creativity always trumps*. The brand and the creativity applied to the brand by the one person whose name is synonymous with the brand is the brand's essence and, ultimately, its only real asset.

"Even at the risk of losing financial gains, you must be able to accept that the brand and the energy fueling the brand must always be considered the key or dominant side of the equation. Any trade-off, where financial and commercial decisions take precedence over the protection of the integrity of the brand, and you weaken the brand."

In other words, fashion companies are really bad at verbalizing things like mission statements, or the DNA of brands and delineating instances where design should overrule business and vice versa. Things are just understood. Or, intuited. Or not. Trickier yet, these non-articulated basics change with the times. That's

CAREER GPS

If you want to be in design, don't start in sales, human resources, public relations, production, or accounting. Those would be dead ends for a designer.

However, if you want to be in *sales*, it could be very useful to start in another department—design or production—to get the big picture of the brand. Even if PR is not your ultimate goal, it could be a great career.

YO, BOSS: DON'T KILL THE GOLDEN GOOSE!

Remember the story of the goose that laid the golden egg? Fashion is a golden egg situation. Just note what often happens when investment companies buy fashion houses, which has been the case at some of the world's most brilliant fashion brands (like Valentino, Calvin Klein, Helmut Lang, and Jil Sander). The founding designer exits the company, and a new creative team is put in place, which, by definition, is not as visionary, driven, or powerful. Ironically, the "luxe" and fashion magic that the investment team was so hungry to lap up and parade about is neither appreciated nor understood by them. The new management put in place often does not "get" fashion and tries to "streamline" the process. Brands exposed to linear-thinking, nonbrand believers can live on for decades, but their mojo, cool, value, and mystique are continually, steadily evaporating.

why the existence of a *living, breathing designer* usually makes for the most dynamic and exciting as well as frustrating and inefficient of fashion entities.

"If business people start making commercial decisions that do not protect the integrity of the brand, you will eventually destroy the brand," continues Pesaro. "With coffee and toothpaste, you do not protect the brand to this degree. In the fashion industry, you have to protect this intangible. In everyday decisions—even at the cost of losing commercial opportunities—you must protect that brand.

"This is also what gives fashion the incredible advantage over nonbranded products. Why can some companies charge hundreds of dollars for a pair of socks or a T-shirt and another company charge only a few dollars for their socks or T-shirt? Fashion companies have this unfair advantage. The brand and the brand personality are really the essential thing distinguishing the brand.

"When Armani purchased up all the shoe companies around Venice, the people who worked at these companies had excellent shoe experience but not brand experience. For them it was a culture shock. They understood product, but not image."

Q. Based on your experience in fashion, do you think people are either born with the "fashion gene" or not? A. "People on the business side of fashion are not necessarily born with a fashion gene. It is just an intellectual understanding of the industry. If you are in any responsible role in the company, you need to understand the economics of fashion. And to be able to adopt your thinking to the fashion industry's brand-centric view of the world."

Q. Is it an asset in fashion to hold a MBA degree? Are more MBAs entering the ranks of fashion management? A. "Being an MBA isn't adding a great advantage. Or, rather, perhaps it's an advantage, but it is not recognized as an advantage. As soon as possible, you must build a CV that shows that you have been with—even for a summer—Chanel, say, or any other large, immediately recognized, global luxury brand."

Unlike other businesses, in fashion you don't get an MBA, go work at McKinsey & Company, then get offered a big job at Prada, D&G, or Hermès. That doesn't happen. The tools you get from an MBA would be useful in the fashion industry if the fashion industry were more developed than it is, insists Pesaro. "The nature

RUNNING THE STORE: RETAIL ECONOMICS FOR BIG BRANDS

You've decided that your entrée into fashion is retail sales. You're ambitious so you'll use your job at Victoria's Secret to upgrade to Banana Republic, then Max Mara, and, eventually, to Louis Vuitton, Armani, Dolce & Gabbana, or Chanel. Then you'll use your cunning and good energy to begin climbing the ladder within that luxury brand in *retail management*, one of the fastest-growing and most important areas of the fashion business. Understanding a bit about this business, particularly how companies view their stores, will separate you from the pack. Robert Pesaro, former Armani executive, explains:

> Stores for brands are a tough business, especially given that the people selecting the location and the size of the stores don't typically understand the economics of those decisions. If the brand is wrong about the size of a store, either too big or too small, or are wrong about the city or the neighborhood, its location, if they negotiate a lease that is disproportionately expensive for the sales you will earn in that location—if they make a wrong decision on any of these factors, it will be very, very hard to make money.
>
> So often, the prestige of a location—say, Madison Avenue in New York City, Monte Napoléano in Milan, Sloane Street in London—unfairly overshadows other considerations. Of course, competition is tough, and communications in a world where so many brands are fighting for space in many various media, retail must be done right. And done right the first time.
>
> If a small company opens one store on Madison Avenue and one store on Faubourg Saint Honoré in Paris, it'll be killed. Only a big brand with hundreds of stores and a serious infrastructure can compete in these locations. It is easy for a company to become disenchanted with stand-alone retail stores but, in the long term, to be successful, it is a brand's backbone.

of this industry is that it has been more of a crafts enterprise. The fashion industry is somehow behind in many basic areas—in logistics, budgeting, financial controls, in human resources—in all normal areas of modern business."

Q. Why does it seem from the outside that fashion functions a bit like a high school clique? A. "Fashion is a very incestuous industry. Companies try to steal people from competitors. People constantly change their jobs within the industry.

"You have to be part of it to move up in it. There is very little outside influence in fashion. It is inward looking, and it is, in fact, a very small world. Management tries to hire people who already have experience in the industry from companies that are respected and possibly in competition with their own brand. There is huge value associated with already-existing connections. Because of that, the headhunters are working almost exclusively within a closely defined parameter."

Q. How did you get your Armani post? A. "The CEO with whom I had a previous working relationship hired me at Armani. There are a lot of these situations."

Q. What's the most promising fashion career path that a person could follow? A. "Retail management, which is becoming the most important channel in fashion. And only people who have come up the ranks, who understand the discipline, and have run their own stores can eventually succeed. This is an

FASHION ADVERTISING

Major brands often create their own advertising internally to protect their image. The following agencies have thrived partially because they function almost like internal agencies for their key fashion houses:

- *AR New York:* Started by ex-*Vogue* creatives Alex Gonzalez and Raul Martinez, this cool agency counts among its clients Banana Republic, Jimmy Choo, Elie Tahari, and Jones New York (www.arnewyork.com).
- *Baron & Baron:* Founded and creatively managed by the prodigiously talented Fabien Baron, Baron & Baron is longtime home to fashion accounts like Calvin Klein, Hugo Boss, and Burberry, as well as Balenciaga, Michael Kors, and Miu Miu (www.baron-baron.com).
- *Laird+Partners:* Trey Laird, formerly in-house creative head for Gap, now oversees that brand's advertising as well as the advertising for Donna Karan, DKNY, Juicy Couture, and Nautica (www.lairdandpartners.com).
- *Lloyd and Company:* Doug Lloyd worked with Tom Ford in the highly successful mid-1990s Gucci renaissance, and retains that brand as a key client. Others include Jil Sander, Yves Saint Laurent, Estée Lauder, and Max Mara (www.lloydandco.com).

exciting career. For a brand to be good at its own standalone stores is the equivalent of holding one's destiny in one's own hands: You decide what product to sell at what price and to what extent you should sell to outsiders, like department stores."

Q. Why are department stores a "necessary evil" for fashion brands?
A. "Selling clothes and accessories to Saks Fifth Avenue gives young companies the advantages of bigger exposure and distribution. At an established company, however, the opposite might be true since, in a wholesale or franchise setting, you lose control of the situation: People who do not work for the brand are making decisions about how the brand will be presented, whether it is easily found, how customers will be treated, and when is the appropriate time to put the collection on sale, as well as which other brands you will live alongside on the selling floor. You give up creative control. This situation can tip the balance in favor of commercial over the protection of the brand."

Q. Which companies do the best job of balancing the corporate side of the business (structure, finance, revenue flow, profits, guarding of brand image, retail strategy, licensing, and personnel) with the creative side (designing an innovative, newsworthy product, maintaining the quality of the product, injecting excitement into the advertising image, establishing an intriguing consumer dialog, and creating a unique retail vibe)? A. "Armani is not bad—even if a dictatorship. At end of the day at Armani, the business decisions privilege the creative side, as it should. The excitement, of course, is all there.

"Dolce & Gabbana, Prada, and Gucci, and most of the successful fashion companies have been successful because they also favor the image side of the brand. It's one of the things that most successful companies do get.

"Beyond the actual collections, there's the *panamontata*, the image and public

RING THE BELL, RALPH

You can almost count on one hand the number of publicly-traded fashion companies. Prada has long hinted it may do an IPO (initial public offering) and be traded on the stock market. At a public company such as Gucci, Polo Ralph Lauren, or Liz Claiborne (part of the Jones Apparel Group), you will be driven to live more in the short term, with an eye toward quarterly results. The pressure is palpably more relaxed in a private company, where the team is focused more on midterm results.

> In a licensed business: at least 20 percent of budget.
> In your own brand: at least 8 to 10 percent.

voice of a brand—the fashion shows, the actors' wearing the clothes, the exclusive events, the ability to get people to be excited about a brand—that all strong fashion brands understand."

Q. Is there a difference in the profile, experience, and education of retail talent versus brand talent? Is switching from side to side accepted and seamless? A. "*Retail people* hardly ever acquire the complete brand talent or vision. Even if eventually they reach the corporate level. Their mentality is that they are hired guns and they live by commission.

"*Brand people* are capable of existing in this all-important image and communication arena. Where you don't need to be an MBA but where you need to understand the DNA of the brand."

Getting the Big-Business Picture at a Fashion House

There has long been a struggle between the shoe and bag brands that want to be taken seriously for clothing, and, the reverse, clothing houses who want to create signature bags and shoes. Very few are successful in both because there is a DNA for bags and a separate DNA for clothing. The "perfect" balance, in terms of revenues, would be:

Shoes and handbags: 40 percent
Apparel: 60 percent

The companies that started out in bags or shoes, like Gucci, Ferragamo, Coach, and Prada, have made enormous efforts with only limited success to make it in the world of apparel. Conversely, companies known for their apparel, like Polo Ralph Lauren, Calvin Klein, Armani, Donna Karan, struggle to be known for shoes and bags, where profit margins are higher. Either way, making it on the "other side" isn't easy.

BILLY DALEY | Worldwide Director of Public Relations, Events, and Advertising, Bottega Veneta

"You're interviewing *Billy*?" one fashion editor gushed to me. "He's my *best* friend. We practically *live* together." That I heard this line spoken numerous times over the process of writing this book tells me that the fast-talking, fast-thinking, Hollywood-handsome Billy Daley really *is* the most superb public relations guy everyone says he is. Palling around with fashion editors, knowing what looks they want practically before they actually even describe them, is just one aspect of his hard-to-define, on-the-firing-line job. On a daily basis, he keeps his Italian Gucci Group—owned brand informed of happenings in the fashion, retail, and celebrity worlds. Billy runs the label's PR department that is charged with the responsibility of sending out the appropriate bags, shoes, and dresses to be shot by magazines and newspapers. He also writes the press releases for the label (writing, by the way, is the most essential skill in PR)—usually after he's had his coffee while reading a stack of dailies, but still long before anyone else has shown up for work. Ironic that a guy named Billy Daley lives for the dailies and has read them all before anyone else has shown up for his or her daily day at work.

BACKGROUND

Born in Boston, raised in Wayland, Massachusetts, Billy is the youngest of four children of an investment banker father and a homemaker mother in a traditional Irish Catholic family.

"My childhood dream ranged from being an actor to owning a bar. Fashion as a career never crossed my mind. But when I got to New York, I sort of ran with the idea."

EDUCATION

Billy attended kindergarten through twelfth grade at the public school in Wayland, after which he had one year of additional studies at Gould Academy in Bethel, Maine. Afterward, Billy entered Lake Forest College (LFC) in Lake Forest, Illinois, four years later graduating with a double major in French and international relations.

BEST YEAR OF MY LIFE

"Since I was not an amazing student, my time at Gould was set up so that I would learn to be more prepared for college and be independent. I learned how to do my homework, study, and 'prepare for things.' The school had so many facets beyond education: For the first time in my life I went camping, pressed cider, sheared sheep—a real outdoor moment. I even completed an eight-day winter mountaineering course with Outward Bound. Gould was two miles from Sunday River Ski Resort, so I skied every day after school that winter. It was truly a special school with a very unique approach to learning. Given that I never really excelled at school, it was a great place to learn."

EXTRACURRICULAR FORESTER
"I did a newspaper column for the college paper. It was called 'In The Know,' and it was about film, fashion, TV, and trends. And I had a radio show. I was a shape shifter."

BILLY, *NOT* BILL
"I have always been Billy—my father is 'Big Bill,' and I am 'Little Billy,' yet he is five foot nine, and I am six foot one. When people call me 'Bill,' I correct them right away: I like my Y."

WHAT THE *C* IN WILLIAM C. DALEY STANDS FOR
Cushing, as in Cardinal Cushing, who married his parents and baptized his older siblings. "Many fashion folks think I must be related to Babe Cushing of the Cushing Sisters—but, alas, that's not the case. Cardinal Cushing died the year I was born [1970], and my parents wanted to honor him by giving me Cushing as a middle name."

JOINING J. CREW
The summer after his freshman year at LFC, Billy took a job at the J. Crew store in the Atrium Mall in Chestnut Hill, Massachusetts, and he would continue to work there over summers and holidays throughout college.

"I *so* wanted to work at J. Crew. My mom knew a manager, and that's how I got my job. It was in Loss Prevention, but I was so busy checking myself out in the mirror to see if I had enough layers that I didn't do too much to prevent shoplifting."

MORE J. CREW
"When I graduated from college, I wasn't recruited by the United Nations, so I went back to J. Crew. I didn't know what else to do. I liked the energy and environment there—though I really didn't love selling clothes."

NEXT STOP, EMPORIO ARMANI ON NEWBURY
"I waited on this woman at J. Crew, who was wacky and cool, and we got along. She asked me 'Do you like Armani?' I said 'Wow.' She gave me the manager's number at the new Emporio Armani store on Newbury Street, where I wound up getting hired. They kept me on the jeans floor."

FLICKERS OF A FASHION FUTURE

"A girlfriend asked me if I wanted to move to New York. I came for a weekend and ran into my friend Matthew Hunt. We'd gone to college together. He was working at Isaac Mizrahi. He told me he had liked my column at school and thought it was funny. He told me I should get into fashion."

ARMANI? VERSACE?

"When I moved to New York, I was naïve and thought that Armani would simply transfer me to one of the label's NYC stores. But Armani said I couldn't just expect to get a job there. So I walked up and down Madison Avenue with my résumé. I ended up getting a job at the Versace men's shop."

SHOWROOM VOLUNTEER

"Right before I started at Versace, Matthew asked if I could come down to Isaac Mizrahi's showroom and help stuff envelopes for the show. At the end of the day, Dawn Brown, who was the director of PR, asked me if I could come back the next day."

THIS IS A JOB?

"Then I find myself backstage at Isaac's show, drinking champagne, calling Shalom and Amber to get in their places for the lineup. Why didn't anyone tell me that this was a *job*?"

ISAAC INTERNSHIP

There wasn't a paying job for Billy at Isaac Mizrahi at that point, but he was offered an internship. "I went in on my days off. I cleaned up the showroom, compiled the press books. I was a twenty-four-year-old college grad doing coffee runs and interning for free. I didn't ever think I would be hired, but I was 'gaining experience and paying my dues'—two phrases I heard over and over."

ISAAC'S COFFEE ORDER

Billy had it written on a Post-it and repeated to himself: A grande decaf skim latte, no foam, flat lid. "I only got it wrong once."

BILLY'S COFFEE ORDER?

Milk and two Splenda. "The funny thing is I get my own coffee, and always have. If someone gets my coffee now, I buy him or her coffee in exchange. 'I buy—you fly.'"

BILLY'S NUMBERS AT VERSACE

"I hated selling clothes. I would do the windows, fix the displays, update press books—ANY-THING but sell the clothes. The manager, Dita, who was Romanian, came over to talk to me. Monday and Tuesday, I'd sold nothing, she reminded me. Wednesday, I was at Isaac's, and so far on Thursday, I'd sold nothing. She wasn't going to fire me, but she wasn't happy. She said, 'Belee, you need to sell something so you can eat and pay rent. A tie? A fragrance?' Two minutes later, Elton John walked in with David Furnish and dropped $30,000 with me. All Dita could say was: 'You are a lucky mother fucker.' I went back to fixing the windows. I had made my month's goal in thirty minutes."

IGNORANCE IS BLISS

"I was living in a one-bedroom apartment with a female friend. We slept on twin beds with a tapestry between the beds for privacy. I had less money, but it seems like I went out more, and everything was new and fun. I was still wearing my plaid shirts, baggy khakis, and blucher mocs."

LUNCH

"After interning for a year, Nina Santisi [Isaac's right-hand person; the producer of *Unzipped*, the Douglas Keeve documentary on Isaac; and longtime vice president of PR] said, 'Hi hon, what are you doing for lunch today?' There was a lot going on. The film. A secondary line. An eyewear launch—Isaac was hot, hot, hot. She offered me the job of PR coordinator."

DELIGHT-MARE

"I wanted the job, but was projected to make 30 percent more at Versace. Dawn said to me: 'What are you thinking? You need to take this job. You can expense cabs, lunches, maybe some dinners. We'll make it work.' I took the job scared shitless that I couldn't handle my bills."

WHAT I LEARNED FROM ISAAC

"You have to respect the cloth. And that fashion PR is a profession, and a pretty cool one at that."

LOVING IT

"Oh, my gosh! This was fantastic. I learned about fabrics and about techniques. I learned about organza, gazar, taffeta, cotton piqué, soutage. I'd get yelled at for calling things by the wrong terms. It wasn't just a pretty dress anymore—they were clothes—'important' clothes. It was all new and exciting.

"I held showroom appointments with Grace Coddington [creative director at *Vogue*] and dressed Gillian Anderson from *The X Files* for the Emmys. I was over the moon with happiness—working twelve hours a day and living for it. My friends in banking were total nine-to-five kinds of workers, and they didn't understand why I worked so long and hard. But I didn't mind—I was all 'Well, you're not going to fashion shows or magazine parties, are you?' At the time I didn't realize what a punk I was for thinking that was what it was all about."

LIVING IT

"Amy Spindler [the late *New York Times* fashion critic] gave Isaac a bad review for the first real show I'd worked on [spring 2006], and I fell apart. Dawn Brown told me: 'I can't deal with Isaac crying *and* you crying.' Dawn is a hardass, but I learned so much from her. Talk about taking your job personally? It was not like I had designed the clothes, but I was that passionate. I was living a dream that I never really knew I'd had."

BEING RECRUITED

"At Isaac, I'd been promoted from PR coordinator to PR manager at the same time I started being scouted by companies like Polo and Prada. After some bad business and the closure of divisions, we all saw the writing was on the wall for Isaac."

GOING TO THE GAP

Billy was recruited by Gap to be the senior manager of global public relations. "Three weeks into it, I hated it. I had gone from freeform to being 'in a box' at a big corporation. I started in June and started to get antsy in July. I went from pulling for major fashion stories for *Vogue* and *Bazaar* to pulling for 'dressed to grill' stories for *Family Life* magazine."

Billy managed to stick it out at the Gap for ten months before accepting a job with Dolce & Gabbana as the senior manager of special events and celebrity dressing.

FROM CORPORATE TO COCKOO

"Dolce sent me to Milan to do the seating for the shows because I knew everyone. But the company was in chaos—there was no president and there was a high turnover in New York. They were overdoing evening gowns and expecting Gwyneth Paltrow to wear a six-inch fur miniskirt. Italians are tough, but this was cockoo town. At one point I was even doing their trunk shows [a sales or retail function, not PR]."

On the upside, Billy got more direct exposure to working the celebrity side of fashion PR and to doing business in Europe.

GETTING PUSHED OUT = BEST THING THAT EVER HAPPENED TO ME

At six feet one inch tall, Billy normally weighs 175 to 180 pounds. Under the stress of an untenable job situation, his weight dropped to 165. "I was miserable. I wanted to jump, but

I got pushed. I signed off on something without Milan's authorization and was forced to resign. It was like I had peed on the Christmas dinner table.

"I was out of work for four to five weeks. It was an eternity for me. But it was the best thing that ever happened to me because this is when I learned to appreciate my friends and see my private life as separate from my work life and the PR me."

KCD

"They asked me to do resort appointments for Chloé, as a freelance project, when Stella McCartney was still there. I was hired a month later. I started working on the production side of the business with Julie Mannion, as the senior manager of production—doing castings, creative direction, planning events, and working backstage at fashion shows in New York, Milan, and Paris. After a while, I'd find myself drifting over to the PR side of things. While I was working on budgets and custom furniture made for a huge event, I found myself jumping in to help people write better press releases.

"At one point, Ed [Filipowski, who together with Julie are the fashion firm's partners] asked me what was wrong. I told him that I loved the company, but I hated what I was doing. Ed and Julie had made a huge investment in me in terms of salary and compensation, and I said that I was probably not returning their investment in my production capacity."

ESSAY ASSIGNMENT: "WHAT I LIKE ABOUT PR"

"Ed and Julie made me write an essay about what I like about PR. Then they sat me down and told me I'd be the first person who has ever gone from production to PR in the history of KCD and that they were putting me on Versace."

THE NEXT 6.5 YEARS

"I got the marquee account. It was daunting and terrifying and amazing. I worked on Versace for three years as the North American press representative for all things Versace—women's, men's accessories. I even got to work at the Couture in Paris—it was amazing."

VERSACE (*ANON*)

"No one could be less Versace than me. It was so far from what I was. But I believed in it. It was an amazing vision. Donatella is a tremendously generous woman, and no matter what was going on at the time, she made a point to be friendly and kind to me. It was a challenging time for her and the company, but when you believe in something, it is easy to work hard."

KCD = FASHION GRAD SCHOOL

"If I equate my time at Isaac with 'fashion college,' then my time at KCD was my master's. It was the first time I realized that fashion PR was more than just sending the samples out to shoots. It was about writing strategies and thinking proactively, planning events with a seamless flow—we excelled at putting together the *right* invitation list, making sure that events had prepress and postpress.

"Ed and Julie made sure everything went well. Yes, we were wearing all KCD black, hustling, doing all of the KCD procedures. But in the end, Ed gave me tremendous freedom. Once I got my feet solid, he would let me run with it. He trusted me to figure it out. But both of them taught me so much about details that I still carry with me today."

MICHAEL KORS

"I got a call to come in to interview to be the vice president of global communications for Michael Kors—and I freaked. I had always admired Michael's designs and his take on 'American sportswear.' He was funny and smart and a no-nonsense guy. Similarly, the clothes were chic and to the point. Never fussy, silly, or extraneous.

"Michael is a very intense, driven man. He works very hard and expects those around him to work just as hard. I have always thought I was hard working, but I have never worked as hard as I worked for Michael. I worked there four years and the brand tripled in size."

MOVE TO BOTTEGA VENETA

"The universe gave me a push. I'd worked with Tomas (Bottega designer Tomas Maier) on a show when I was at KCD. It was a role that evolved once I became available. The Gucci Group is very focused and strategic. It's daunting learning a new corporate language and dealing with luxury in this world."

BILLY DALEY'S DAILY BIG DEAL

The crises never stopped crossing Billy's desk. One blow-up involved a Michael Kors sheath dress that had been made for Michelle Obama, but was incorrectly identified as Azzedine Alaia because Ikram Goldman, the Chicago-based store owner who acts as the gatekeeper to Michelle Obama's closet had so dramatically altered the silhouette of the dress, that it was mistakenly credited to Alaia by the White House press secretary.

PR ≠ BFF

"I don't confuse being the PR person with being the designer's or the CEO's BFF. He's my boss. I report to him. Sometimes I can do Dean Martin to his Jerry Lewis when we're with editors—he tells the best stories. I set them up for him. But it's a business relationship. I never forget that."

BILLY'S RULES OF FASHION PR
"PR is not hard. It is about common sense and being a decent person. Most of all it's about cultivating relationships and maintaining them. Don't bullshit. Call people back. Be direct. Write a good thank-you note."

SWANS VERSUS BEES
In hiring PR people, "Designers usually want a look, and I want someone with passion. Someone who *needs* to read *WWD* every day. Someone who will pick up the phone and call editors to resolve an issue instead of waiting for an e-mail to come in. It's hard to find the right people. There are people who are all about task completion, and there are people who can do PR while thinking about 'what can drive the business.' I have never been above doing grunt work—I even still pack samples and clean up the showroom if need be. My team needs to be able to 'get dirty' because there aren't enough staff for people to be sitting at the desks waiting for the menial tasks to get done."

MANTRA
"Keep moving forward. Grin *and* smile."

WORST TRAIT
"Sometimes I have a terrible temper. When I have an outburst, I flog myself the minute it's over. It's like there is a surveillance video on loop in my mind that plays it over and over. I see for myself that I was an idiot. I always take the time to acknowledge the outburst and apologize because it's my mistake. Then I address the issue and try to explain the reason for the outburst."

FASHION PR
"I love what I do. I can't imagine what else I would do. But talking about dresses does not define me."

FAST-TRACK KIDS
"They work for a year and want to be a PR director. They don't understand the concept 'You are *not* ready.' It's this attitude: 'Can you believe? She's like twenty-eight, and she's still a PR manager?' At twenty-four, I wasn't paid, got coffee, and worked eight to eight. I still work eight to eight. They [interns and assistants] want to come to meetings with Michael before they know what *collate* means."

BILLY'S SECRET WEAPON

"I got in this habit of getting to work early, on average between 7:45 and 8 a.m. It started because I lived on the Upper East Side and I didn't like to deal with the crowded 6 train at 9 a.m. So I'd have my coffee at my desk—literally waking up there—read all the papers, return faxes, use the free 800 number long-distance line to call my mother. That habit has stuck with me. It's something that has helped me. I can get focused and map out my day.

"Once it's 9:20 a.m., the phone goes, the e-mails come in fast and furious, and it's a full-on chaotic day. But from 8 a.m. until 9:15, it's for me—not for anyone else."

HOW CAN YOU READ EVERYTHING?

"You learn how to skim. I read or skim *WWD*, the *Times*, the *Post,* and *Daily News* every day and a bunch of fashion news websites and blogs."

SHOULD KIDS STUDY PR OR COMMUNICATIONS IN COLLEGE?

"That's more of a giant agency thing. When you're inhouse PR, you don't send a release for a shoe. We send *the shoe*."

PR INTERNS

"Doing editorial sample pulls and schlepping bags is part of the job. Some PR kids don't get that it's not a good idea to send a dress to a magazine on a wire dry-cleaning hanger. And that there should be a working zipper and no stains. They don't know to use a Kors flocked hanger, a clean garment bag, and a label. It's all about how the magazines perceive the garment—if it is sent with care and presented beautifully, then it will be treated with the same respect (hopefully). But if we send things out haphazardly, we send the message that we do not value this dress."

JOB SATISFACTION

- "When people say thank you. I don't need an Hermès coin purse or Miho flowers. A simple thank-you. Because people rarely take the time to look back and reflect. And when someone does take the time to acknowledge, it is very, very nice.
- "Knowing that a bag sold really well because of a magazine credit puts the process into a business perspective. We see Michael Kors as the next great American brand, so we need to make sure that every press effort achieves a specific purpose, whether it be a branding opportunity or a sales opportunity. Or hopefully it will be both."

SITTING AT THE MONKEY BAR WITH SIMON AND YASMIN LE BON, JESSICA ALBA, AND BLAKE LIVELY

"Yeah, that kind of stuff is fun. A random surprise and wacky bonus, but I never forget that it's work. These celebrities are not 'friends'—they are business associates, and creating good relationships with them clearly helps, but one needs to keep it all in perspective."

PR: EXPENSE, NOT REVENUE

"The way PR is viewed is that we spend money and don't make money. It's a hard job because whatever you do—a spread in *Vogue*, Michelle Obama's and Cameron Diaz's wearing Kors—it's never enough and it's never over. One is only as good as his or her last hit, so it's a cycle, and it gets daunting and tiring. But being driven and passionate will help you get through the tough times."

"BILLY DALEY IS A GOOD PR"

"When I heard through a friend that Anna Wintour had said something complimentary about me, I was on a high for about an hour. Then I moved on because praise is nice and in PR your reputation means a lot, but the work you do means more."

EGO CHECK

"In an Irish Catholic family, you're not allowed to have an ego. When I call my mom and tell her how tired I am or how much I had to travel, she teases me, saying, 'Poor you, going to fashion shows, poor you, partying late with Tom Brady and Giselle. That must be *very* hard.'

"To my face, they seem to be not impressed, but I know my dad revels in the fact that I came here on my own and figured it out. My dad's never had to get me a job. But he knows what I am doing and pays attention. He will even say, 'I saw that girl in *that* dress—what's up with that?' But the translation of that is more like, 'I saw your work in the press and it was good.'"

BILLY DALEY PR?

"Start my own agency? No. I quite like knowing that there is a 401(k) and that the copier will be fixed without my intervention. I like getting up and going someplace. I like working on one brand and all of the things that go on with that. To be honest I am not sure I have the business acumen to do it, and I don't like the idea of going out to hustle clients. I think when I am done, I will open up a wine bar or a flower shop, or, who knows, I'll be sixty-five, still be stressing about not having enough front-row seats at a fashion show."

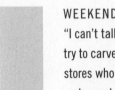

The Business of Color

Those deep purple tulips catching your eye? They don't *just happen* to grow that way. There's a clever botanist in a Dutch lab who developed this shade with the knowledge that it is the precise hue that will send positively powerful stimuli to your early-twenty-first-century brain at this precise season, encouraging you to admire them.

Similarly, there are branded fashion shades that unfailingly trigger a great warm rush of happiness: Tiffany blue telegraphs *great gifts*! Chanel black and white telegraphs chic; Fendi yellow signals Lagerfeld via Rome and all the combustible exuberance inherent in that combo; Hermès orange communicates a stratospherically high level of luxury, above all other brands. These colors didn't *just happen* either. Clever business people long ago settled on these specific hues to help symbolize and trigger instant recognition of their brands. Valentino red does the same. "Owning" one's own standard shade that withstands the passage of time is a rare and lofty achievement.

Everywhere you look, colors are being selected for you. Ask a graphic designer friend or an art teacher to show you the Pantone book, which is composed of the endless number of standardized Pantone colors. The book consists of small "pages" that are perforated so that a square sample of each individual color may

CODE NAME "PINK PURSE"

It's the outrageous, courageous color chosen for ads and media imagery, but the producer and agency know full well that they will *not* sell a lot of them. Regardless if it's orange, purple, or chartreuse, color specialists call the image color the *pink purse.*

be torn out as a "chip" for easy reference or attached to a visual to use as a guide in production, color correction, and printing. Flip through it and notice which colors have the most little color squares missing from its pages. You are holding a record of the story of color in life and in fashion. You are also holding the last physical remnant of designing pages by hand, precomputer era.

Like fashion itself, color doesn't stand still. Individual shades travel through complicated phases. A "new" color emerges, call it apple green. At first, it feels foreign and weird, then, in time, your eye adjusts, and you identify this color with things edgy and cool. As more time passes, this green is accepted as "in fashion," and you eagerly pay full price for a J. Crew apple green spring raincoat. Within two or three years, however, you lose the positive association with this once "hot" green. Pushed farther and farther to the back of your closet, the raincoat begins to feel more "gag me" than "buy me." When your little sister tries to borrow it, you disown all responsibility, sneering: *You're not going out in that perky green, are you? You'll look like a leek!"*

Color is a compelling, defining force in our lives. To be in fashion, you have to understand color and feel intrigued by its possibilities. Fashionistas get that there's a color strategy behind the vibrant violet-blue Ralph Lauren uses in this fall's cabled cashmere jumper (maybe he's even named it, something aspirational like "Windsor"). It so inspires you that you save your money to buy the cardigan at full price. You know that Windsor didn't exist last season, and you sense it's the only thing you really need to make you feel *this season*. In fashion, so to speak.

As with the tulips, there's an equally potent color strategy at work behind the jumper cables your dad picked up at Kmart last winter to stick in your trunk in case your car wouldn't start one winter morning. Not surprisingly, Windsor didn't beat out red and black. Someday, however, it might. If you look at the most successful brands in our orbit—Apple, Target, Volkswagen, IKEA—all of these companies grasp the power and magic of color far better than their competitors. And Chrysler's new electric GEM car is cleverly trading off Apple's color success: It comes with its own iPod docking station and is actually being produced in the exact shade range of Apple's iPod.

Some forward-thinking experts, including Leslie Harrington, Ph.D., the head of the Color Association, believe that there's a bright future for young people in the field of color. "So many professions now are developing specializations. Color has been seen as just part of what designers do. But that's becoming more difficult to do."

In the past, Harrington explains, color was considered to be a purely intuitive decision. Today, however, there is a blending of well-informed "intuition" with actual research and understanding of consumer behavior intermeshed with a company's image, branding goals, and strategies. "When we do color forecasting, we are mining social, political, and global forces. It is becoming so much more complicated out there."

People who do color forecasting independently realize the time and resources it takes. Others, including companies as diverse as Calvin Klein, Inc., large textile mills, and Burton Snowboards commit the resources to join forecasting services like the Color Association for the answer.

GETTING IT RIGHT: COLOR CASE STUDIES

1. BURTON CARES ABOUT COLOR

This groovy Vermont-based snowboard maker combs through color forecasts not as an end solution but for inspiration so that they can do the countertrend. Subversive and spot on for their counterculture high-altitude tribe.

2. APPLE VERSUS IBM

Apple broke the color taboo in technology. "I have a feeling that they stumbled upon it," muses Harrington. "They realized that the norm was no color. Their whole platform was computers for the home, whereas IBM was office environments. Apple launched the iPod in five colors and probably said to themselves, 'Wow, that worked, let's do it again!' You can tell that worked for them because they went from five to eleven colors." The sad reality is that most companies would've nixed the concept from the start, saying that it would be impossible to manage so many stock-keeping units (SKUs).

3. VW VERSUS HONDA

When VW reintroduced the Beetle in the United States, they put it in that weird green in the advertising. "They knew they wouldn't sell that green bug. But if you think about the person who does buy a Beetle, he or she has quirkier color sense than most people. Rather than try to appeal to the masses, they zoomed in on this audience to the nth degree with the colors and the place to stick a cut flower (more color). Then they were surprised that they did sell some of those green guys too."

Why Business Types Need Color

For designers, color is an intuitive, subconscious element of their work. Something fundamental, yet inseparable from the whole. You, as forward-thinking sellers and future fashion executives, understand that color is a most powerful *branding and selling tool;* and you will seek to separate it out and build beautiful strategies around it. To bring color to life. But, how best to do this without losing your shirt? Learn from those companies who've done it best (see case studies, page 262) and educate yourself on services that provide color intelligence.

"Color will separate the business winners from the losers," says Leslie Harrington. "It already is. This is about business. This is about competitive and strategic advantage, reputation, and brand value in the eyes of the consumer. If you get color wrong, you lose."

Forecasting the Shades of Our Lives

"We forecast twenty-four months ahead," explains Leslie Harrington of the Color Association, the oldest and most prestigious color-predicting organization on the planet. "The seafoam green in our palette for spring 2013? It was decided in spring 2011."

How Color Is Predicted

"We select a group of designers to make up our fashion committee. They represent a mix of well-known and unknown designers. We also look to balance people who work in designer fashion with those who work in mass or in more specialized footwear, activewear, and accessories areas to produce a real cross-cut of the marketplace. They bring to the table what they think is going on—usually not something they've already sent to production but what they're working on. Sometimes they all show up with the same electric blue. We try to determine where that is coming from. Other times, they have nothing that matches so we explore the reasons behind that.

"At the same time, we are watching the runway shows. We can track that same electric blue color Nicole Miller used on her runway for fall, then watch as *Vogue* uses it in its pages. If that does start to happen, we usually build on it going forward. It's always intuitive and very creative. It's the same way many designers work. When there's no action like that with another color in our palette, we also try to understand why."

Why Color Scares Companies

Companies would love to put a science around color so that they could manage it and put in their frameworks and processes. But the cool thing is that color cannot be managed that way.

Also frightening to purely business types? Disparate entities (Gucci, Apple, and a fabric stall at your local flea market) using completely different frames of reference eerily strike on the exact same shade at the exact same moment. "Unconsciously we are being guided by signals in society and popular culture," explains Harrington.

Color Decision Rights

"If you're a designer, you make the decision," says Harrington. At Target, usually the buyer is making the color calls. The problem with this structure is that buyers are naturally very risk averse when it comes to color. "If they can produce only four colors, which one are they going to drop? Not the black, gray, or navy—they'll cut the new muted green neutral."

If the color is right, it will sell; if the color's off, it'll land like a big obvious mistake on the sale racks. Here's a color conundrum: We all know if designers

---

COLOR ASSOCIATION INTERNSHIP PROGRAM (WWW.COLORASSOCIATION.COM)

The Color Association internship program is small and highly competitive: Only one intern is accepted for every twelve-week stint. Says Leslie Harrington, "We often have international interns from India, the United Kingdom, Sweden, and Japan. The international appeal of this program attests to the fact that it is hard to get real color learning. They come across the globe to get it."

FORMALIZING A COLOR EDUCATION

In conjunction with FIT, the Color Association is in the process of developing a color certification program, the first of its kind.

COLOR COLLEGE: EXECUTIVE LEVEL

Harrington explains: "What happens when you've been in this business for four years and you need to know more, and you realize you are not up to speed. The topics I am teaching in this class are for these professionals: It's the big picture of color strategy and of color and branding."

don't add breadth to their line, things won't sell. But stores, especially today, are hesitant to invest in unproven shades. They need to understand the basic role of color: Will it play the role of color per se (more risky) or be a new ground color or neutral (a lot less risky)?

"If consumers are hesitant to invest, they may instead choose to buy the gray blouse over the white one, hoping to try to use it to update their wardrobe rather than buying another black or brown suit."

Color and *Project Runway*

"Almost every time the judges critique, color comes up with a comment like this: 'I am really disappointed that you didn't do something more interesting with color.'"

Color and the Red Carpet

"When you look at the awards shows, they talk about *the color* of personalities' dresses. They always talk about color."

Companies Starting to Get It

"Companies are becoming much more aware that both their bottom and top line performances are linked to color strategy. With a down economy, companies rely more on innovation: Innovation will force us to do more with less. If you need to breathe new life into an existing product, color is a great thing to consider."

Color as a New Business Frontier

Futurists predict that 50 percent of the jobs our children will have don't exist today. The field of color and business may well be a new frontier. Says Harrington, "In the future, businesses will require more innovative, creative thinkers, not more analytical thinkers. MBA programs mold students in a way that is becoming obsolete. Building business awareness into MFA programs or more innovative thinking and visual stimulation into MBA programs makes sense." (Harrington's reference is to a cool book called *A Whole New Mind, Why Right-Brainers Will Rule the Future* by Daniel H. Pink.)

Color Career = Right Brain + Left Brain

What's fascinating about this whole field of color is that it is a blend of right- and left-brain thinking—a blending of the traditional MBA and MFA training. Harrington suggests that "to be successful in business, you'll need conventional business tools as well as an understanding of human behavior and dynamics. Interestingly, computers actually feed off both sides of our brains. Completely in step with their times, kids today, born and raised in the Internet era, are naturally attracted to careers that aren't totally right brain or left brain focused."

The Way You Learned About Color? All Wrong

Thanks to computers and digital images, the light theory of color (in which there are various sets of primary colors) is replacing the traditional teaching of red, green, and blue as primary paint colors from which all other shades are created.

Remember: Color TV Was Invented Only Sixty Years Ago.

Perhaps more than any other innovation, color TV had a huge impact on the world of color. For most of history, the colors people could buy and wear were limited by our ability to manufacture them. Wearing and living with color diversity is, in itself, a modern phenomenon. Take, for example, purple. Throughout history, purple was the color of nobility because the pigment could be produced only by using masses of crushed mussel shells as dye, rendering the color prohibitively expensive. Then, in 1856, a British college student named William Perkin was fooling around in his chemistry lab at school and struck on a way to distill coal so that it would produce a carbon-rich tar that proved to be a suitable fabric dye. It was the first new color in a generation.

Color Challenged for Its Greenness

At same time, color will increasingly be challenged for its possible negative effect on the environment with a call to account for which dyes, potentially harmful, helped create any particular shade.

Color Arbiters Are Everywhere

Everything we buy has a color, and we had to make a color decision in order to purchase that item. And someone in the manufacturing world has made a decision about that color: You name it—snow shovel, juicer, jeans. Today, cotton is even grown in color.

ROOPAL PATEL | Senior Woman's Fashion Director, Bergdorf Goodman

One way to get to know Roopal Patel is to read her "fashion show round-ups," blogs that she updates from Milan and Paris during show season. These casual missives feel like notes from a friend rather than a dictate from an intimidating, luxe retailer. You quickly learn what she likes (she diplomatically omits her dislikes) and, thanks to her edit, develop a short list of what you'll want to buy next.

Another way to get to know Roopal is to log on to www.Style.com to scan her sixty-nine-image slide show. A stunning Roopal in a black one-shoulder dress by Narciso Rodriguez. A hip Roopal in a headband, fur neck scarf, and black Marc Jacobs short dress. How is it that Roopal, not an actress, an heiress, or a socialite, gets paid to wear designer gowns, attend A-list parties, and sit in the front row at all the fashion shows? She'd tell you it was "destiny and fate." We'd add something about discipline and starting at the bottom and working your way up. Oh, and watching Elsa Klensch on CNN as a girl.

BACKGROUND

Born in the United States, Roopal grew up in Muttontown, New York, a small community on the north shore of Long Island near Oyster Bay. She is the oldest of three children. A doctor specializing in cardiopulmonary and geriatric medicine, her father practices at Mount Sinai. Her mother, who once ran her own travel agency, now has a more leisurely life, focused on her family, yoga, and golf.

KEEPING THE TRADITIONS

Both of Roopal's parents were born and raised in Kenya, where their families, Indian emigrants, had moved. (Both Kenya and India were once under British rule.) The couple met at university in India. While her parents speak Hindi, Gujarati, and Swahili, Roopal speaks only Gujarati.

EDUCATION

High school: Old Westbury School of the Holy Child
College: NYU Stern School of Business

ACHIEVER FATHER

An irrepressible student, he just received his MBA at the age of 55. He is also a big supporter of the Indian community.

STYLISH ACHIEVER MOTHER

"My mom ran her own travel agency and, when my parents would go out, she wore the most amazingly elaborate saris in colors like fuchsia, orange, and turquoise with over-the-top jewelry. Watching her get dressed when I was a kid taught me to love the art of dressing up."

CHILDHOOD EXPECTATIONS

"To do well in our studies. The dream for all three of us was to be doctors. Beyond that, the idea was that we would choose a profession, be it business or law."

CHILDHOOD DREAM

To be a dancer. "I loved Martha Graham, the Joffrey ballet, Bob Fosse."

A VERY LESSONED GIRL

Roopal studied dance from the age of four, and she also took tennis lessons and played the flute for many years.

FASHION ORACLE

"I'd wake up and watch Elsa Klensch on CNN. That's how I learned about Gianni Versace, Giorgio Armani, and Donna Karan.

"I grew up with *Vogue* and liking to shop. But I had no clue that if you weren't a designer you could make a living in fashion."

RETAIL FRIDAYS

While at NYU, Roopal had no classes on Fridays so she took a job at Urban Outfitters, folding sweaters, sweeping the floor. "It was fun."

Next, she sold jeans at the Diesel shop where she met a woman who invited her to intern at her showroom over the summer. "That's when I realized there was this whole other world of fashion."

SIMPLY CHIC SHOWROOM

"It was really fascinating to see the collections and the process that needed to happen from showroom to store." During this time, Juicy was launching from the showroom, and Roopal actually modeled the brand's first T-shirts for stores.

NEXT STOP: JUSSARA LEE

"It was a new company so I wore many hats. I was doing mailers. Helping with the fashion show at Bryant Park. I learned that sales wasn't my calling. And I saw how much I liked to be stimulated by many different things happening simultaneously. I felt suffocated looking out of one person's window.

"At the time, I had no idea how important this education would be to what I do today. I learned about advertising, marketing, public speaking, presentations."

JOB TIP

"I was lucky. Destiny and fate played a very big part in my career. Our Bergdorf buyer at that time told me that there was a position open in the fashion department. I met them and got the job. It was the first time I knew what I wanted."

FASHION APPRENTICE

"I worked in the fashion office for three years. Lillian Wang [now Von Stauffenberg] truly taught me so much of what I do today: how to develop a new designer, how to screen new resources, how to translate a designer's vision into retail, how to put together a trend presentation."

Roopal laughs when she recalls, "Back then, I would sit with boxes and boxes of slides. It took me seven days. Today, I can put together a presentation on the computer in one hour."

ONE YEAR AT CLUB MONACO

Roopal left Bergdorf to join Club Monaco in visual merchandising. Ralph Lauren had just purchased the brand, and big expansion plans were under way. "It was exciting. We opened fourteen stores that year. I was able to be a part of those store openings. I saw how the LA store needed to be different from the Detroit stores and the South Beach store. You could go in and redefine the whole store. I liked the high-low dressing element, the company, and the environment."

STYLE.COM, ROUND 1

"The site was just launching. At the beginning, it was set up as a partnership with Neiman Marcus. I was hired as the person who acted as the conduit between Neiman's and *Vogue*."

BAD SURPRISE ENDING

"Unfortunately 9/11 happened. At which point Condé Nast let a lot of us go."

JOBLESS AFTER 9/11

"This was the first time I was let go. I didn't look at it as a sign of failure, but it shook me up and was something I didn't expect in my career.

"It was also a nice break. I had met Peter Som, and I really liked what he was doing.

"I started working with Peter out of his apartment. I just did everything: casting, merchandising, and making model cards. I also consulted with Club Monaco during this time, working on their home stores called Cabane, which were based in Toronto."

STYLE.COM, ROUND 2, WITH CANDY PRATTS PRICE

"And then Candy called one day. We had briefly overlapped at Style.com. She told me that she had some projects for me to work on. Candy also has her pages and trend stuff. I worked with her on those.

"This was a really amazing and really educational time for me. I learned so much from Candy and owe her a lot. Obviously she is old school, and 99.9 percent of the time she was right. I thought it was weird that my projects were running out, and she didn't say anything about next steps." The reality was that Candy had already lined up Roopal's next step.

CALL FROM CANDY'S FRIEND

"Then one day I got a call from Robert Burke. I knew Robert and Candy were really good friends. I thought he wanted to talk about what Christmas present to get her."

DESTINY AND FATE

Robert Burke hadn't called Roopal to talk about Candy's Christmas present.

"He said that they'd had this position available for two years. We just hit it off immediately. It was instantaneous. Robert Burke hired me to be the fashion director of Bergdorf Goodman."

DREAM-COME-TRUE JOB

"I was twenty-nine years old. It was my dream come true. I always wanted to come back to Bergdorf in some capacity, and the nice thing is that Bergdorf Goodman was changing at the time with so many renovations."

SIX YEARS LATER: DREAM-COME-TRUE JOB

"Every day it's an honor and a privilege. I feel blessed by my career. It's a dream."

TERRIFIED TO GET DRESSED ON THE FIRST DAY AS BG FASHION DIRECTOR?

"I didn't feel a pressure to dress in a certain way. I believe that you have to be who you are. I am who I am, and I wear what I want to wear. If something is eight years old, I don't care. If I still like it, I wear it. I don't preach. I don't dictate trends. I don't create ideals on a false level. I believe if you don't feel comfortable in something—even if it's the most expensive, exquisite couture gown—you shouldn't wear it. For me, I have many insecurities in life; dressing just isn't one of them."

THE ART OF GETTING DRESSED

"For me the art of getting dressed is really important. I take great pride in it. It's one of my great joys.

"It's part of being in this position to see how clothing and fashion can make such a difference in your life. You can put on a beautiful dress and feel beautiful. A beautiful color can make you feel so much more beautiful.

"You feel like a rock star when you wear Donatella Versace. Narciso Rodriguez knows how to give you that perfect 360-degree view. Every angle is perfect. Marc Jacobs puts that little bit of whimsy in every piece."

THE TRANSFORMATIVE POWER OF FASHION

"It is very rewarding if I've helped make one designer's dream come true or if one woman finds a gown that changes her life. That is satisfying for me."

JOB PARAMETERS

"When you go to the collections, it's a big mural. We try to simplify that for women. My job is to simplify the message."

Roopal does that through her e-mails to customers and by editing the BG magazine and other mailers (alongside creative director Aidan Kemp).

WHAT ELSE DOES A FASHION DIRECTOR DO?

Roopal does a trend presentation to sales associates four times a year. She screens new designers. "I try to work directly with designers and try to see as many new designers as possible."

SPECIAL DISCOVERIES

"Kate and Laura Mulleavy called and called and called. They sent a book, and, wow, it was really amazing. They had eight pieces, and I asked right away, 'Can you make some more?'"

Thanks to Roopal, Bergdorf launched the Rodarte label. "Kate and Laura are going to be major. They are already major, and they are lovely people. They are my friends. When you collaborate like this, it's not just work."

Another random meeting led to the introduction of Derek Lam's collection to Bergdorf. "There are so many moments like that."

THE MAGIC OF BERGDORF GOODMAN
"Everyone here is open-minded. I've never heard anyone say, 'No. That can't be done.' That's the beauty of working at Bergdorf Goodman. 'No it can't be done' *is not said here.*"

FOREVER INDEBTED TO
Robert Burke. "He taught me so much of what I know. He's the reason I'm here. Robert took the risk to hire me."

ROOPAL'S BLOG = A MORE PUBLIC ROOPAL
"The blog is still new—we've done it for only two seasons. I have a lot of fun doing it. But I still see myself as an inside girl inside the company. Jim Gold [BG president and CEO] is a public face. Linda Fargo [senior vice president, women's fashion director] is a face. I'm not."

INTUITION
"So much of fashion and so much of runway is intuition. The first sixty seconds of a runway show tell me whether it will be good or amazing."

IT LOOKS LIKE FUN, BUT IT'S STILL W-O-R-K
"Just because you're in fashion doesn't mean you aren't working. No, it's not brain surgery. And the whole point is that fashion is fun. But people forget: You are working just as hard as anyone else."

FAVORITE TIMES
"Riding on the back of Christian Louboutin's moped around the alleyways of Paris." Also, meeting Mr. Valentino: "I was so much in awe of him. There have been so many amazing moments."

HOURS: 24/7?
"At the same time, this job demands a lot of travel and socializing. A lot of work things are after hours."

CAREER VERSUS REAL LIFE

"Lately I have made more of a conscious effort to slow down and find a balance in my life."

DIVERSITY ROLE MODEL?

"I never in my life wanted to be the poster child for Indian-Americans. When I walk into a room or a party, I never think of myself as Indian or dark or different. I just think of myself as Roopal."

YET, ISN'T IT AN INDIAN-AMERICAN MOMENT?

"I am friends with [Indian-American] women like Padma and Rachel Roy. It makes me happy to see their successes."

WHAT HER PARENTS DIDN'T UNDERSTAND

"There were moments when they did not understand. Like when I was making $35,000, and my dad mentioned to me that all of my friends were making $80,000 and $100,000 salaries. I said, 'Dad, don't worry. One day it will be major.' "

HOW THAT'S CHANGED

"Now my parents will call me up when they read something about Jack and Lazaro [of Proenza Schouler] or Jason Wu. It's just funny."

SECRET PASSION

Star Wars. "My brother bought me the *Star Wars* encyclopedia for Christmas, and it was my favorite gift. Most people don't know that I'm a total *Star Wars* junkie. I'm addicted. For me, George Lucas is the biggest celebrity."

WHERE ROOPAL SPENDS HER FREE TIME

"I'm a downtown girl. I do things there."

WHAT YOU WON'T CATCH ROOPAL WEARING ON THE WEEKENDS

Sweats, gym clothes, ripped jeans, her boyfriend's clothes. "I don't wear makeup on weekends, but I don't do the slob girl thing. I still believe in art of dressing."

PAMELA BAXTER | President, Christian Dior, Inc., United States, and President, LVMH, Perfumes and Cosmetics, North America

The story of Pamela Baxter's amazing life and meteoric career has the makings of a great Hollywood screenplay. The film would open circa 2010 with a day in the life of the U.S. president of the House of Christian Dior. Wearing next season's hottest silhouette (and played by a freshly bobbed Kate Hudson, who conveniently wears Pamela's same Dior size 36), Pamela jets off from New York to Paris for a breakfast with her boss, LVMH chairman and arguably the most powerful man in fashion, Bernard Arnault, before taking in the Dior couture show at his side in the front row. After the final model does the bridal turn, Pamela slips backstage to greet Dior designer John Galliano (played with crazy aplomb by Johnny Depp) with a hug and a kiss.

Then, flashing back to her unlikely beginnings on her father's South Dakota ranch in the mid-1960s, we see glimpses of her rodeo successes contrasted with her charming townie existence living in a hotel with her mother (Goldie Hawn) so that the pixie, high-spirited Pamela could wear real shoes and girlie clothes and attend grammar school. Life is beyond beautiful for the young heroine until a hunting accident (enter scary music and dark clouds) leaves her father dead and forces her to rewrite her dreams and ambitions. The in-between parts win the Dior-couture-clad Hudson an Oscar. Absent in Hollywood that evening, however, would be Pamela Baxter due to a prior commitment: She's off on her latest spring break scuba adventure with her grandchildren.

BACKGROUND
Pamela grew up in Mobridge, South Dakota (population 3,574), a town founded only a hundred years ago, earning its name from the railroad bridge built there to cross the Missouri River, that is, "MO-bridge." The area is rich in Native American history with the remains of numerous Mound Dweller and Woodland Indian villages.

ANNIE-GET-YOUR-GUN UPBRINGING
The barrel racing champion at the Sitting Bull Stampede in 1965, a summer rodeo still held today, Pamela lived a townie-rancher life, dividing her time between the Brown Palace Hotel on Main Street, where her mother preferred to live and was more convenient to school, and her father's ranch, sixty miles outside of town, where she perfected her riding skills.

CHILDHOOD AMBITION
To be a prima ballerina. "But I realized at around ten that, coming from Mobridge, that probably wasn't going to happen."

FIRST PAYING JOB

Painting fences on the family ranch. "I used my money to buy clothes." (A habit that's definitely stayed with her, especially now that Pamela's office is just an elevator ride away from Manhattan's biggest Dior boutique.)

EDUCATION

After her father died in a hunting accident when Pamela was eighteen, her dreams of attending Stevens College in Columbia, Missouri, and studying dance were dashed. Instead, she attended the University of South Dakota, in Vermillion (hitchhiking into Sioux City on the weekends for excitement). Years later, Pamela completed a business degree at UCLA.

FIRST BEAUTY JOB

By hanging out with the cosmetic girls on her breaks decorating the windows of the original Eddie Bauer store, Pamela was able to nab a temporary job working behind the Revlon counter at Bon Marché in Seattle, while the other girl took time off to go to Greece. When that girl stayed in Greece, the job was Pamela's. "I went from counter manager to makeup artist, and the rest is history."

IN HER STABLE

In fashion, the Christian Dior label and boutiques. Her beauty brands include Dior, Givenchy, Guerlain, and Acqua di Parma as well as the independent brands Fresh and Benefit.

GLANCING INTO HER CRYSTAL BALL

Pamela intends to significantly increase the U.S. market share of Dior's worldwide business and make her mark on the fashion business.

WORST JOB EVER

Waitressing in college. "I was so bad they made me stay in the kitchen and peel potatoes."

EARLY CAREER HIGHLIGHTS

National Makeup Artist Program, then West Coast training director for Charles of the Ritz, Borghese account executive in Los Angeles, then regional sales director for Aramis.

CAREER RISK TAKING

At the age of forty, with a successful career in sales, Pamela took the risk to move to New York City and try her hand at marketing.

THE NEXT BIG RISK: ON MEETING M. ARNAULT

Fighting off complacency after twenty-five years at the Estée Lauder companies and looking to do something new for the last decade of her career, Pamela spoke to a headhunter acquaintance about the possibility of finding a spot at a fashion brand. The headhunter said fine, she'd think about it, if Pamela would agree to meet these guys from LVMH beauty first. Soon after, the headhunter asked one last favor: Would Pamela agree to meet M. Arnault? Pamela was never serious about taking on the job of heading the troubled, overdistributed, and gray-marketed stable of French luxury beauty brands of Dior, Guerlain, and Givenchy. But she was totally intrigued to meet the big *fromage*, Bernard Arnault.

PAMELA GAVE IT TO THE SKINNY FRENCH GUY STRAIGHT AS A SOUTH DAKOTA HIGHWAY

Thinking he'd never take the drastic measures Pamela saw as essential, "I gave it to him straight. I said that I came here just to meet him and that I didn't want the job. That things did not look good to me. That to fix his business, he would need to shut down at least one-third of his distribution, and that that would cost him $30 million to $40 million. The concept was to downsize before we could grow in the right luxury markets. He didn't bat an eye."

WHY SHE TOOK THE JOB

"I loved M. Arnault. He was so passionate and articulate about the Dior brand. Here is someone who can convince you to commit through his own convictions and vision." Plus he agreed to support her plan.

MENTORS

All from Pamela's twenty-five years at the Estée Lauder companies:

Bob Nielsen: "He took a chance on me. I'd been working in marketing for only two years when he made me VP of marketing for Aramis."

Leonard Lauder: "Patient and scholarly, he loved to teach. We would take these trips together once or twice a year, and everyone from field VPs to account executives from all different brands would pile into a van. We'd spend three days visiting stores, looking at the merchandising, the competition, and the look of the beauty advisors. He was always teaching us what to look for."

Jeanette Wagner: "There are a lot of women in cosmetics, but not many have reached her level. She was definitely a female executive in a man's world. And girl power is something she's given to me."

CAREER CHANGER

STARTED IN: **BEAUTY**
SWITCHED TO: **FASHION**

It's rare in fashion that you start at the top. But that's what Pamela Baxter did when, after working in beauty sales and marketing for twenty-five years and then heading the turnaround of the Dior beauty business in the United States, she took the reins of the Dior fashion business as well. That was what she had said she was aiming for when she first met with Bernard Arnault, CEO of LVMH (parent company of Louis Vuitton and Dior). Who knew? The barrel racing rodeo champion from Mobridge, South Dakota, running one of France's most esteemed fashion houses.

PROUDEST OF PROFESSIONALLY

Fulfilling her goal of taking on Dior fashion from a beauty background and training
Signing the first fragrance licensing agreement for Estée Lauder with Tommy Hilfiger, then
    launching the hugely successful Tommy fragrance
Heading the first Crème de La Mer team for Lauder

Most of all, however, Pamela says she is proudest of her management abilities: "Knowing who is right in what job, putting the right person in that job, and letting him or her grow."

PROFESSIONAL MANTRA

"It's all about the people. You have to find them, hire them, educate them, and then let them go."

HER ADVICE TO SOME FUTURE PAMELA BAXTER

"You cannot get a better education than I had, starting behind the counter. I developed myself around sales and marketing, and I was smart enough to know that I'm no genius at operations and finance. I find good people for those areas and give them lots of freedom and credit."

NOT ABOUT ME, ME, ME

"I've deliberately stayed under the radar. And if I'm hit by a car tomorrow crossing Fifty-seventh Street, there's a succession plan in place so that the business will not miss a beat."

BEST AT

"I never throw a résumé in the trash because I remember how hard it was to get a job out of college. I try at least to start a conversation with the person, be it on the phone or over e-mail, or I direct him or her to the right person. If you get the right people in place, business just happens."

WORST AT

"I don't have a lot of patience. I want things to happen fast so I'm not good at waiting."

FRENCH LESSON

While Pamela runs her business the way she knows best, she's had a business culture shock at LVMH. "Where we celebrate success, they look for the downside. Where we trust intuition and enjoy taking risks, they tend to analyze and choose to not make a change as a means to avoid mistakes. We encourage an entrepreneurial spirit with our teams. The French are very hierarchical."

WHO MOST ROCKS HER WORLD

More playmate than traditional grandmother, Pamela, a girlish sixty-ish, earned her scuba certification alongside her two grandchildren, David, nineteen, and Azure, seventeen. And she takes them on diving expeditions twice a year.

WHY SHE SOMETIMES SKIPS COUTURE IN JULY

See above: two weeks this month are reserved for diving in Anguilla.

PERSONAL PASSIONS

Eating good food and collecting and drinking good wine.

HER ROCK

Partner and husband of twenty-seven years, John Hines.

WHY SHE'S "AUNTIE PAMELA" TO MARY J. BLIGE

John's nephew is married to the singer.

GIVING BACK

Pamela works tirelessly raising millions of dollars for charitable causes at industry events like the Dream Ball and the March of Dimes.

ANN WATSON | Vice President Marketing/Communications, Club Monaco

Ann Watson made her climb up the retail ladder look like a cakewalk. Straight out of Syracuse University, she beamed herself to New York City to begin her career in the executive training program at Macy's. The Texan who oozed confidence and warmth pounced on a worthy mentor, and she devoted herself to learning her craft so that she would be qualified for the next higher level. And the next and the next. But life interrupted her bright plans. After winning her dream title at Saks Fifth Avenue, the 9/11 tragedy struck along with a painful personal loss. On top of that, her job was eliminated.

Instead of scrambling for her Next Big Job, Ann chose to take time off for her own spiritual quest, wandering the Far East. The life balance that she found on her travels sounds cliché, but, for Ann, it was profound. The yoga she practices now provides her a sharper fashion and life point of view. Her lifelong struggle with dyslexia—something she's only recently spoken about—makes her more sympathetic to others who've faced challenges. The teenage car accident that squashed Ann's dream of becoming a ballerina now strikes her as a critical life lesson. Ann Watson still makes everything look easy, but the beauty of that is that it *wasn't*.

BACKGROUND
Born and raised in South Texas, Ann is the daughter of a stay-at-home mother and a rancher/entrepreneur father. She attended St. Mary's Hall, a small all-girls boarding school in San Antonio.

MODEL MOM
As a young woman, Ann's mother had modeled for Mr. Stanley Marcus. "Neiman Marcus was always near and dear to my heart."

CHILDHOOD DREAM
To be a ballerina. "I was accepted into the Houston Ballet Academy at a young age and could not wait to get to the American Ballet Theater. Ballet gave me a place to express myself and to truly feel a sense of personal achievement at a very young age as well as creating a structure of self-discipline that has served me ever since."

CREATOR VISUALIZER CRITIC SELLER

CHALLENGES

"I am dyslexic. I was lucky enough that my mother found it at an early age. It's something that was passed down from my mother's side of my family."

Ann's mother found her excellent support at a time when little existed. "We would make flash cards, writing the word 'dog,' put glue on top of the letters, sprinkling salt on top to create a texture. The more senses I involved in the learning process, the greater the retention."

HOW ANN POWERED THROUGH

"You simply realize that this is not a hindrance and that you just learn differently. The way I see things, Einstein and da Vinci were both dyslexic and creative people.

"I never told my teachers in college until finals, when I needed extra time. I didn't like to feel different.

"I got all my school books on tape. One of the ways I got through college was that my roommate was a great editor, and I was good at getting down the ideas. So I'd write our papers, and she'd edit them. And we'd both get A's.

"In my career, it taught me that you cannot stereotype people. In society today, we call it a *disability*: I think of it as an *ability to think differently*. To think 'outside of the box.'"

EAST COAST EXTRA CREDIT

During high school, Ann was drawn to the East Coast, spending one summer studying art at Phillips Academy in Andover, Massachusetts, and two summers studying art at RISD.

WHY SHE ATTENDED SYRACUSE UNIVERSITY (SU)

"At least it was in New York State. My father wouldn't let me go to college in New York City because he said I needed a campus."

Ann started at SU in the fine arts program, but found it "too isolating." She switched to the Newhouse School of Communications, ultimately graduating with a BS degree in retail management.

FROM FRIDAY'S GRADUATION TO MONDAY'S START AT MACY'S

"I couldn't wait to start! I remember calling [SU career advisor] Jarvis Jefferson, saying: 'I know I'm not supposed to start for a month, but could I please start [the Macy's executive training program] on Monday?'"

WHY MACY'S?

"They had the best reputation at that point. Ed Finkelstein was still there. He had started out working in the stockroom and rose to the top job, which inspired me as it meant that Macy's really supported its people. It was creative, innovative, and merchant driven. The bar was raised pretty high. Macy's was the first culture I wanted to be a part of—not only because Macy's was part of New York City's culture but also because Macy's had been a big part of defining retailing in America. There was also a seismic shift going on: It was 1988, Campeau and Macy's were battling it out for the Federated Department Stores, and Donna Karan had reinvented the power suit and the way a modern woman's wardrobe could express not only power but sensuality as well. I knew Macy's with its incredible history and reputation was the place where I could be part of the action and make a difference."

STALKING HER FUTURE MENTOR

"I watched Joan Kaner walk the floor at Macy's and interact with buyers and sales associates. She said what she had to say, and she didn't scream, which was *not* the norm in the 1980s. I told myself I wanted to be like her. So one day I followed her back to her office and blurted out, 'If I could choose any mentor, I would want it to be you.' Then I was embarrassed at what I'd done and turned to run off. Joan said, 'Miss Watson, come back here. Please come sit down and tell me *who* you are.'"

DON'T WAIT FOR A MENTOR TO CHOOSE YOU

"It really makes a difference. Choose somebody you want to work for, and you will learn from him or her. From that that moment on, I chose my jobs based on the person I wanted to work for."

"MY OWN OFFICE?"

One year later, Joan Kaner left Macy's to head the Neiman Marcus New York fashion office, and soon after, she asked Ann to join her there.

"I was twenty-four years old. Joan took me on a tour of the offices. She said, "And this will be your office." I felt like *Working Girl*. 'Oh, my God! I made it!'"

Ann held this post for four years. Her title was: Neiman Marcus, New York, Fashion Merchandising Counselor.

NEXT STEP: VIEW FROM THE OTHER SIDE

"While at Neiman Marcus, I had visited Escada and had suggested that they make their evening wear into its own collection. At one point they called and said, 'Ann, we want to do what you suggested, and we want you to run it.'

"That's how I came to launch Escada Couture, which gave me my first glimpse of what a global company was like. Going to Munich was like going to the United Nations. Escada had partners from every country in the world for one week every season under one roof. It was fascinating to hear about the nuances of each market. And in the role, I traveled to every small specialty store in the United States. Having the connection with the customer has always been so important to me; it is where the 'juice' is!"

Ann's position: Escada USA, National Sales Manager, Escada Couture, which she would hold for two years.

BACK TO NEIMAN MARCUS

Joan Kaner lured Ann back to take on the role of senior fashion editor. This stint lasted three years, before Saks Fifth Avenue recruited Ann.

NEXT STOP: SFA

"I had always dreamed of this job. I always envisioned the fashion office as the hub of the fashion cycle in creating the merchandising and communications strategy for the store. I wanted to integrate the fashion office into the corporate structure and into marketing. It was a perfect challenge."

THE MARK OF A GREAT BOSS

When Ann told her boss of this great offer and resigned, Joan Kaner showed no disappointment or resentment. "She told me she was proud of me and that she fully supported me."

At thirty-four, Ann became vice president, fashion merchandising, women's, Saks Fifth Avenue, New York, which was that "ultimate job she'd always wanted" but where she would remain for only two years.

JUMPING OFF THE RETAIL LADDER

"When you first start in executive training, you see your path laid out ahead of you: First you are a buyer, then the divisional merchandising manager (DMM), then the general merchandising manager (GMM), then president of a company. When I first joined Joan at Neiman's, I went off the traditional retail career track.

"There was no fashion office ladder—the fashion office was something you achieved later in your career. I didn't even know in college that there was a fashion office or a fashion director. There is a common thread, but, corporately, it's separate. The fashion office is communications driven and consumer driven. It's about how to connect with women through fashion and beauty. It's about how to distill a larger cultural trend into a single, exquisite bangle."

MOMENT OF TRUTH
"My stepmom died with so many regrets. When I lost her, I made myself a promise that I would go and do the one thing that I had regrets about: I had not really traveled the world and explored other cultures. Then 9/11 happened. I realized that it was time for me to go do something for myself. Saks was in its third round of layoffs, so everything coincided."

FIVE DAYS LATER?
Completely relieved with how things had evolved, Ann picked up her last paycheck, bought a plane ticket to Cambodia, and found someone to sublet her NYC apartment.

AND SINCE I'M IN THE NEIGHBORHOOD . . .
Ann traveled and studied throughout Cambodia, Vietnam, Thailand, Tibet, China, Japan, and India over the course of a year.

ANN WATSON'S FIVE GREAT LESSONS FROM THE EAST
1. To really follow your dreams and realize that things do not happen *to* you. They happen *for* you.
2. To trust your instincts. That if you listen to yourself and trust yourself, you will be guided in the right direction.
3. That beauty is an innate language that all women speak, whether it's a peasant in India laying pebbles to make a new road or a diplomat waiting for a private jet on a tarmac.
4. That people with so much less than you are truly happy and unbelievably generous to strangers. That money does not make you happy. Actually, it is giving that makes you happy.
5. That life is all about the little moments, not the grand gestures. Be still enough not to miss the moment.

PROUDEST OF
"My year away. My self-exploration as a person. Seizing the opportunity that came my way. It gave me life experience I wouldn't have had otherwise."

WHAT WON'T BE WRITTEN ON ANN WATSON'S TOMBSTONE

That she met all of her career goals.

MISTAKES

"All of my mistakes have been made through impatience."

EXTENDING KINDNESSES

"I have been fortunate enough that in almost every role I've had, I've had a relationship with young designers. I've had the chance to help young people. When someone calls and asks me to meet with his or her daughter and talk to her about a career in fashion, I always make time. I make time to visit schools like Parsons and SCAD and the University of Chicago."

ADVICE TO YOUNG CREATORS

"Go sit on the steps of Alber Elbaz [Lanvin designer, Paris] until he lets you in.

"You have to learn the craft. Young people get caught up in the conceptual before they master the skills. You have to understand how to take it apart and put it back together. Rei Kawakubo [Comme des Garçons], who is one of our great conceptual designers, is the most amazing master tailor."

WHAT ANN LOVES ABOUT FASHION RETAIL

"It is the only medium that is absorbing and reflecting pop culture at the same time.

"Nothing moves as fast as fashion retail. By comparison, the hotel and media businesses are slow. It's one of the rare platforms that allows creativity within a fast-paced business, fosters the entrepreneurial spirit, and feeds off direct contact with consumers."

DAILY WALKABOUT

"I am constantly in stores. I live with my customer. I see her making decisions, trying things on, coming out of the dressing room. I interface with her day in and day out."

SYRACUSE MOTTO THAT ANN EMBODIES

Knowledge crowns those who seek her.

ANN WATSON'S ADVICE ON YOU HOW *YOU* SHOULD START IN RETAIL

"First get the foundation down. You can put that foundation down only with a big company. If you want to be in retail, explore the training programs at Saks, Neiman Marcus, Macy's, and Bloomingdale's.

"At the end of the day, this is a people business. It's about building relationships. And the best place to build relationships is at a retail company. The people I grew up with in the business now have jobs as the publisher of *In Style* or the president of Valentino. They are now all top dogs."

SNAPSHOP: KEY U.S. FASHION RETAILERS

Listed below are eight places where you can start your retail career:

1. *Barneys* is fully owned by Istithmar, a Dubai-based investment group, with stores in key U.S. cities. It is the coolest of the big stores, with the edgiest designers and most original product mix (www.barneys.com).
2. *Bergdorf Goodman* is the most posh of specialty stores, with one luminous location, on Manhattan's Fifth Avenue at Fifty-seventh Street. It is fully owned by the Neiman Marcus group (www.bergdorfgoodman.com).
3. *Bloomingdale's*** is part of the Federated group, which is publicly traded. This is the store that invented "shop-u-tain-ment," with in-store events and themes (www.blooming dales.com).
4. *Henri Bendel* is owned by The Limited, which is a publicly traded company. It has recently decided to sell only beauty and accessories, eliminating its fashion trade (www.henri bendel.com).
5. *Macy's,*** like Bloomingdale's, is a Federated store, and, like Bloomingdale's, it is a "department" store, which means that it sells kitchenware, housewares, appliances, furniture, and so on. The Herald Square flagship is a sprawling, often overwhelming and impersonal, urban destination (www.macys.com).
6. *Neiman Marcus* is privately held by the Texas Pacific Group and Warburg Pincus. Founded in Dallas and still headquartered there, Neiman Marcus exudes an over-the-top Texas luxe and exuberance (www.neimanmarcus.com).
7. *Nordstrom* is a publicly traded company, but Nordstrom family members are still in its executive ranks. It is famous for treating its salespeople with great respect, who, in turn, treat customers in a kind, unpushy manner. Seattle-based and West Coast dominant, Nordstrom was founded by a Swedish immigrant as a shoe store (www.nordstrom.com).
8. *Saks Fifth Avenue*** is a publicly traded company, and it attracts an urban sophisticated shopper. When the economy took a nosedive, Saks was the first store to take dramatic markdowns and roll sales racks into its designer boutiques (www.saksfifthavenue.com).

**Postcollege executive training programs that are worth exploring.

CHRISTELE WIELGUS | Corporate Director of Visual Display, Prada

Her title contains the word "corporate," but there is nothing corporate about Christele Wielgus. In fact, if you were to meet her, as I did for coffee on Mercer Street one day, you would probably take her for an artist, an actress, or a dancer. First, there's the way she dresses herself, combining vintage and homemade pieces with luxe current items in stunningly original ways: brocade Prada silk pajamas with purple python cowboy boots; an Asian flea market colorful padded coat worn over a narrow black skirt and crisp white blouse. Then there's her more-than-waist-long dark wavy hair—more nineteenth-century than twenty-first—and the way she applies red lipstick, more for effect than an attempt at prettiness. Yes, Christele screams *original*, and that's the precise quality fashion houses desire in their visual merchandisers: someone with the ability to separate his or her presentation from all others; to curate the season's line so that it comes across as cooler, chicer, artier, more outrageous, or more elegant than all others; to communicate throughout the stores and its windows references that have the power to elevate the brand above the commercial to art. A tall, and extremely physical, task. One that Wielgus seems destined to do.

BACKGROUND
Christele was born and raised in a small town one hour from Paris, the younger of two sisters.

CHILDHOOD DISCIPLINE
Christele studied ballet for twelve years.

INSPIRATION AND ALTER EGO
Christele's mother studied couture millinery in Paris, and she had her own fashion label and custom clothing boutique for ten years before marrying Christele's father and having her two daughters. Christele feels extremely close to her mother: "It's a total connection."

A friend of Christele's, photographer Martha Camarillo, has taken a portrait of Christele and her mother, and hopes to film a documentary about their relationship.

FREE FARE TO PARIS
As Christele's father worked as an engineer/draftsman for the Syndicat National des Chemins de Fer (SNCF), the French national train system, Christele's mother would take advantage of free train fares to take her daughters to visit Paris at least twice each month throughout their childhoods.

CHILDHOOD DREAM
To work and live in Paris.

EDUCATION
Finished high school and passed her Baccalaureate; then, moving to Paris, completed the equivalent of a BFA program at L'Institute Supérior des Arts Appliqués de la Mode (LISAA).

MARGIELA MODEL, ETC.
Once she had her degree, Christele spent many years searching for the right career fit. Among her many roles was a fashion week gig with Lolita Lempicka and a turn as a runway "model" for Martin Margiela, the famously reclusive Belgian fashion designer who always used friends or acquaintances instead of professional models for his presentations.

PETIT BATEAU
In the end, Christele took a job as a sales associate at Petit Bateau (the French fine cotton brand) near the Place Madeleine in Paris. "I was doing the windows without realizing that this job had a name."

MORE EDUCATION
Institute Français de la Mode (www.ifm-paris.com); Paris, master's degree.

THREE MONTHS AT RALPH LAUREN
After writing to apply for an internship, Christele spent three months working at the original Paris store of this most American of designers.

SIX MONTHS AT SONIA RYKIEL
Here Christele, thinking she'd taken a job as a design assistant, was drafted into working as a fit model for the iconic French designer one day when the normal fit model was late. "The young designers were afterward very rude to me."

DANCING FLAMENCO FOR SHOP GIRLS AT PRADA
As a sales associate at the Paris Prada shop on the Rue de Grenelle, Christele would dance the flamenco on the sales floor to amuse her colleagues. During this period, when not dancing, she became friends with a guy who was a manager at the store.

BIG BREAK
Christele got her first job in her eventual field as assistant director of visual merchandising with the French designer Thierry Mugler, a post she would hold for two years.

NEXT STEP: YSL
During the four years Christele worked as the European coordinator of visual merchandising at Yves Saint Laurent, she worked at the end of M. Saint Laurent's career, for the entirety of Tom Ford's stint designing there, as well as at the beginnings of Italian designer Stefano Pilati's era at the house.

"I always teach my boys. You have to understand what you are seeing. We spent a lot of time at the YSL archives." At the end, Christele found herself starting to "feel bored," and she sensed that, with a change in management, she would no longer be in favor. "I am always full of intuition for these things. When I don't feel comfortable, I know it is not my time."

THE MOMENT CHRISTELE HAD BEEN WAITING FOR
During Christele's time at YSL, the Prada manager she'd fallen out of touch with reconnected with her and asked her to move from Paris to Hong Kong, where he'd since relocated, to be the head of visual display there for Prada. "I wanted my own city. This was the chance for which I had been waiting many years."

PRADA HONG KONG? OR PRADA PARIS?
When Christele went to Milan to meet with a Prada fashion coordinator to discuss the job, it was unclear to her which job was being discussed. Apparently, there'd been a crisis in Paris, and she was being considered for a role there. Christele, however, was ready for a bigger change.

PRADA HONG KONG? OR PRADA SHANGHAI?
When Christele arrived in Hong Kong, there was some discussion about whether she should head the visual merchandising in Shanghai instead. Ironically, Christele's sister and her family had at the same time just moved to Shanghai, ruling it out as a destination: "I wanted my own city."

IN LOVE
"The first six months were difficult. But then I'd fallen in love with Hong Kong. I wanted to stay in Hong Kong."

SUMMONED TO PRADA TUSCANY

"But after a year and a half, I was asked to fly to Terra Nova to meet with Prada executives."

Christele was permitted to fly business class for the eighteen-hour flight from Hong Kong to Rome. She then traveled to Florence, which is nearby Prada's Terra Nova factory where much of the manufacturing for the brand is done.

"NO. I NEED A SHOWER"

Christele arrived in Florence and had budgeted thirty minutes during which time she would go to her hotel to shower and dress for the interview. The office called to ask if she could come early for her 2:30 p.m. appointment. Christele responded that she would do her best to arrive quickly, but, no, she absolutely needed to pass by the hotel for a shower.

CAREER MANTRA

"You *can* say no."

"DO YOU LIKE THE UNITED STATES, YES OR NO?"

Te piace la U.S., si o non? Christele had traveled from Hong Kong to Terra Nova, Italy, essentially to hear this question in a meeting of only several minutes. Almost twenty-four hours of travel for a fifteen-minute meeting. "That is just the way they do things at Prada. Face to face."

HELLO, U.S.A.

As director of visual merchandising for the United States, Christele directed a staff of eight people, two of whom oversaw the wholesale side of the business, managing the look of the brand at specialty stores like Bergdorf Goodman and Neiman Marcus.

WHAT CHRISTELE IS WEARING TODAY?

Deep purple python Prada boots, Prada silk pajamas, a coat that her mother designed and sewed from vintage couture fabric.

WHAT CHRISTELE IS DOING TODAY?

"A floor move—redoing floor displays every [three weeks] in the SoHo, which is a major undertaking that looks something like a military operation."

HOW CHRISTELE WORKS

In one sweep she changes the way one of her people had put sweaters on a table, and then she removes two items from a rack of eighteen, and instantly makes it. She literally flies inside the store adjusting piles of sweaters here, luggage there. Assistants, cameras in hand, record her every move.

WHY CHRISTELE EATS A SANDWICH AND A QUICHE FOR LUNCH

Visual display is a physical job. Moving, unpacking, loading, pushing racks. Walking the sidewalks outside the store to see the windows from all angles. Christele rarely sits down.

PASSION OUTSIDE PRADA

Flamenco dancing, which she continues to practice two to three days per week. "I thought about Tango, but you need a partner. I needed something where I could go to classes and dance on my own."

FASHION DREAM NUMBER 1

"Of course I am interested in creating a concept store. To find an idea and build it up."

FASHION DREAM NUMBER 2

Or to realize her own bag line, made from vintage couture fabrics. "I want to create something. I do feel I need someday to do my own project. To be free and independent."

CHILDHOOD DREAM REVISITED

After her stint in the United States (and after being interviewed for this book), Christele has now happily returned to Paris with Prada to continue her visual merchandising work.

HOT JOBS: STARTING YOUR OWN STORE?

Then you'd better *really* stand out. Be all about something in particular. Something you live for and love. Here are a few retail entrepreneurs with strong points of view.

BE ALL ABOUT FASHION

Among the first and most seismic fashion concept shops in the world was Colette (213 Rue St. Honoré, Paris) where guest curators and high/low mixings keep this address a mecca for fashion pilgrims. www.colette.fr

The Italian fashion hub is undoubtedly 10 Corso Como with its gallery, book shop, restaurant, and store loosely collected at the end of a courtyard. The brainchild of Carla Sozzani, this high-minded bazaar is now faithfully re-created in Tokyo and Seoul and in the beginnings of the fashion label, 10 Corso Como. www.10corsocomo.com

In Los Angeles, fashion meccas include Fred Segal Hollywood www.fredsegal.com and Santa Monica www.fredsegalfun.com

BE ALL ABOUT SKATEBOARDING

Established in 1994 by James Jebbia in downtown Manhattan on Lafayette Street, Supreme continually expresses its cool through collaborations with designers like Thom Browne, photographer Larry Clark, artists like Jeff Koons, Damien Hirst, and Takashi Murakami. The kidney-shaped skate bowl in Supreme Los Angeles is a natural theater for groovy guys making moves. www.supremenewyork.com

BE ALL ABOUT SERVICE

One swimsuit store in São Paulo, Brazil, delivers a selection of suits for women to try on at home. Understanding that the bikini shopper isn't loyal to a single brand because fits and styles change from season to season, the Selection of Unbelievable Beachwear (SUB) store carries a rich mix of swimwear brands, from Rosa Cha, Brazil's most famous swim brand, to Agua de Coco, Vix, Fernanda Niemeyer, and Jo de Mer.

BE ALL ABOUT PARTYING

There's a new Berlin venue that's a groovy sneaker, T-shirt, and coffee shop by day and a happening disco by night. And, Paris' Techtonik store feeds off a teenage desire to party, selling Techtonik clothes in a nightclub setting with a DJ booth, booming music, and a disco sidewalk scene.

FASHIONISTA SURVIVAL GUIDE

No Such Thing as Superficial

Woody Allen has said that showing up is 90 percent of life. I'd adapt that statement in one critical way to fit our fashionista world: Showing up *looking chic and appropriate* is 90 percent of fashion.

All of this seems terrifically obvious to me now, but I was paralyzed on the style front when I started out. Hopefully my years of conscious observation can now help you to get it right. So here it goes: an annoyingly specific guide to the personal care, grooming, feeding, and dressing of a well-put-together creative professional whose future is bright.

Clothes: The Essential First-Year Wardrobe

I will spell out for you the perfect wardrobe to get you through year 1 in a creative work setting. (These guidelines are a bit different for Visualizers, whose work settings often take them outside of the office.) The premise here is that you are working hard, living off your own salary, keeping your head down, and not trying to wage a clothing competition with the designer, fashion director, or editor in chief. What I'm suggesting is a very limited wardrobe. A uniform. Pulling this off well takes a lot more style than an excess of expensive (or inexpensive) clothing.

First, make this commitment to yourself: What you wear in all other aspects of your life and what you wear to work occupy two completely separate compartments. In a perfect world, you'd have two closets. In your imperfect teeny apartment, make one part of your closet for your work world only. This simple organizational act will speed getting dressed in the morning, help you in the proper care and maintenance of your clothes, and make downtime feel all the more delicious. So, everything else discussed here is your professional wardrobe, okay?

THE ESSENTIALS
- Black trousers—one cotton or linen pair for summer and one wool gabardine pair for winter
- Black, gray, or navy pencil skirt (to the knee)
- Black V-neck sweater
- Gray cardigan
- Crisp white blouses
- Black and white cotton tanks and tees
- Tailored black coat to knee
- Classic tan or white trench coat
- Warm dark-colored parka that covers your derriere
- White jeans (pressed, no stains, proper fitting, *not* the ones you wear out for a burger with friends)
- Cute, cheap rain boots

WHERE TO PUT YOUR $$$
- One great pair of high simple black sandals.
- One great pair of midheel black or brown suede boots.
- One great bag. Here something vintage borrowed from your mother or grand-

THE CARE AND FEEDING OF SHOES

Before even wearing your new shoes, take them to a reputable shoe repair shop (Shoe Service Plus on Fifty-sixth Street between Fifth and Sixth Avenues is the best in Manhattan) to have black rubber half soles glued to the bottom of your soles. Otherwise, one giant rainstorm, and they'll be mush. I have had Manolo black suede boots for twelve years. Proper upkeep, and by this I mean *maniacal* care, ensures that my boots always look brand new. Told you I was a nerd.

mother would be très cool, like an old Vuitton, Gucci, or Chanel; otherwise, use a not-so-$$$ vintage bag you find at a vintage store or flea market.

- Black or gold ballet flats: Chanel, Tory Burch, or J. Crew, or any cute knock-off brand.

Accessories

If you are starting out, I'd strongly urge you to *keep it simple* even in the accessory department. Skinny hoop earrings always look right. A good gold or silver watch is a necessity. The most basic badge of responsibility is a watch: Always wear a watch when you are working. Pearls can work if the rest of your look isn't too prim. Save serious bling—diamonds, fake diamonds, and heavy-duty gold necklaces—for another part of your life. It's distracting in the workplace.

It's cool to inject your look with one shot of surprising color via belt, bag, T-shirt, and shoes. Add something a little jarring to catch the eye, like magenta, forsythia yellow, silver, or lilac.

PAYBACK FOR KEEPING THINGS SUPERSIMPLE FROM THE START

- You won't look like a fool.
- You won't blow money on stuff that you'll never wear.
- You won't create the impression that you are privileged or an air-head or a fashion victim.
- You will look really smart and pulled together.
- You will be able to make slight adjustments in your look as you adapt to the official office look.
- You will slowly gain access to sample sales and other means of acquiring Important Items for not a lot of money. Take advantage by picking up a bag, jacket, or trousers. Add item by item to your wardrobe, making sure it is something that works with your core stuff.
- You can start to comb vintage shops for cool, inexpensive add-ons.

Don't Forget the Fit of Your Clothes

Most people buy clothing, wear it, tire of it, then throw it out or give it away. The entire process may take less than six months. It's high-speed consumption.

I believe in making clothes mine. I tailor anything that doesn't fit exactly the way I'd like it to. This is time-consuming and costly, but it is really the right way to go. The difference between a shoulder that fits and one that flops, or a skirt that hugs your hips just so and one that drably hangs too wide, is substantial. Inexpensive clothing, like something from Zara or H&M, can look instantly more expensive if it fits you properly.

RULES TO DISREGARD
- *Don't wear black and navy together.* Actually, black and navy together *is* chic. Red and brown or camel is another cool combo.
- *Horizontal stripes make you look fat.* No, they don't. Fat makes you look fat.
- *Wear white only in the summer.* This rule flopped over and died long ago. Whatever the season, it's smart to have a pair of white trousers that work.
- *Your bags and shoes should match.* Not so. Matching bags and shoes is almost always a bad idea, and it shows a total lack of style.
- *Match whenever possible.* This is no longer a good idea. Dressing "outfitty" in general—stockings to match a color in your blouse, blouse to skirt to sweater—looks 1980s' department-store-style daft.
- *Wear glitter at night, not during the day.* Such traditional rules about daytime and nighttime dressing have fallen as well. It's cool to wear a little sparkle by day and almost always cooler to underdress by night.
- *You shouldn't wear the same thing twice in one week.* Forget that rule. When a fashionista loves something, she lives in it and lets it define her.

RULES TO FOLLOW
- Don't wear a suit jacket with its pants or skirt at the same time unless it's a very proper or dressy event. In fact, a dark suit or velvet suit with a shimmery blouse is a great black-tie, tuxedo type of look.
- Don't wear a tight top with a tight bottom—only one half can be tight; otherwise you risk looking tarty.
- Don't leave the house until you feel good about what you're wearing.
- Plan tomorrow's look today to lessen the stress of putting an outfit together in the morning.

Underwear Matters

So do your socks. In the course of a day at a retailer, designer label, or fashion magazine, you could easily be asked to whip off your clothes to try on some look or another. Just keep it simple and clean.

THE TRICKY BALANCE

I do not wish you to be a lemming, trying to imitate the behavior and habits of those around you. Nor do I wish for you to be the target of mean sketches or sidelong glances—that is, the innuendo that says, "She *really* does not get it." You have to find your way between these two extremes.

Too tan skin = you vacation too much = you spend free time and $$ at the tanning salon.

Too white teeth = tacky and blinding to the eye = you don't see what's wrong? = you don't have a good eye.

No moveable facial parts = Botox OD = you're not comfortable with yourself.

Too small nose = you hated yourself as a teen and/or your mother hated your face as a teen = plastic surgeon overdid it.

Leg Cover

Bare, tan, moisturized, skinny legs are always good. Fishnets come and go, but black and tan shades in as-small-as-possible diamonds always look good. Opaque black tights, plain or with texture, are better than sheer. Footless tights with ballet slippers work if you are under thirty regardless of how fit you are. Sheer nude shades *always* look stupid.

Manicures

Yes. A $10 Occasional Habit + Home Touch-Ups. I'd never attend an important meeting without first having a manicure. And interviewers are trained to notice nails. Does she gnaw her cuticles? Are the nails so long she couldn't possibly type? French manicures telegraph "tacky." Red is good for a midlevel job, but it might send the message that an assistant spends too much time on upkeep. Nails and hand gestures say everything about the girl: Is she nervous? Conniving? Hyper? Recently engaged? Unkempt? Unhygienic? Secure? Confident? Together?

The no-brainer shade of choice: something like Ballet Slipper, Sugar Daddy, Pretty in Pink, or simple clear polish. English people think they can do these things themselves at home. Maybe you can do it, but I don't even try. Take the twelve minutes and spend the $10.

It's standard practice at cheap nail salons to cut clients' cuticles, but if you can avoid having your cuticles cut, you'll be better off in the long run. Say "push back, don't cut." Establish a relationship with "Kelly" at the corner nail salon. Ask her real name. Remember it, and she'll remember you. Be nice and tip well ($2 to $3 on $10 manicure).

Hair

Long straight hair is not a style. Call it "natural" if it makes you feel better. It is *de rigueur* for interviewing at Apple or Google or for freelancing at home in Seattle for a software company. It is also okay for the Peace Corps, Vanderbilt Medical School, or the Iowa writers' MFA program. It is not fine for the real creative business world where looks matter.

If you cannot afford a good salon, find out which is the best salon in your area. Then call there and ask when it conducts its "training" nights. You'll get a great cut for next to nothing with the top guys overseeing everything.

Pedicures

This is a monthly salon ritual for the six months when you're not wearing sandals and a twice-monthly ritual for the six months you are.

Best to skip polish altogether over the dormant season to let your toenails breathe, losing any yellowish tinge constant polishes creates. Always keep toenails short and square (long toenails are beyond gross!). Unlike your hands, where strong color can be distracting, you can have fun with toe color—dark red, pink red, blue red, orange red—and color always makes the foot look happy. "Notice me!" your little toenails scream.

SERENITY-INDUCING FASHIONISTA SOAK

You've had a tough day? Endured the wrath of a Super Bitch while your boyfriend broke up with you via e-mail? Feel a cold or flu coming on? Pour a whole box of Epsom salts and two giant bottles of hydrogen peroxide into the hottest bath water you can stand. Soak for fifteen minutes. You'll thank me later.

Eyebrows

Pluck, don't wax. But don't tweeze yourself unless you are certain about what you are doing. There are definite trends in eyebrows. Bushy brows were big in the eighties; a supernarrow brow look has more recently taken hold. Try to avoid either extreme, instead finding what best suits your face. At the very least, pluck hairs in between your two brows. Not many of us can pull off the unibrow Frida Kahlo effect (but if you are among the few who can, GO FOR IT!) as well as any obvious errant hairs above or below your brow.

Once on the sidelines of a Patrick Demarchelier photo shoot, Kevyn Aucoin took it upon himself to give me an eyebrow lift. He attacked quickly, depopulating all the hairs of my brow below an imaginary but all-important line horizontally across my face. His weapon? The most pointed Tweezerman tweezers I'd ever seen and a furious, almost violent plucking action. Tears rolled down my face as I tried to remain chipper, professional, and grateful. This hurt more than childbirth or the time I broke my nose waterskiing. This pain belongs in a class of its own.

Two days later, when the skin finally calmed down, I got it. To match my small-boned face, Kevyn had created a lighter, narrower brow, giving me a lady-like line that I've since been able to retain myself. I never let it get so dramatically out of control that I cannot find Kevyn's original shape. Besides, that would hurt too much. I remain grateful to Kevyn.

Your Body, Ultimately, Is All You Have

I have always been obsessed with exercise. I did power aerobics back in the day with Molly Fox and Jeff Martin. Then, like the other cool people, I switched to the Romanian maniac trainer Radu. I pounded and grunted alongside beautiful people like Cindy Crawford, Tony Radziwill, and his cousin, John F. Kennedy, Jr. When my then boyfriend commented that my legs looked like those of a "soccer player," I converted to the softer, more feminine Lotte Berk religion, source of the long and lean. Next came Pilates. Highly effective after a cesarean. My belly had never been flatter or stronger. Now I'm into Ashtanga yoga, the type-A prescriptive version. To be in my forties and doing splits, headstands, and jumps that I couldn't have done in my twenties feels good.

So go ahead. Belittle me as the "Forrest Gump of exercise." I did follow the trends. Or accuse me of being shallow and superficial to spend time daily on my body. I'd say you should try it for yourself. Exercise is great for my self-image, it has kept my mood good, and it makes me feel powerful and strong.

On the investment front, strict adherence to exercise has been a key factor in staying the same size for all of my adult life. The size 38 pale pink bouclé Chanel dress and bracelet-sleeve jacket I scored at a sample sale fifteen years ago—as well as lots of other Chanel treasures—still fit. I love dragging out my own vintage stuff and refitting my jackets for today.

Makeup Bag

Go visit a MAC store or a Bobbi Brown makeup counter at an hour when they are not busy. Ask for a good office day look. Then, if you can afford it, buy these six most important products to use on your face:

1. The perfect concealer and/or foundation
2. Blush
3. Eye pencil
4. Mascara
5. Powder
6. Lip color

If you are very clever, you can try to re-create those products at your favorite discount drug store. The trickiest part is matching skin tone shade, so if you can buy only one great product—make it concealer or foundation that matches your skin tone.

THE STUFF YOU PULL OUT OF YOUR BAG MATTERS

Status lipstick. Hermès (they only make one), MAC, Bobbi Brown, Dior, YSL, Chanel.

Status compact. Ditto.

Status fragrance. Find something that makes you happy and stick with it. Some of my favorites: Chanel No. 5, No. 19, or Cristalle; L'Air du Temps by Nina Ricci; Joy by Jean Patou; Fracas; Annick Goutal's Charlotte; anything Jo Malone or Marc Jacobs; Lauren by Ralph Lauren; Hermès Eau Sauvage.

Splurge Beauty = A Skin Care System That Works for You

There's nothing more beautiful than clear skin. There's nothing more distracting or upsetting than pimples popping up every time you have your period or you are dealing with a little stress. I never had pimples before I was in my twenties. Then, while working like a dog in my first jobs, well, stress = acne.

Devote the time and money necessary to find a skin care system that works for you, whether it is Neutrogena, Clinique, or Proactiv, whatever. Nothing else matters more than clear skin. Once you find something that works for you, don't play around with other products. Stick to the one that works.

The key to finding your own smooth skin holy grail is sticking to a routine long enough to allow it to work—say, six to eight weeks. The next magic product is sure to be screaming out at you, tempting you away. Don't listen. Stick to what's already in your bathroom. Be absolutely religious about your routine—whether it's cleansing, toning, moisturizing, or splashing, whipping, and slathering—and you will, well, . . . thank me later.

Life in a Four-by-Six Gray Cubicle

You've finally made it! Your own office! Well, sort of. Maybe it's a prison-cell-sized cubicle, but, at least, you have visual privacy. What do you do with it? How do you make it your own? Can this paltry space express your best fantasy of yourself, your dreams and aspirations?

The first objective must be to clean out the detritus of your workspace's previous lives. On this count, be ruthless. This chore is to be done after hours because it is not directly connected with the business of the office, within the first two weeks of your occupancy.

What is an editor? Someone who decides what to keep and what to toss. Someone who decides what words and pictures fit nicely or provocatively together. You are now the editor in chief of your own desk. Practice editing. Make it work visually and functionally, and from a public health point of view!

THINGS TO KEEP
- Inspiring international magazines.
- Dictionary, thesaurus, Associated Press style manual, Strunk and White.
- Usable office stationery.

DESK DRAWER LIFESAVERS

These are items that live in your desk:

Small flat mirror for teeth check. Life at deadline-driven creative places means eating two, sometimes three meals a day at your desk. You don't want to walk into a meeting with spinach marring your smile.

Toothbrush, toothpaste, floss, and a small bottle of mouthwash. In their own zip-up opaque container for discreet trips to bathroom.

Comb and brush. It takes a second and makes a difference.

Tampons, Aleve, Tylenol, Motrin, Excedrin, Tums, decongestants. Stocking up on an assortment of over-the-counter basics assures fast friends and fewer headaches.

Lip balm.

Hand cream. Anyone working with papers all day long ends up washing her hands with the harsh soap dispensed at most offices. This leads to superdry hands so you need to keep your own personal tube of hand cream handy.

Lint remover. Masking tape–style roller.

Makeup. A separate zippered fabric bag should contain at least the following essentials: concealer, mascara, eyelash curler, pink blush, lip gloss, and/or lipstick in a daytime shade of pink or plum or sheer red. And if you have oily skin, a nice light compact of face powder.

Fragrance. Keep a fresh and light scent for quick spritz pick-me-ups during the day.

Sewing kit. For the emergency stitching up of a falling hem or the reattaching of a popped button.

An extra pair of stockings or fishnets.

An extra pair of shoes. High heels if you normally wear low, low if you normally wear high.

Gym gear. You never know when the opportunity might arise.

- A complete set of one year's back issues of the magazine you are working for or catalogs of books your company has published or recent ads your agency has produced. This is the historic memory of your job.
- Impersonal supplies: stapler, new box of staples, scissors, paperclips.
- Pens and pencils not previously gnawed upon or otherwise contaminated.

THINGS TO TOSS
- Anything to do with food or food consumption: straws, Chinese takeout mustard, soy sauce, fortune cookies, napkins, sugar, plastic forks, pepper packets, Burger King ketchup packets, and so on.
- Anything of a personal nature the previous occupant left behind: comb, brush, cosmetics, vitamins, menus, and so on.
- Glass vases (see below).
- Pencils and pens previously used; some would call this spendthrift, but this is about a fresh start so I'd toss out all supplies not coming fresh out of a box.
- Business cards with someone else's name on them (duh!).

Dumping Ground

Most offices have a bin or designated dumping ground where you can leave books, tapes, CDs, T-shirts, and glass vases for other people in the office to retrieve and use as they wish. Find out where this depository is and use it, often and generously. When I was a beauty editor, we had periodic closet sales, selling lipsticks, compacts, creams, and so on for $1 each. The proceeds, as much as $2,500, went to homeless women's shelters. The leftover products from the sales also were sent directly to homeless women's shelters.

Take note: There are often forced office clean-up weeks when the business manager has a Dumpster installed in a central location. Don't let the invitation to organize your workspace get more personal than this!

Acceptable Personal Touches

Strong personalities of the creative inevitably break through even the most formatted office settings. Some nice touches I remember from my earlier *Bazaar* days included these:

- A completely out of place, odd antique wooden chair sat in the lifestyle editor's office.

- The features editor, Susan Kittenplan, had on her wall a large framed letter from her teaching days at Dalton. The letter was from her kindergarten class writing to wish her well and say goodbye. That struck me as wonderful.
- Celebrity wrangler Maggie Buckley had two fabulous orange trees in her office, sent to her by Anna Wintour after Maggie defected to *Harper's Bazaar*. A generous and beautiful gift that continued to grow and bear fruit for years, somehow telepathically reminding everyone that Anna and her magazine continued to grow and flourish, thank you very much, without any one of us. Maggie also had a calendar that showed the phases of the moon, which I found weirdly comforting.
- Liz Tilberis' large white denim Shabby Chic sofa was the key design element in her room. The inviting comforting side of her personality. Her large glass-topped Corbusier desk communicated the hard harsh reality of life and business. You knew how serious the encounter was to be depending on whether you were invited to sit on the sofa with Liz or directly in front of her, on the cold metal chairs.
- I managed to score two black leather Barcelona chairs for my office at *Bazaar*. They looked great and, when pushed together, served as a minisofa when during my pregnancies I needed to lie down. Don't think they made it into the new Hearst Tower, but these iconic chairs look good almost anywhere. *Note:* Skip knock-off versions of this item; they don't make it.

The exception to personalizing a workspace comes with people in the art department. There's precious film to edit and scan. Layouts to approve. They don't have room in the workspaces or probably their brains for extra images or things. One art director friend of mine has a simple office fantasy: a clean white office with a single flower in a vase. After many years in the business, that's still her fantasy.

Basic Work Space Rules

1. *Minimize personal effects.* What is fine and normal is a small, framed picture of your hunky boyfriend or a framed drawing that your nephew drew. Pet pictures always work. A good black-and-white shot of your family's dachshund on your desk shows a sense of humor and humanity. Endless sorority

pictures, wedding pictures, boyfriend- or girlfriend-on-vacation snapshots, husband- or wife-looking-his-or-her-best seem maudlin and sentimental. Ditto work pictures. Besides, unless you are fabulously interesting, your personal life is probably better left a mystery, no?

2. *Express your creativity with one or two great items.* The framed print of a great (not personal) photograph, a cool "found" not-office-y chair, a white or chartreuse beanbag chair, a sketch, a lamp, a tree, a sculpture, a carpet, a chalkboard with colored chalk, a bulletin board that you've transformed from a utility item into an inspiration board (see below), or a well-designed office chair that you've found or scavenged.

3. *Keep the office clean and hygienic.* No food = no rodents. Don't kid yourself, there are little cockroaches, mice, perhaps even rats, in almost every workspace. EEEEEEEK!

4. *Completely clear your desktop at least once daily.* No matter how muddled or messy or how many layers you accumulate over the course of a day, don't leave at night before you can see the actual surface of your desk. A good practice is to clear off the desk before you leave. Spray your desk along with your germ-ridden phone with your own handy-dandy Mrs. Meyer's Lavender Countertop Spray. This little ritual makes starting the next day so much easier. (And great for inexpensive holiday gifts, www.mrsmeyers.com)

5. *Practice good phone hygiene.* I am going to ask that you do something you've probably never done before: Smell your phone. Go ahead. Inhale deeply and sniff it up close. Pretty gross, right? The black plastic ear and mouthpieces contain millions of bacteria-filled globules. The seemingly innocuous headset of your phone is your enemy. It contains the olfactory imprint variously of earwax, Chanel No. 5, and Elizabeth Arden Eight-Hour Face Cream. No one other than you is responsible for the smell of your phone. Get it? The office cleaner might pass his or her dust cloth over it twice a year, but no one ever cleans it. In a perfect world, a plastic canister of Clorox wipes would occupy the spot next to your Mrs. Meyer's and be used to rid the phone of its nastiness on a regular basis.

6. *Be actively inspired.* You need a place to express your ideas, whether it's a big blank black book, a small black blank book, or a bulletin board. Something that is not directly related to the day's assignment but represents your bigger dreams. Your own personal inspirational inspiration. When Jackie O died, I bought a hard-cover sketchbook with a brown tie closure. I glued my favorite stories and images about her—one of the last century's greatest cultural icons—into this book. Besides living out my own personal tribute to her, I created a reference of sorts that I still refer to.

7. *Hang up your coat.* Always. Whether it's somewhere in your own space or in a communal closet, it's just civilized and shows self-respect. If there's no hook on the back of your door, find a way to get one screwed in. Then buy or borrow a nice wide wooden hanger. Voilà!

8. *Make sure you have a locked drawer.* It's easy to get lulled into the false sensation that all is good and safe when you are comfortable at your place of work. Make sure you have a safe place to keep your wallet and use it. I can't tell you how many times, especially around Christmas, people had their purses, wallets, or other valuables stolen. This seems to happen mostly in the middle of the day, though leaving jewelry, cash, or credit cards in your desk at night would be stupid. If your desk doesn't have a locked drawer or cabinet, ask nicely for one. If you are not heard, then insist. Every office manager can find a way to achieve this for his or her staff.

9. *Almost-dead flowers.* How pathetic are the stacks of moldy vases on top of shelves and counters at every magazine office I've ever visited. Afraid no one will ever send you flowers again? Get over it. Give the vases away. The instant your blooms droop, whisk them straight to the garbage.

Meeting Etiquette

Take notes. Since the creative brain is a fickle, famously lazy organ, I find that having paper and pen around me at all times is useful. Every time you walk into someone's office, you automatically should have a pen and notebook in your hand. Ten million new concepts will be flung at you fast and furiously every single day.

It's not possible for you to remember everything. Find a notebook you really like, then use it. Somehow my Mac and my iPhone don't channel the creative juices as effectively. Napkins, placemats, blank spaces in the newspaper or *New Yorker* have also worked in a pinch. If you are always writing or drawing, you might actually be a writer or illustrator.

Write notes. Nothing can replace the elegance of a handwritten note on personal stationery. I'm addicted to e-mail, IM, text messaging, like you, I'm sure. Nevertheless, call me cavegirl but I believe there are occasions when pen and paper are still essential. If a colleague loses a parent or a pet, write a simple note of condolence: "I am thinking of you in this time of pain. Yours, sincerely . . . " That's it. *Basta. Finito.* If a colleague gets a promotion, has a baby, or gets married, write a congratulatory note: "Dear Abigail, Such terrific news! You completely deserve this giant happiness!" If your boss gives you flowers for your birthday, write a note thanking him or her: "Dear Henrietta, Thank you for thinking of me on my birthday. The flowers are gorgeous!" Keep your own stationery in your desk for times like these. Nothing makes a better impression. Write in your own personal scrawl with a thick navy, black, or red felt-tip pen. Make it your signature look.

Make yourself interesting by being interesting. Go to movies when they first open. Go to art exhibits. Read reviews of movies and exhibitions. Read newly released books. Read *The New Yorker.* Read *Vanity Fair.* Go to concerts. New restaurants. Travel to Havana or Maputo, not just the Hamptons or Malibu. Creative businesses feed the culture, and, at the same time, they function as a mirror of our life and times. Consciously insert yourself into your times. **Be culturally engaged**.

Soak it up. So much institutional intelligence enters naturally through one's pores. Listen, watch, learn. How is the phone answered? When do people take lunch? Is there an afternoon lull? When do people start leaving in the afternoon? What time does the boss leave the office? How late do most people stay in the office? Do people dress or act differently on Fridays? Do people dress or act differently when the boss is out? Does the art department have different rules from fashion and features? What are they, and why is there a difference? Do a group of assistants order lunch together? Eat lunch together? Make sure you are not left out.

This will sound cruel, but think about it: A sick or elderly tiger is forced to break from the pack and is eventually left behind to die. It's not so different in creative offices. Don't be the odd guy out.

Similarly, you should study the creative energy of the place: How does that person sound so brilliant and original? Why is everyone talking about Goya? Or Andy Warhol? Or Mod? Man Ray? Whatever the hot topic in the air, don't let it float by before you take it in. No matter how many other zillions of things you have to do, lap it up. Immerse yourself in it. Or at least take ten seconds to Google it, for goodness' sake.

Suck it up. There is sucking up and sucking up. Appropriate sucking up means smiling and greeting your boss or bosses. Getting to work on time. Always being available and cheerful for little jobs or chores. Acting professionally and responsibly even when you are feeling awful and you have so much to handle that you could scream.

Gag-me sucking up. This is an insidious attempt to affect one's fate or status by ingratiating higher-ups. This behavior includes giving inappropriate gifts. Trying to impress a boss with your famous friends, access, or connections. Evidence of this sad behavior was once found at a communal fax machine in the *Bazaar* fashion department. A midlevel fashion editor had faxed a handwritten letter to a fashion director, who was shooting on location. In the letter, the editor sending the fax complimented the director on her abilities, her unique eye, her unparalleled talent. The faxing editor then wrote how grateful she was to work for the director. Yuck and inappropriate and desperate. This editor had previously seemed formidable, tough, and independent. After people read her fax, this editor suddenly seemed small, unattractively political, and weak. And the whole office knew about it.

Fashionista Holidays: How to Survive

Christmas is fast approaching, and you're paralyzed over the idea of office gift giving. How could you possibly give something of meaning or value to the Queens of the Universe who free of any charge have the latest shoes, bags, clothes, perfume, makeup, car service, and fancy lunches?

Be real. If you are an assistant, it's great to give something special that you make: cookies packed in a nice tin or strawberry-rhubarb preserves that your mother makes. The more homemade looking, the better.

But if you, like me, don't have domestic talent, buy something supersimple. Almost generic: yoga tights, a simple but useful item of clothing that that person seems always to be without on Wednesdays at 6:30 p.m. when she's on the way to yoga studio. This is everything a gift should be—thoughtful and sweet.

Tasteful Secret Santa or Office Gifts
- Gift card to Starbucks, Jamba Juice, movie theater
- Gift certificate for a manicure, pedicure, or blowout near the office
- Canvas L.L.Bean tote with initials or first name stitched on front
- Monogrammed terrycloth slippers
- Cute key ring

When you're the boss, gift giving is much easier: You pass along some amazing graft you've received to your deserving assistants. This reveals the inequity inherent in the fashionista world order. The starter fashionista assistant has a bigger gift-giving burden than her fashionista boss. But a good boss looks out for her charges. I once bought a pair of Chanel motorcycle boots for my assistant, Heidi Chen, at the Chanel editor's sale. The cost was embarrassingly small, something like $50, but the gesture was grand. Heidi acted like she'd won the Lottery.

How *Not* to Get Fired

Essential Information for Those Who Are New to the Office Environment
Use good fashionista phone etiquette. Turn off your cell phone when you are at the office. Answer all incoming office calls with a cheerful and helpful tone. In your first days on a job as an assistant, ask your boss for the names of people she wants

1. to be put through to her (that is, Karl, Marc, sick parent, husband, babysitter, key friends, her bosses) regardless of what's she's doing
2. only to know they are on the line so that she may decide what to do
3. not to speak to (Take messages.)

When calls come in belonging to the third category, try your best to get specifics. Go beyond just taking down a name and number to find out what the person needs and whether you could possibly resolve the issue yourself. In your early weeks at a job, quickly review these calls at the end of the day with your boss to ensure that she approves of the way you've dealt with issues. A smart boss cannot waste his or her time screening calls. A boss has the prerogative to allow calls to jump to voice mail. *You* do not. Check yours and your boss's voice mail often.

Practice Good E-mail Etiquette

I've been fired by e-mail (so lame). I've been broken up with by e-mail (loser). I've intercepted e-mails in which other people have said both amazing and gross things about me.

The danger with writers (like *moi*) is that we put too much of our writer-ly selves into the medium. We think we can have real conversations. Settle real issues. So the advantage I have as a writer in this medium—the ability to express myself quickly and clearly—is more than canceled out by my assumption that everyone else wants to *really* communicate with me in e-mail. Most don't. And anyone working in a big company would be smart not to try to achieve real communication.

I know I don't have to tell you *how* to e-mail—you've been doing it, like, your whole life. But it would be smart of you to tune in to these really specific, but rarely articulated rules regarding e-mail in the workplace.

DON'T TICK OFF COLLEAGUES IN E-MAIL BY:

1. *Failing to be clear.* Write your e-mail and then read back through it before sending. Check that you are responding to what was asked of you in a clear way. Eliminate any words that are superfluous to this communication.

2. *Failing to be succinct.* Don't go on and on about how you *feel* about staying late this Thursday evening or what you *would* be doing if you didn't have to come into the office on Saturday. Sounds brutal, but no one cares. Always keep messages to the fewest lines possible.

3. *Generating e-mails to those above you on the food chain.* Unless you have been instructed to do so, do not e-mail anyone above you on the masthead. If in doubt, don't do it.

4. *Perpetuating chitchat.* Never respond to the following "last word" or "closure" e-mails: "Thank you," "Have a nice weekend," "See you then," or "Great." If you answer this type of e-mail, your superiors are likely to wonder, "Is she *that* bored?"

5. *SENDING ALL-CAPS MESSAGES.* First, it's impossible to read all-uppercase messages, especially on a portable device. Second, all caps translates into uncontrollable rage, regardless of what you actually write.

6. *Making personal, critical, insulting, or nasty comments.* Don't write anything in an e-mail that you wouldn't want to see posted on the office bulletin board with your name attached.

7. *Overemoting.* No %-) (braindead). No :* (blowing a kiss). No :-0. No LOLs, BTWs, WTFs, FYIs, or OMGs. In your personal life, these symbols are cute and normal. At work, where everyone is time crunched, they're annoying.

8. *Using TM speak or making mistakes.* Text messaging lingo and word shortenings have no place in workplace e-mails. Avoid any of the following: u (for *you*); urs (for *yours*); cuz (for *because*); and pls (for *please*). Proofread e-mails before you send them to be sure the message is clear, the spellings are all correct, and the tone professional. Save important e-mails that you are crafting in "draft" the evening before you are expected to send the message. That way, in the clear-headedness of the morning, you can give it one last critical read.

9. *Reply all.* We're all guilty of hitting "reply all" when we really should be clicking only "reply." At work, you can safely assume that "all" do not care what you think. But, most important, don't dump unnecessary e-mail on your colleagues.

10. *Assuming everyone sends and reads e-mail 24/7.* Many serious fashonistas turn off their cell phones and/or BlackBerrys when they are on assignment interviewing a personality, in Milan or Paris at the shows, or on a shoot. They do so because they cannot be distracted from the very important task at hand.

From a work standpoint, nothing else really matters as much to them or to the company.

It's important that you understand people's different roles in your work structure and that you respect their changeable abilities to communicate, in turn. Conversely, for a publisher or advertising salesperson *ever* to turn off his or her PDF would be sacrilege.

No matter where you work, it's so uncool to generate new e-mails in the middle of the night, on the weekend, or in the middle of a holiday. It's fine to answer already open conversations, as necessary, in as terse a manner as possible. Otherwise, put messages in a queue and send everything Monday morning like a sane person.

How to Avoid Sending E-mails You'll Regret

Put your outgoing e-mails in a queue, which means you have to go through a separate action to send them. That way, if you are peeved or tired, you can write what you *really* think in an angry, ALL-CAPS message, and then, the next morning, having gotten it out of your system, delete it. Deal with the subject calmly, and in person.

Who Pays for Wireless?

To function in the modern work world, you need to be able to access e-mail remotely—even if your employer isn't paying for it. And more and more, employers are *not* willing to accept charges for mobile devices, especially for junior staff. Suck it up and get a BlackBerry or an iPhone. The freedom it buys you will be worth it.

Workplace Privacy: Who's Reading Your E-mail?

If your company *wants* to read your e-mail, it *will* read your e-mail. Don't feel protected by writing notes on your own personal Gmail account or on Facebook. Since these messages are sent through your firm's servers, they can be read just the same.

TEN THINGS *NOT* TO DO VIA E-MAIL

1. Accept a job.
2. Resign from a job.
3. Express disrespect for your boss.

4. Display disrespect for your company.
5. Bash someone else's work or contribution to a project.
6. Bash a coworker.
7. Talk about getting laid, drunk, stoned, high, toasted, lucky, or arrested the night before.
8. Communicate career interest in a competing company.
9. Write so much that your boss or colleagues will have to scroll down more than one screen.
10. Use keywords like "breast," "penis," "sex" (you get the idea) prominently in your messages. These words are often triggers in corporate software designed to uncover possible issues of harassment.

When to Go Offline

When you find yourself getting negative or personal. Don't write negatively about anyone via e-mail. If a negative conversation about someone has to take place, walk over to the coworker's desk and chat face-to-face. Or pick up the phone and call the person's cell phone.

iPod Etiquette (Hint: It's an Oxymoron)

Unless it's 9 p.m. and you are the only soul left in the office, or unless it's Sunday morning and you stopped by to finish a story, you shouldn't have even one ear plugged into your iPod. It reads *insolence*. Sorry.

How to Know When the Job Is Working Out

In creative businesses you'll know right away if things are working for you. Your review happens every morning at 9 a.m. when you log in to your computer.

1. You are occasionally thrown a bone. Example: You're asked to attend a business lunch or go on a press trip for the company.
2. Bosses or managers include you on e-mails or sometimes drive by your work space to say hello or thank you for a job well done.
3. You sometimes get invited to extra meetings at the office.
4. You sometimes get invited to business social events.

5. You get, and can easily articulate, your company's basic mission, and you understand your role in helping to fulfill that mission.

Yes, people talk about "emotional" intelligence (fashion people tend to have loads of it), but perhaps we all should learn to develop our "work" intelligence. That's our internal meter on how well you are fitting in with the culture of the place. Do things "click" for you there? Or is everything a huge effort? Are you swimming against the current? If you sense that you are not fitting in, you should start looking for another job. That day.

Listen to your own instincts. Are you working with people you admire and want to learn from? Are people generally happy in your office? Is your boss happy with you? Deep, deep down, are *you* happy?

FASHIONISTA FINISHES: TEN GOOD WAYS TO GET FIRED
Ever wondered what you need to do to get yourself auf wiedersehen'ed from a job it took you months to score? Depending on your work environment, any combination of these infractions can lead you down that path. Most of this is common sense, but here you have it.

1. *Not being punctual.* All creative work functions on serious deadlines. Taking deadlines lightly isn't cool, even if it's NOT a life or death situation. If your boss asks for a letter by Friday, give it to her on Thursday so you can have it to her mistake free Friday morning. Regardless of whether you believe your task is important or that it will significantly change another's life, do it when it's asked for. If your boss can trust you to get little stuff done on time, she'll eventually trust you to do more important work, like attending a press conference she cannot make or a film screening. The Real Deal won't come to you unless you prove yourself on getting the cappuccino order right. Is that why you went to college? No. But that doesn't matter anymore. This is real life.

2. *Calling in sick on an occasional Monday or Friday, then showing up with a gorgeous tan from your weekend in Miami.*

3. *Working shorter hours than your boss.* Come in late and leave early.

4. *Looking and acting bored.* Show attitude. Roll your eyes. Play solitaire on the computer.

5. *Refusing to do something someone kindly requests of you, stating that it's not part of your job.*

6. *Lying, cheating, and/or stealing.* Ideas. Money. Pens. Lipstick. Yogurt from the communal refrigerator. Next season's shoes. From others. From the supply closet. From the fashion or beauty closet. From anyone.

7. *Writing and sending personal text messages and e-mails chronically during working hours.* Chatting on your cell phone. Don't kid yourself: Your boss will know. Your colleagues will know. Some companies actually monitor employees' electronic communications so your boss's boss's boss will know.

8. *Gossiping.* Talking disparagingly about someone's homemade dress. Imitating the receptionist's Brooklyn accent. Pondering the apparent lack of sexual activity in the lives of your superiors. Mentally taking apart their outfits as mundane or trying too hard. Sure, these activities can break the tension in a day. Give you something to laugh about. And, indirectly, they can make you feel superior. It's always harder in life to be generous. Kind. Good. To look for the best in everyone. Smile at people. But ultimately, if you spread a little kindness, you will live a longer and healthier life, have kind and loving children, and find peace and happiness. (See pages 64–65 on the appropriate sharing of confidential information.)

9. *Being miserable to colleagues in an effort to get ahead.* Say disparaging things about coworkers to higher-ups. Chitchatting with someone from the *New York Post* or *Women's Wear Daily* about a person on the staff you don't like. Grounds for swift and immediate firing. Loyalty is everything in business. Even if you don't feel as though you belong right away, act discreetly because you cannot trust others to do the same. Be someone who can be trusted. This is not a zero-sum game: Your success is not predicated on the failure of someone else. In fact, if you bond together with other bright, hard-working assistants, chances are you'll all look better and all help each other career-wise down the road.

10. *Letting the daily buzz overwhelm you, so you never explore what your real job could be.* There's the 75 million phone calls, thousands of e-mails, and piles of unopened mail. All of those things make up the flurry of everyday life, but it's unlikely that the flurry is the sum and substance of your Real Job. Don't let that adrenaline of the daily buzz blind you to the bigger picture of your role. So what *is* your bigger mission, anyhow? If an intern can do your job, you don't deserve the job. Details and mania can take over anyone's life. Find ways to get the little important stuff done more efficiently so that you can do more of the "senior" thinking. Find ways to make the department run more smoothly, so you'll have time to report or write or go on a photo shoot or think up some new approaches to this page or ad or segment that you don't like.

P.S. Sex and drugs are both activities that would seemingly get you fired. It's strange that I've never heard of anyone in a creative business getting fired for doing drugs, though I'm sure lots of people probably engage in some forms of illegal substance abuse. Suggestive, or in any way inappropriate or sexually loaded, language (mostly from straight guys to straight women) apparently gets you fired and sued faster than you can say "ciao."

Fashionista Detox: Fifty-Three Ways to Stop Acting Like a Fashion B*#@ch

You play the role. You look the part. You act the part. You walk the walk, albeit teetering above the rest of your world in your four-inch-high Saint Laurent Tribute patent sling backs. Your face is concealed behind your hefty black Tom Ford Marcella sunglasses. You're slinging the 36-centimeter white Balenciaga python bag, the sample to the model that doesn't go into production for at least four months. You aren't supposed to be *friendly* or *kind* or *caring* when you're dressed to kill, for heaven's sake. Or are you?

I believe the most dazzling fashionistas on earth can actually play many roles at the same time: style queen, compassionate mother, supportive wife, listening friend, loving sister, caring neighbor, loyal citizen, fair boss, cool colleague, serene yogini, helpful stranger. Sometimes it's disarming to others if you behave in a normal, courteous way when you are dressed as if you have just walked out of the pages of a magazine. Sadly, this is a challenge for most fashionistas. When dressed for fashion combat, not many fashionistas can find it in themselves to smile and say good morning on the elevator, make small talk at the doughnut cart, inquire about how the receptionist's husband is feeling after his surgery. Nevertheless, it's something to aspire to. Here are some pointers for when you find yourself at an elevation so high that there's no oxygen left in the air to feel human.

1. Spend a few days with your parents, siblings, nieces, and nephews. Offer to help them with chores or errands, drive them around town, or do them little favors.

2. Adopt a stray or rescued pet from the pound during your summer or year-end holiday. Avoid hiring a trainer so that you will have primary responsibility for your new pet, at least until show season. Refrain from choosing cliché fashionista names like "Coco," "Karl," "Helmut," "Chloé," "Twiggy," "Marc."

3. Don't wear black for a month.

4. Commit to a fashion blackout holiday: no magazines, no *WWD*, no shopping, no cities. Pack only exercise clothes, flip–flops, and sneakers. No labels. For best results, explore a visit to an ashram that requires a vow of silence or a spa that provides guests with uniforms.

5. Read a section of the Sunday newspaper you usually skip.

6. Volunteer at a soup kitchen. Wear flats. Make eye contact. Smile (and mean it).

7. Do a weekend seminar in yoga or TM without your fashionista posse.

8. Offer to tutor a kid in reading or math at a nearby school. Don't be late. Don't reschedule.

9. Make a date with your best pal from high school or grade school (assuming he or she does not carry any of your career traits). Try to focus at least half of the conversation on your friend's life.

10. Become a Big Brother or Big Sister, and follow through on your obligations.

11. Join the Peace Corps. No, really. Go to Africa. For two years.

12. Check in on an elderly neighbor. Offer to run errands for him or her. Bring yellow tulips.

13. Let yourself eat a doughnut, a slice of pizza, or some ice cream once in a while.

14. Light a candle before you go to sleep at night, keeping it safely away from Pratesi bed linens and Scalamandre curtains. Practice deep breathing. Imagine that you are inhaling peace and love, exhaling anger and stress.

15. Enroll in a class for a language you've always wanted to learn. Practice with tapes as you drive and walk around. The more obscure (Icelandic? Swahili? Finnish?), the better.

16. Make your own coffee one morning.

17. Make your own lunch and bring it to work in a brown paper sack. Make one for your assistant too.

18. Pitch a tent and sleep inside it. Even if it's in the middle of your living room.

19. Set up a badminton net in your apartment. Organize tournaments among friends.

20. Schedule a monthly Scrabble date with friends.

21. Plan a winter weekend visit to an ice hotel. (Not just a James Bond prop, they exist both in Sweden and Switzerland.)

22. Join a bridge club.

23. Don't buy, borrow, or in any other way acquire any new personal effects for one month.

24. Stop Twittering and FBing for forty-eight hours.

25. Read (or reread) *Madame Bovary*.

26. Read a few pages of Proust.

27. Don't say "genius," "heaven," or "brilliant" for a week.

28. Plant a tree, a bush, a flower, or, at least, some lavender.

29. Declare an *i'm not so vain day*. Avoid mirrors and makeup for twenty-four hours. Do physical exercise (a walk, run, spin class, swim, fencing, ballet, Pilates, boxing) before you go to work.

30. See an exhibit at a museum you've never entered. Buy the headphones to help you focus. Be in the moment.

31. Do a load of wash on your own.

32. Iron a favorite top. (Where *is* your iron?)

33. Connect with a teacher, professor, or mentor who has inspired you, and let him or her know it.

34. Stop sending work e-mails after hours and on weekends.

35. Don't look at your wireless device during meetings, lunch, or dinner.

36. Suspend iPhone or BlackBerry activity for a twenty-four-hour stretch on weekends.

37. Get outside! Cancel your fashionista vacation to Capri. Schedule an adventure bike trip or hiking trek to Montana. (See www.backroads.com.)

38. Take a bath.

39. Offer to babysit for a friend. Or, if that's too scary, offer to visit the baby.

40. Go to the zoo.

41. Take a figure drawing class at an art school.

42. Limit yourself to two cappuccinos per day.

43. Finish a book.

44. Go to the post office to stand in line to buy stamps.

45. Go sit quietly for a few minutes in a mosque, church, or synagogue.

46. Ride a bicycle for transportation.

47. Let your critical eye take a nap: Try to go for eight hours without thinking or saying anything negative about other people's clothes or shoes.

48. Buy a MetroCard. Take the subway to work.

49. Take up knitting. Craft dramatically long striped scarves (choose signature colors like lilac and brown) for all your fashionista BFFs at Christmas.

50. Take the interns to lunch. Listen to their ideas on improving stuff in the office. Ask them what they most want to do professionally, and give them your thoughts on next steps.

51. Grow good karma. Think positive thoughts about your archenemy. Find an excuse to call someone with whom you have had an awkward relationship, and clear the air. Buy coffee for the stranger behind you in line.

52. Be decisive. Instead of letting invitations or e-mails pile up, respond immediately.

53. Pick up your own phone when it rings. It's so much easier and more human to deal with stuff in the here and now. Say *Hello!* not *What?*

INDEX